P9-AQB-852

HURON COUNTY LIBRARY

3 6492 00503295 5

307.12160971133 Ber

Berelowitz, L.
Dream city.

PRICE: $40.00 (3559/cl   )

Dream City

Dream City

City

VANCOUVER AND THE GLOBAL IMAGINATION

LANCE BERELOWITZ

DOUGLAS & McINTYRE
VANCOUVER/TORONTO/BERKELEY

Copyright © 2005 by Lance Berelowitz

05 06 07 08 09 5 4 3 2 1

All rights reserved. No part of this book may be reproduced,
stored in a retrieval system or transmitted, in any form or by
any means, without the prior written consent of the publisher
or a licence from The Canadian Copyright Licensing Agency
(Access Copyright). For a copyright licence, visit www.
accesscopyright.ca or call toll free to 1-800-893-5777.

Douglas & McIntyre Ltd.
2323 Quebec Street, Suite 201
Vancouver, British Columbia
Canada v5t 4s7
www.douglas-mcintyre.com

Library and Archives Canada Cataloguing in Publication
Berelowitz, Lance, 1956–

   Dream city : Vancouver and the global imagination /
Lance Berelowitz.
Includes bibliographical references and index.
ISBN 1-55365-103-0
1. City planning—British Columbia—Vancouver—History.
2. Architecture—British Columbia—Vancouver. I. Title.
HT169.C32V35 2005   307.1'216'0971133   C2004-906460-6

Library of Congress information is available upon request

Editing by Saeko Usukawa
Design by George Vaitkunas
Front jacket photo of Concord Pacific Place by Shannon Mendes
Maps by Eric Leinberger (except where noted)
Derek Lepper photographs copyright © 2005
Printed and bound in Canada by Friesens
Printed on acid-free paper
Distributed in the U.S. by Publishers Group West

We gratefully acknowledge the financial support of the
Canada Council for the Arts, the British Columbia Arts
Council, and the Government of Canada through the Book
Publishing Industry Development Program (BPIDP) for our
publishing activities.

The quotation from *The Waste Land* by T.S. Eliot, published
by Faber and Faber Ltd., is reprinted by permission of the
publisher.

The quotation from *Polaroids from the Dead,* published
by HarperCollins Publishers, Inc., copyright © 1996 by
Douglas Coupland, is reprinted by permission of the author.

The quotation from *The Corporation: The Pathological
Pursuit of Profit and Power,* published by Penguin in Canada
and Free Press in the United States, copyright © 2004 Joel
Bakan, is reprinted by permission of the author.

Modified extracts of some of the text that Lance
Berelowitz wrote in collaboration with City of Vancouver
staff for the brochure *Vancouver's New Neighbourhoods:
Achievements in Planning and Urban Design,* produced
by the Vancouver Planning Department (Larry Beasley,
Co-Director of Planning; Ann McAfee, Co-Director of
Planning; Ralph Segal, Senior Urban Designer), are used by
permission of the City of Vancouver Planning Department.

Images from *A Plan for the City of Vancouver,* commonly
known as the Bartholomew Plan (1929) and a "Civic Centre"
voter flyer c. 1946 (both documents commissioned by the
predecessor Vancouver Town Planning Commission) are
reproduced by permission of the Vancouver City Planning
Commission.

Pages ii/iii: The downtown peninsula and False Creek.
Jeremy Woodhouse / Photodisc
Page vi: The Coal Harbour waterfront walkway. George
Vaitkunas photo
Page xii: The downtown skyline and the Stanley Park
seawall. George Vaitkunas photo

To Shelley, who first had the temerity to suggest that I might be the person to testify in public about Vancouver and who kept the faith.

Contents

It will be noted that no mention has been made of any human foresight having been exercised in the control or direction of the growth of this British Columbia metropolis. Its history is that of Topsy, it just growed. —ARTHUR G. SMITH, CHAIRMAN, VANCOUVER TOWN PLANNING COMMISSION, FROM THE INTRODUCTION TO *A PLAN FOR THE CITY OF VANCOUVER,* 1929, BY HARLAND BARTHOLOMEW AND ASSOCIATES

Acknowledgements

I ALWAYS KNEW there was a book to be written about Vancouver, from the first time I laid eyes on it. For this Vancouver, the place itself, must be credited. I just didn't know how to do it. Several people helped guide me along the way.

Without his knowing it of course, Reyner Banham first suggested the way with his inimitable treatment of Los Angeles, that alter ego to Vancouver (even if we deny it). His book *Los Angeles: The Architecture of Four Ecologies* was a seminal influence on my way of looking at and writing about Vancouver, and remains the most intelligently written modern critique of any city in the West Coast littoral. Students of Banham's work will, I hope, find something of his spirit of inquiry resonating throughout the following effort at deciphering this city.

Robert Gretton at *Canadian Architect* magazine was the first editor in Canada to grant me public space to air my views on this preposterously optimistic city. His faith in the view of a newcomer gave me the confidence to continue writing long after that view became that of an insider and also led to my first award for writing in Canada. Subsequent editors at *Canadian Architect* generously allowed me to elaborate on these views. I am grateful to them all.

Detlef Mertins and the other organizers of the Royal Architectural Institute of Canada's first national forum on "The Architecture of Emerging Public Spaces" (1988) and the resulting publication *Metropolitan Mutations*, provided a valuable opportunity to develop some of the initial themes amplified in this book, and public exposure to these ideas. The resulting positive feedback from professional peers, including Joost Bakker, Ken Greenberg and Stephen Fong, further encouraged me to conclude that my pursuit of understanding the *genius loci* of this city was not entirely idiosyncratic.

Many local designers, critics and Vancouver observers supported me in this work along the way, both directly and indirectly. My thanks go out to those who have indicated that there was something worth writing about and that I might be the one to do so. This includes academic colleagues at the University of British Columbia, practising architects and planners, and other confreres. In particular, my thanks to Chris Macdonald, Director of the UBC School of Architecture, who took the time to read an early draft of this story and pointed out several shortcomings. Professor Graeme Wynn of the UBC Department of Geography also read the manuscript and provided detailed comments on some of the early chapters, specifically with respect to my loose understanding of the city's geographical and environmental setting. And Professor Rhodri Windsor Liscombe tried to strengthen my tenuous grasp of the city's extraordinary modernist history, while not always concurring with me. Any remaining historical inaccuracies or misattributions are no fault of theirs.

Stephanie Robb generously and patiently explained why the Vancouver Special house deserves its name. David Beers demonstrated why I consider him to be one of the sharpest editors going, as well as his friendship beyond the call of duty, by reading the manuscript, giving acute advice and, not least, opening some important doors.

City of Vancouver Planning Department staff, led by the ever-gracious Larry Beasley, helped in ways small and large, sometimes without knowing it. In particular, John Madden provided useful development statistics. Dan Campbell was generous in his assistance with City maps and graphics. While this book does not always agree with some of my City colleagues' usually more rosy assessments of changes on their watch, I have nothing but admiration for their professionalism and dedication to the task. They certainly can take some credit for the urban planning successes the city has seen. They should also know that any criticisms between these covers are made in a spirit of constructive critique.

My publisher, Scott McIntyre, proved a wily negotiator and an even more persistent champion of this project. I owe him a large debt of gratitude for believing in this book and for convincing others to believe in it as well, thus securing its viability. Scott is something of a national treasure and every author should be so fortunate to have such an enthusiastic publisher. The rest of the team at Douglas & McIntyre were all terrific. Special thanks to my tireless editor, Saeko Usukawa. The gifted eye of designer George Vaitkunas has resulted in a far more handsome book than I could have expected.

Eric Leinberger applied his enviable cartographic skills to the suite of maps he created especially for this book. Derek Lepper added the magic of his photography.

The Canada Council for the Arts made this work possible through a generous grant from its Visual Arts—Architecture program as well as production support. The Canada Council performs a nationally critical role in enabling artists, designers, writers and critics to contribute towards building a Canadian visual arts culture, for which we should all be profoundly grateful. I am.

Finally, my deepest thanks and profound gratitude to my wife and partner, Shelley Craig, who always had more confidence than I did in the relevance of my observations to others, and who cajoled and encouraged me to do something about it.

Lance Berelowitz
Vancouver, 2004

Introduction

VANCOUVER HAS EMERGED as the poster child of urbanism in North America. In recent years, through a series of locally grown strategies, Vancouver has consciously willed itself into becoming a model of contemporary city-making. Like the most vivid of dreams, the city is reinventing itself: something curious, perhaps even miraculous, is happening here. The visitors—mostly from American cities seeking to find the key to their own urban renewal—come in steady droves, eagerly shepherded around town by local planners, politicians and academics. They go away suitably impressed. Barely a month goes by without yet another magazine article or news report praising Vancouver's urban virtues.

And it is easy to be impressed by the obvious: the city's spectacular setting, the intimate and apparently happy cohabitation of wild nature and built fabric, the tightly packed gleaming new condo towers downtown, the public waterfront, the vibrant neighbourhood high streets, the neat parks and lush, tree-lined suburban streets. The place seems to work.

But how did Vancouver get here, and is the attention deserved? How much of Vancouver's experience is applicable to other cities, particularly those in the United States? Why are places such as Shanghai, San Francisco and even Toronto now hiring Vancouver architects and planners to fix their cities? In short, what are the keys to understanding Vancouver's unique sense of place and its relevance to the rest of the world?

To answer these questions is to look into the heart of this city of dreams, to dig beneath the surface impressions and unravel fact from myth, cause from consequence. In short, this is writing as a form of urban archaeology. Or perhaps, to offer a more suggestively West Coast genre, it is a detective story.

Vancouver has propagated a number of myths about itself, now well established and accepted in the public mind. Yet it is a city of paradoxes. Dig deeper beyond the obvious, and the reasons for Vancouver's success seem more often to do with historical happenstance or a kind of invented authenticity. Or simply having made fewer mistakes as a result of being so remote and so much later in its development than almost any other major North American city. Ironically, Vancouver's very isolation and relative lack of political and economic power have meant that it was largely bypassed by the worst of North American "urban renewal": freeways, elevated and underground pedestrian systems, huge shopping malls, big-box retail, oversized curvilinear dead-end streets in place of the traditional street grid.

Certainly, metropolitan Vancouver does have many of these symptoms of "modern" North American town planning, particularly in its outlying suburbs and bedroom communities where in fact the majority of its residents live. But there is a kind of virtuous *cordon sanitaire* around the City of Vancouver itself: almost no freeways transgress its municipal boundaries or violate the regular street grid, and a grand total of just two major shopping malls besmirch its neighbourhoods.

There is a certain irony in American cities looking to Canada to remember what the United States taught us about city building and have now forgotten themselves. Think of Daniel Burnham, the Olmsted brothers, Harland Bartholomew and John Nolen, all of whom had an effect on the layout and form of many Canadian cities. In Vancouver's case, both Shaughnessy Heights and the British Properties were developed under the influence of these giants of American town planning. And Vancouver's vaunted, now late lamented, urban and interurban streetcar system was directly modelled on similar ones in Los Angeles and other American cities.

And—just as Los Angeles is for restless Americans—Vancouver has always been whatever newcomers want it to be, the perennial immigrants' city of the imagination: Dream City. Yet it is really the place itself that has seduced the imagination of émigrés and visitors alike.

Of course, back in 1985 when I first arrived in Vancouver, I knew none of this. But I had my suspicions …

Dream Sequence—Arrival
When I stepped off the plane from London in 1985, it was immediately apparent on my first exposure to Vancouver that this was unlike any other city I had visited or lived in as an adult, and something to write home about.

Not about the obvious seductions of Vancouver's admittedly ravishing natural setting or its apparent culture of beach and body beautiful, though these certainly appealed after a decade of full-throttle Thatcherism had rendered away the charms of a by then dispiritingly mean—much less Great—

Britain. Nor about the high culture available out here at the edge of the known world. Compared to London or Paris, where I had lived for the past decade, there wasn't much evidence of that. Rather, it was a dream-like blend of the disarmingly innocent and the refreshing yet tantalizingly familiar—a recapitulation of the old with an invigorating newness—that seduced. And there were intriguing signs that this was a city marching to its own drum, inventing its own unique urban form.

In short, Vancouver, on first inspection, seemed like a fantasy dream.

There is no other arrival experience quite like it. You land on an estuarine island at the mouth of the largest remaining salmon-bearing river in the world. Stepping out of the airport terminal, your olfactory senses are immediately assailed by the powerful smell of salty sea ozone wafting in from the surrounding water, mixed incongruously with the odour of jet fuel. Looking up, you are quite likely to spot one or more bald eagles circling off the intertidal zone that almost surrounds the airport. Other equally exotic avian species are a part of the landscape: while you are unlikely to know this, you have landed right in the midst of the Pacific Flyway, one of North America's most significant migratory bird routes.

Vintage Beaver and classic Twin Otter float planes buzz as they lift off the protected river waters that form an additional runway surface along the southern edge of the aptly named Sea Island.

The original terminal building itself—until recent major renovations diluted its exuberant if touchingly naive expression of faith in technological progress—seemed caught in 1985 between a lost world of air travel experienced as public drama and the prosaic reality of late twentieth-century mass tourism. From the terminal's upper level portal, the long view is ringed by snow-capped mountains, including the improbable but unmistakable silhouette of a glacier-clad volcano, a diorama of nature that is at once tantalizingly close yet reassuringly distant.

As you drive off the airport island over a gently rising bridge, you may glimpse a lone figure down in the flat green fields off to your left. He is moving languidly, improbably practising what appear to be golf swings. He is. Jets float down over the bridge on their final approach, skimming low over the golfer's head. He takes no notice. Over towards the airport perimeter fence, a small crowd of cars is likely to be clustered at the end of the runway, folks with binoculars and short-wave radios in hand, thermos flasks of coffee on the car hoods: Vancouver families on a typical day's outing, watching the planes come in.

As you crest the airport bridge, Vancouver is laid out before you. It seems to float, poised between mountain and sea, a light confection hovering between the temperate rain forest of the Coast Mountains and the convoluted inlets of the Pacific Ocean.

As you travel into town over the whaleback of the Burrard Peninsula, a dense cluster of slim towers emerges ahead, rising in shimmering layers in front of the mountain backdrop.

Compared to the bigger cities of Europe or Asia or even North America, everything seems somehow diminutive, improbably languid, neat and uncrowded, a dream-like simulacrum of messy urbanity. And yet more than two million people live here, in one of the most compact urban centres in North America. So there's the thing, the maddening contradiction that is Vancouver at the beginning of its second hundred years: a city that seems to have emerged out of its surrounding wilderness chrysalis-like, seemingly almost fully formed yet so young, so unlayered. And with a unique sense of place.

No wonder I began to write about the place within days of arriving.[1]

THIS NARRATIVE attempts to capture the essence of Vancouver's sense of place—its *genius loci*. It is not a definitive monograph of Vancouver's urban geography and history of settlement. Nor is it a comprehensive review of the architectural heritage of the city. Such models have already been well provided, foremost amongst which are perhaps *Vancouver and Its Region* by Graeme Wynn, Timothy Oke, et al., with respect to the former, and *Exploring Vancouver* by Harold Kalman, Ron Phillips and Robin Ward, for the latter. Rather, it is an attempt to make some sense of the special setting and urban forms that have shaped this young city and continue to influence its emerging design. It is selective, focussing on those clues and features that in my view contribute towards deciphering the puzzle that is modern-day Vancouver.

Vancouver is little more than a century old. Until about 1885 the only intimations of the future city were a sawmill, a church and a smattering of wooden houses in a clearing on the southern shore of an otherwise largely untrammelled Burrard Inlet, though parts of the forest around the inlet had already been logged. That was it. In a city as young as this, the traditional historical chronology approach seems churlish, if not downright irrelevant to understanding the forces that have shaped and continue to shape it. This is instant urbanism, compared to almost any other city in the developed world (with the notable exception perhaps of Los Angeles, most of which

Top An aerial view of
downtown Vancouver in
the 1980s, before Expo 86
and the redevelopment
of the False Creek basin.
Allen Aerial Photos,
courtesy UBC Department
of Geography

Bottom An aerial view of
central Vancouver in 2003,
showing the redevelop-
ment of the downtown
peninsula after Expo 86.
Derek Lepper photo

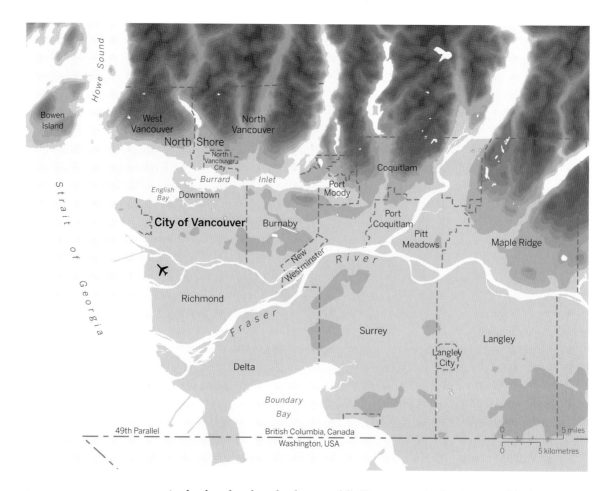

Vancouver and its
regional context.
Eric Leinberger

is also barely a hundred years old). Vancouver is also inseparable from its natural setting, and the story of its urban form is as much about setting and context as it is about built content. Thus, this book does not offer the detailed chronology of events typical of a historical monograph. Put another way, the oblique observation is often more revealing than the formally linear historiographic approach.

How best then to understand this very different model of urbanism? Just as earlier historians learned the languages of antiquity in order to read the classic texts in their original, and as architecture critic Reyner Banham realized that in order "to read Los Angeles in the original" he had to learn to drive,[2] I have taken up Vancouver's favoured form of locomotion, which has largely involved lengthy walks along the city's waterfront edges, taking time to raise my eyes and gaze at the surrounding panoramic views, sniff the sea air, smell the flowers, commune with the birds and generally perambulate as if I lived in the very best place in the world. But is it a city?

Much like Vancouver's typical urban perambulator moving tangentially along the edges of the city, observing and experiencing it obliquely and individually, readers are encouraged to take whatever path and sequence appeals to them in the following chapters, in whatever order catches their fancy. The structure of this story will be familiar to Vancouverites: it is a simulacrum of the city it describes; discrete trajectories of non-linear experience, whose proximity and juxtaposition reinforce their separate meanings.

Some vital statistics[3] to keep in mind as we begin our perambulations:

Greater Vancouver has some two million inhabitants.

Greater Vancouver is made up of twenty-one separate municipalities and one electoral area, which together form the Greater Vancouver Regional District (GVRD). The ones to which I refer in this book include the City of Vancouver itself, New Westminster, Richmond, Burnaby, Surrey and, on the North Shore, North Vancouver and West Vancouver.

The City of Vancouver has around six hundred thousand residents—approximately 30 per cent of the total metropolitan population—who live on about 129 km^2 (50 square miles),which is less than 2 per cent of the total Greater Vancouver land base of 6571 km^2 (2,537 square miles). However, the amount of land suitable for urban development is much less, only about 1441 km^2 (556 square miles) because of protected watersheds; local, regional, provincial and national parks; agricultural land; forests and land that is too steep to develop.

And a note on nomenclature:

"Vancouver" and "the city" (lower case) refer to the general Vancouver conurbation. "City of Vancouver" and "the City" (capitalized) refer to the Vancouver municipal corporation.

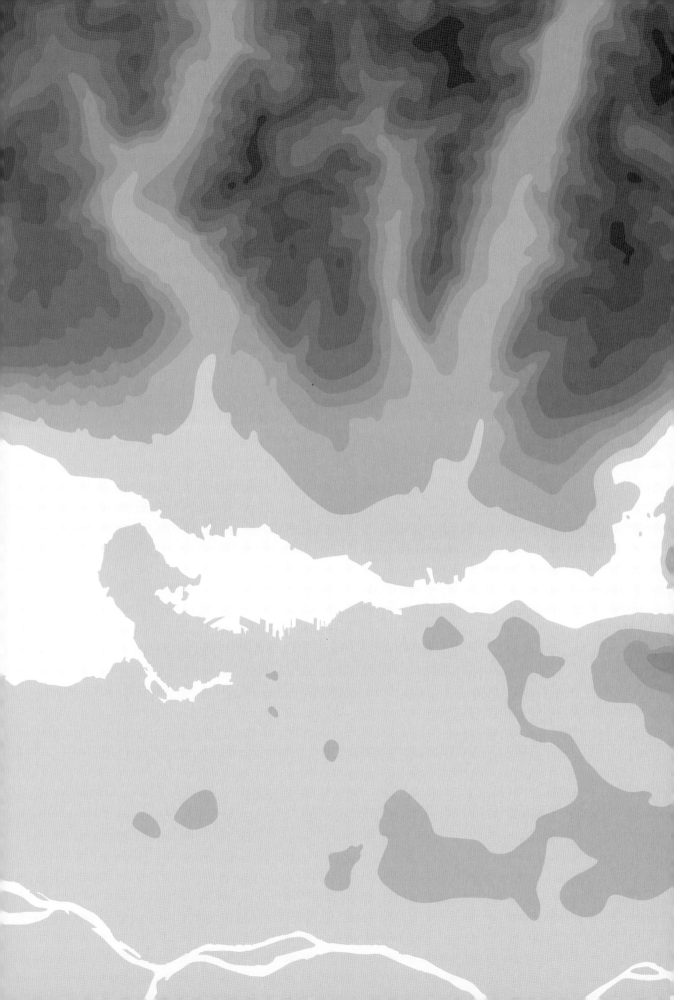

The Elemental City

1

THERE IS SOMETHING very elemental about Vancouver, a defining characteristic of place that only a few cities have. Like Sydney, Australia, for example. In his 2001 love letter to his home town,[4] Australian author Peter Carey calls it the city's DNA. He was referring to Sydney's underlying sandstone, and how so much about the place flows from that geological fact. "Sandstone shows everywhere, in the buildings of old Sydney and in the retaining walls of all those steep harbour streets." Carey goes on to explain that because of the sandstone's sedimentary porousness, rainwater drains so rapidly that it leaches the thin topsoil of nutrients. This, in turn, determines the unique local flora, which has adapted to the scarcity of nutrients by protecting its leaves with deadly toxins, resulting in "the distinctive smell of the Australian bush, the high oil content in the plant life, and the inability of the soil to decompose such fallen leaves." All of this makes for optimum fire conditions, which, when one happens, "perfumes the very air of Sydney with …" well, you get the drift. Carey is a better storyteller than I am.

What might Vancouver's elemental DNA be?

In Vancouver's case it is not the underlying geology from which it derives its elemental essence but rather this formula:

latitude + coastal longitude + mountains = precipitation

To put it another way:

**temperature + prevailing ocean winds + vertical barrier =
Pacific Northwest rain forest**

Almost everything about Vancouver springs from this formulation of geographical facts: the quality of the air, the taste of the water, the light, the smells, the colours of the landscape, the food it grows and eats, the very climate and resulting lifestyle. This is Vancouver's *genius loci*. And the city's urban form has responded to these elements.

The city's relatively mild, temperate climate is directly related to its latitude (much farther north and it would be wetter and cooler, like Alaska; much farther south and it would be Mediterranean, like Los Angeles), its longitudinal location beside the moderating influence of the ocean (much farther inland and its climate would be more extreme) and the presence of the Coast Mountain barrier (without which it would be much drier).

The air is soft and moist, carrying the warmth of the ocean rather than the Arctic airstream that skims past farther north, only occasionally sideswiping Vancouver with the tips of its frigid tentacles.

The drinking water, so soft and only lightly chlorinated in comparison with that in many Canadian cities, results from it coming directly from watersheds high in the mountains, which catch the rain and allow it to naturally settle and filter.

The light is soft, filtered, gauzy, misty, reflective, moisture-layered, often grey, sometimes blue but seldom the blinding sharp light of the Prairies or the Midwest or the Mediterranean. This is the light of a temperate maritime setting, a diaphanous Turner watercolour.

The natural smells are those of the ocean, of pungent ozone, rain-washed flora, slowly rotting vegetation, fungi and rich deltoid soils.

The urban landscape is preternaturally green, lush, betokening the febrile growing conditions of the rain forest.

There is one other key contributing element to the physical essence of Vancouver, and that is its location on a combination of glacial till, outwash deposits and fertile soils. After the last major ice age (locally referred to as the Fraser Glaciation), the whole area was covered by silty sand and gravel deposits from the several glaciers and rivers flowing out at the base of the Coast Mountains. Much of Vancouver today is built on the rich alluvial deposits from these and other long-shifted watercourses.

This confluence of factors provided the optimum environment to nurture an abundance of food—from the salmon in the Fraser River to the fields of wild berries—which was part of what first attracted human settlement to this place long before the city was founded. Coast Salish First Nation groups had seasonal and permanent settlements all around the area for several centuries before the arrival of European settlers and colonists.

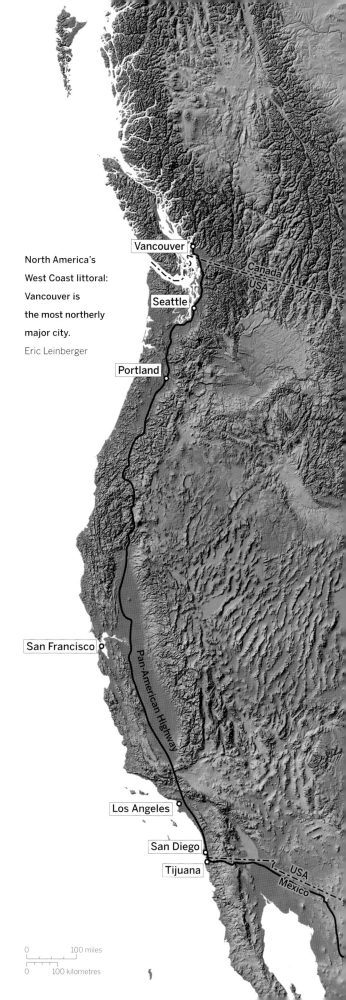

City at the Edge

The Fraser River delta has played an even more elemental role in Vancouver's emergence.

Here, at 49°17' north, the last latitudinal minute, as it were, before the continent plunges into the sea, is Vancouver, the most northerly major city in the West Coast littoral. Just to the north and within sight of the city, the continent terminates in a wild farrago of steep slopes, jagged peninsulas and deep fjords, making large-scale settlement and access by land virtually impossible. But the gentle hump of Vancouver's Burrard Peninsula and its even smoother, smaller doppelgänger that is now the downtown peninsula were created by the inexorable advance of a glacier during the last major ice age just fifteen thousand years ago.

North America's West Coast littoral: Vancouver is the most northerly major city.

Eric Leinberger

Vancouver

Canada
USA

Seattle

Portland

San Francisco

Pan-American Highway

Los Angeles

San Diego

Tijuana

USA
México

0   100 miles

0   100 kilometres

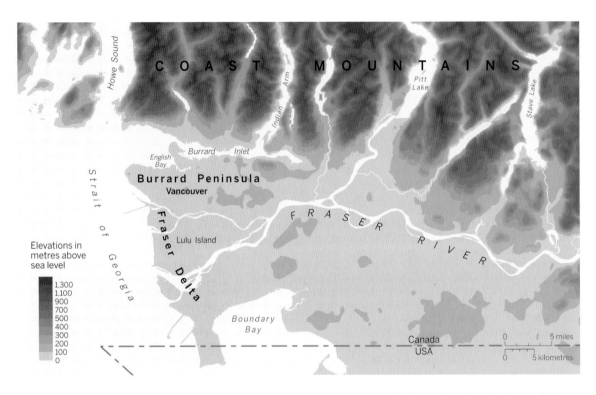

Elevations in
metres above
sea level

1,300
1,100
900
700
500
400
300
200
100
0

Vancouver's topography.

Eric Leinberger

As the ice receded, it left behind smoothed-out land at the base of the Coast Mountains. The gathering force of the Fraser River's waters, depositing its silt and debris, did the rest. Without the Fraser delta, there would be no city here. Vancouver occupies the last available flat land at the edge of the continent: Edge City.

Another sort of edge quality has characterized Vancouver from its beginnings. Significantly, apart from the initial maritime explorers who alerted Europe to these shores, Vancouver was not colonized from the sea but from the land, unlike superficially similar places such as Cape Town or Sydney. It is the terminus, not the beginning, of the modern Canadian story. Its genesis as a city was as the western terminus of the transcontinental Canadian Pacific Railway. It is the last continental stop on a route beginning, metaphorically, in the British Isles, and, geographically, in southern Patagonia, where the Pan-American Highway begins a route that finally runs out of coastal access at Vancouver. Vancouver has always been the city at the end of the line: Terminal City.

Vancouver also has been the locus of a different kind of settlement by an ever-widening diversity of peoples and cultures, particularly Asians, because of its location on the Pacific Rim. It is a city of immigrants. As such, it is becoming the social Petri dish of Canada, leading to a new cultural edginess, one that is much less Eurocentric. Evidence of this cultural shift is easy to find in the city's pan-Asian fusion cooking scene and Asian festivals, in its leading position as a centre for teaching English as a second language and in its high-profile ethnic minority political activism.[5]

The convergence of these two edge conditions, the physical and the cultural, provides the first clues to explain Vancouver's emergent urban form.

Aberdeen Centre mall in Richmond: multiculturalism in the suburbs.
George Vaitkunas photo

2

In the Garden of Eden

VANCOUVER'S NATURAL ENVIRONMENT is a critical factor in shaping the city. Without an acknowledgment of this multifaceted presence, Vancouver cannot be understood or adequately described. Indeed, an entire mythology has been constructed around Vancouver's relationship with "Nature," in parallel with the construction of the city itself.

Vancouver's geographic circumstances have created the abundance of rainfall that marks this city perhaps more than anything else. The Pacific Northwest temperate rain forest with its fertile soils has created a landscape of fecund growth. This lushness, combined with Vancouver's dramatic setting between mountains and sea, and its convoluted land forms interspersed with water bodies, results in something of an earthly paradise.

That claim has of course already been made for Vancouver's southern alter ego, Los Angeles. But if Reyner Banham's dictum for Los Angeles—"to produce instant Paradise you have to add water—and keep on adding to it"[6]—is applied to Vancouver, then Vancouver is already there. Whereas water was all that early Los Angeles needed (and still needs) to grow, Vancouver's missing ingredient is not water but sun.

To turn the formula around, if the Los Angeles equation for unfettered development is:

desert + sun + (water) = growth

then Vancouver's is:

rain + land + (sun) = growth

In Vancouver, you need only add sunshine to bring out its best.

Rain

Vancouver seduces: it leads you along, sullenly taunting you with its seemingly endless grey, introverted days of rain and dankness. Then, just as you feel that you can't stand it anymore and are about to forsake it for another, the clouds lift, the sun breaks through, smiling beatifically on the land, that seductive mountain panorama reveals itself once more, and your heart is captured all over again …

That's the way it goes in Vancouver. Ask anyone. The first hint of sunshine brings out the crowds. City residents emerge and gather in suddenly burgeoning numbers along the urban seawall and beachfront walkways, passing each other in happy conversations, using every known mode of self-propelled transportation: on foot, bicycle, in-line skates, skate board, scooter, wheelchair. There is a sudden sense of reinvigoration. The city comes alive.

Vancouverites have many words for rain, such as mist, drizzle, shower, downpour. Rain is the one constant throughout the year. Its presence and quantity are frequently referred to in casual conversations. Everyone knows exactly how many days it has been raining, how much has fallen and when a new record has been set. Even its occasional absence may be remarked upon, as in, "It's been so long since it rained, eh?" This might be a reference to a two-week interregnum. Longer absences of precipitation are recognized with superficial pleasure and relief, but underlying these is a palpable collective anxiety: there will be a price to pay for all this lack of rain. And there usually is: in dropping water-reservoir levels, increased smog and forest fires. People's choices about where to live are dictated as much by the rain as by price: everyone knows that it rains way more on the North Shore than in Kitsilano, where in turn it rains rather more than in Tsawwassen. This sliding scale of rainfall levels is a kind of shorthand for a local social geography.

Land

The land of the city is a conjugation of soil, forest and topography. In the spirit of formulas for growth, it might be described as:

land = (soil + forest + topography)

Soil

Vancouver's soil was deposited by the last ice age, when glacial till was pushed out of the mountains to form the Burrard Peninsula. Over the millennia, the Fraser River spread yet more alluvial soil across the lowlands, creating the sprawling Fraser Valley. The result is soil of unsurpassed fertility.

The dark soil supported a lush evergreen rain forest where the city itself is today. Farther out in the Fraser Valley, the alluvial soil, plentiful water and just enough sunshine support a thriving agricultural industry. Just a thirty-minute drive past the City limits, numerous roadside farm stalls offer a rolling cornucopia of freshly harvested riches from early spring through late autumn: blueberries, strawberries, raspberries, asparagus, artichokes, lettuce, zucchini, eggplants, beans, peppers, corn, carrots, cranberries, onions, potatoes, pumpkins and more. The Fraser Valley is the city's food basket. Which makes it all the more dispiriting to have to acknowledge, as local academic Bill Rees has pointed out, that Vancouver consumes far more than it produces on its ecological footprint.[7]

Another sign of fecundity is the mysterious eruption of innumerable wild mushrooms all around the city in the autumn. In sidewalks, on boulevards, in play fields, parks and backyards, numerous species of fungi, ranging from the delicious to the deadly, burst out of the moist ground. Vancouverites have long known about the presence of so-called "magic" mushrooms among others and partaken of their hallucinatory pleasures, contributing to Vancouver's Alice in Wonderland reputation. More recent immigrants (who often have long experience in these things) now also lead the way in identifying the more gustatory species such as the golden chanterelle and more elusive morel.

Wild fiddleheads, dandelions, blackberries and salmonberries also grow in profusion all over the city, lending it the almost surreal air of an open-air food market. Vancouver: the Edible City. Today, it is impossible to visit Vancouver without noticing the abundant profusion of local ingredients that distinguish the city's cutting-edge restaurant scene.

Forest

The rain forest adds its own powerful contribution to the urban setting. The abundant rain, rich soils and moderate temperatures combine to create a verdant urban landscape of trees, hedges, shrubs and grass. This implausibly green landscape remains that way all year round, much of it being coniferous. The presence of the rain forest within the city is an unmissable feature, especially to visitors from other, more climatically challenged, cities. It lends a softness and an otherworldly quality to the city, for those whose eyes are open to it.

A classic Vancouver
green street hedge.

Derek Lepper photo

Vancouver's benign climate permits a rather contrived array of plant life to coexist. Among the native conifers is the occasional arbutus tree, at the northern limit of its range, with its reptilian-like, perpetually peeling smooth red bark, outposts of the sizable madrona forests found farther south along the North American west coast. South American monkey puzzle trees, ornamental Japanese cherry trees, various palm trees, fig trees, tenacious rosemary bushes, gnarly old grapevines, even banana trees: all these botanical exotics grow in isolated pockets across the city, often denoting human efforts at domesticating the rain forest and re-creating immigrants' left-behind cultural landscapes. For example, mature Mediterranean fig trees, heavy with fruit in late summer, trace the original settlement patterns of a substantial Greek community in the inner suburb of Kitsilano.

The very air is scented by the pungent smells of the omnipresent rain forest vegetation in various stages of decomposition and regeneration, as well as the presence of the ozone-rich sea. This makes for a heady perfume, quite unlike that of most large cities. Sometimes on foggy autumn days, the salty smell of the sea is almost overwhelming, stretching well back into the urban hinterland from the waterfront edge.

The native landscape has also been bent to the will of the city. Among Vancouver's more extraordinary urban landscapes are the suburban streets lined with impossibly tall rows of perfectly manicured hedges that form vertical green streetwalls. In some residential neighbourhoods, such as South West Marine Drive or around the uplands of Shaughnessy Heights, the streetwalls of clipped, soaring dark green cedar, fir, hemlock, juniper and laurel are tightly compressed to form an impenetrable barrier, a kind of regimented, domesticated version of the surrounding rain forest.

These hedges, whether meticulously tended or riotously unkempt, are anti-social, not to say anti-urban, for they serve to isolate and disconnect the city's public realm—the streets—from the residents of the homes they hide, creating separate spaces within the city. The effect is like moving down a green-walled tunnel, beyond which are the unknown and unknowable private realms. There is very little overlook of the street, no interaction between passersby and residents taking the air on their front porches, washing their cars or mowing their lawns.

Another extraordinary Vancouver landscape emerges every spring when thousands of cherry trees blossom along the streets and avenues.

A uniquely Vancouver urban landscape: the annual spring
cherry blossom snowstorm. Derek Lepper photo

The long spring season of the Pacific Northwest means that the various cherry species that have been widely planted along city streets bloom over an extended period. Eventually, as the trees start shedding, the city happily submits to a sublime snowstorm of cherry blossoms as they swirl in the air, carpeting the sidewalks and covering parked cars. At the same time, across the rest of Canada, the snow is very real.

The pace of natural growth in Vancouver is also noteworthy, if not downright startling. Whereas other regions of this northern country struggle to make trees grow to any significant size in a person's lifetime, here on the wet coast, flora flourishes in a parody of those architectural renderings that show new buildings instantly hung with dripping creepers or screened by mature trees. Vancouver's gardeners are perpetually fighting a rearguard action against the forces of nature. The rain forest everywhere insinuates itself back into the smallest cracks in the urban fabric, always threatening to overtake the built environment. Left to its own devices long enough, the rain forest would largely obliterate the city within mere decades, much as it has many abandoned aboriginal settlements up and down the coast.

Topography

The third notable aspect of Vancouver's landscape is its dramatic topography.

With the Coast Mountains rising up steeply to the north, the sea lapping in from the west and the broad plains of the Fraser River delta fanning out to the south, Vancouver's physical setting is undeniably spectacular. An island-studded fjord (Howe Sound) marks the city's northwestern approaches. The western horizon across the Strait of Georgia is defined by layers of mountainous profiles: the southern Gulf Islands foreground the taller serrated ridge of Vancouver Island. More mountains rim the panoramic long view to the east, piling up towards the interior. And to the southeast, rising some 3285 metres (10,780 feet), the glacier-covered, distinctive volcanic profile of Mount Baker in the State of Washington is a distant yet tantalizingly eminent presence visible from all sorts of unexpected vantage points throughout Vancouver.

A cherished Vancouver
myth: ski in the morning
(*opposite page*) … and sail
in the afternoon (*this page*).
Lance Berelowitz photos

Ocean, archipelago, glacier, volcano, fjord, flood plain, rain forest, alpine peak: these are not your everyday urban backdrop. Views in every direction present stunning natural tableaux.

This dramatic geography has had a profound impact on the form and extent of settlement. Greater Vancouver is hemmed in by mountains to the north and east, by the sea to the west, and by the 49th Parallel (the international boundary) to the south. These natural restrictions (and one artificial line, that unkindest of cuts) have played a significant role in limiting the size and direction of urban sprawl, and the rate of densification. There is only so much flat land available for urbanization, let alone for large-scale industrial manufacturing. As a result, the urban form is more concentrated than the typical North American conglomeration. In addition, the shape of urbanization is mostly linear (primarily in an easterly direction, as most of the remaining developable land is inland up the Fraser Valley) rather than radial, as the city core is close to the edge rather than at the centre of the inhabitable area.

Vancouver's topographic range is dramatic, too, stretching vertically from below sea level[8] to the Coast Mountains, which rise steeply to around 1500 metres (4,900 feet). Beyond them is mountain wilderness. The phalanx of Hollyburn, Grouse and Seymour mountains forms the northerly urban edge of the metropolis. Their altitude plays havoc with Vancouver's reputation as a mild climate haven. With increasing elevation, the climate changes noticeably: what is an abundance of rain down on the city plains turns rapidly to snow up in the mountains. It can be -8° C (18°F) at the top of Grouse Mountain overlooking the city, where it is a balmy +8°C (46°F).

This intimate coexistence of temperate maritime city and alpine wilderness contributes significantly to the diversity of the city's natural ecology and to the mythology of Vancouver as a place of private leisure: commentators often trot out the well worn line about Vancouver being "the only city where you can alpine ski in the morning and ocean sail in the afternoon." Like all such clichés, it has more than a germ of truth. It is indeed possible. Pausing at the top of Black Mountain in Cypress Bowl before throwing themselves down the snow-covered pistes, skiers can look down on the sun glinting off sailboats tacking off Point Atkinson or golfers languorously playing the Gleneagles course some 1200 m (3,900 feet) below.

Sun

Just add sun, as the commercial might have it. Sun is the crucial limiting factor in Vancouver's urban ecology. The sun is in short supply for most of the year. But when it does present itself, it transforms the city. Then, with its beaches basking in the sunshine, Vancouver becomes the closest simulacrum Canada has to Southern California's culture of sybaritic pleasure. Television images dutifully trotted out on the Canadian Broadcasting Corporation news every February show flowers blooming in Vancouver while the rest of the country huddles under its blanket of snow, confirming Vancouver's Lotus Land status in Canadian mythology.

But the myth is something of a chimera, and Vancouverites know this, though they pretend otherwise. The city's indolent beach culture is only really available for maybe ten weeks of the year. But this does not stop Vancouverites from pretending they are living in Los Angeles. People in T-shirts, shorts and sandals sit on sidewalk café terraces (heated of course) throughout the year or drive around in convertible sports cars with the top down in February. They are all complicit in keeping up the Lotus Land myth.

The perpetuation of this partly invented reality also drives major investments in the city's public amenities: the extensive seawall walkway system, the outdoor public tennis courts in every neighbourhood and a plethora of local parks, nearly all of which have children's playground equipment. It has also deluded Vancouver into designing buildings as if this were Southern California, with all the unfortunate consequences that have become familiarly referred to as the "leaky condo" crisis. The sun is what makes the myth plausible. It is the crucial element that completes the city's formula for unlimited growth and contributes to its reputation as a Garden of Eden.

Vancouver's beach culture, a simulacrum of Southern California.
Lance Berelowitz photo

3

In Nature's Way

Chop. Chop. Chop. The blessed forests came down, and interested passers-by watched … then speculated on their past and their future. The forest vanished and up went the city.—ETHEL WILSON, *THE INNOCENT TRAVELLER,* 1944

THE TOURIST POSTCARDS never show it, but not all is benign in this supposed Garden of Eden. Although Vancouver at first gives every appearance of being sensitively in balance with its surrounding environment and of having an ethos of respectful coexistence, it has always had a strong love/hate relationship with nature. Vancouverites tend to over-idealize their place in the world as a natural paradise and to underestimate their impact on it, even as they go about ignoring it, misunderstanding it or degrading it. In fact, the city's growth is founded on the paradox of urban development: destruction of the very things that attract people in the first place.

While Vancouverites pay lip service—and in many cases more than that (Greenpeace was founded here)—to protecting and nurturing their environment, the truth about their cohabitation with nature is often more ambiguous. There are many ways in which this profound ambiguity is manifested.

The View Imperative

Everyone wants a view, and why not? Vancouver's real estate market consistently demonstrates the significant perceived value of having a view of mountains and/or water. Real estate ads routinely call attention to even the most oblique or limited views: a peekaboo view from a tiny top floor balcony increases market value. However, in addition to the direct impact on property values, Vancouver's obsession with the view has distorted the city's built form and its natural ecology.

As with Los Angeles,[9] Vancouver experienced rapacious development of its hillsides, beachside bluffs and steep slopes. There is nothing accidental about this in either city. Yet the most dramatic, most valuable sites that afford the best views are invariably the most ecologically sensitive. But in Vancouver people will pay for the view, and handsomely. A house with a panoramic water and mountain view will sell for at least a hundred thousand dollars more than the same-size house, just down the hill, that does not have a view. This distorts land development in obvious ways. Often, obscenely large homes are perched along the edges of the upland, not only usurping the view unto themselves but also affecting some of the most valuable ecological niches. The edges of intersecting land forms, such as riparian shoreline, bluff and plateau, are frequently the locations of marginal habitats found only in these areas.

Selling the view.

Derek Lepper photo

Another interesting aspect of Vancouver's view imperative is that it often reverses the intuitive logic of orienting buildings towards the sun (that is, to the south, at Vancouver's latitude). Since the mountains and most of the water views are largely to the north, many homes and buildings face north rather than south. This practice also is evident in new high-density areas such as downtown's Coal Harbour, Bayshore Gardens and Triangle West. New buildings are skewed, rotated, stepped in plan and terraced in section, all the better to enjoy the view. But this phenomenon is true also of public open space, especially downtown, where a whole phalanx of such spaces all face north. As a consequence, many of them are in shade for much of the day. In a city with so many overcast days, this is a curiously perverse response to the local environment.

Higher Ground: The Topographic Impulse

Closely related to the cult of the view is the topographic impulse. In Vancouver, topography has always been a shaper of the city's urban form as well as a socio-economic indicator. The high ground has always been sought out by the social elite, and a cursory study of a topographic map reveals a direct correlation between contour levels and real estate values, though it is also true that view sometimes trumps elevation. The most sought after, most expensive real estate in the city is typically also the highest: the heights of Spanish Banks in West Point Grey, Shaughnessy Heights, Quilchena ridge, the British Properties on the North Shore. Among the earliest residential areas was Shaughnessy Heights, located on the ridgeline of Burrard Peninsula due south of downtown. Here was laid out the young city's premier suburb,

Left Buildings skewed and rotated to catch the view.

Right A balloon camera establishing views for siting a new tower.
Derek Lepper photos

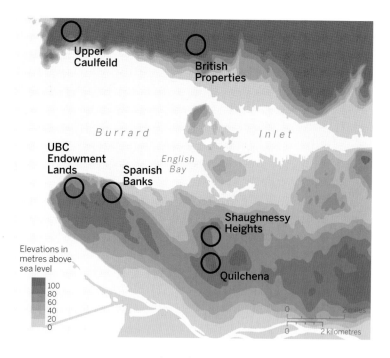

Upper
Caulfeild

British
Properties

Burrard   *Inlet*

UBC
Endowment
Lands

*English
Bay*

Spanish
Banks

Shaughnessy
Heights

Quilchena

Elevations in
metres above
sea level

100
80
60
40
20
0

0   2 miles

0   2 kilometres

Contour levels and
property values:
a direct correlation.
Eric Leinberger

along the lines of the English Garden City Movement.[10] The location was chosen for its views over the surrounding lower land and water and to the distant mountains, as well as for its supposedly better quality air.

What the topographic impulse has meant is that some of the most dramatic natural landscapes have been directly targeted for urban development, and along with that has come significant habitat destruction. It is also radically transforming the physical outlines of the city.

The downtown peninsula's natural eastern and northern escarpments are rapidly disappearing or being largely recontoured by frenetic development. In fact, an entirely new "ground plane" is in the process of being created along Coal Harbour, extending out over what were once intertidal mud flats. The land has been utterly transformed, and whatever ecological values

A new ground plane
being created over the
former escarpment.
Derek Lepper photo

Creating a new topography for the downtown peninsula.

Derek Lepper photo

it once might have had are long gone. The irony is that today there are very stringent safeguards put in place by senior levels of government to protect marine habitats from rampant urban development. By most accounts these appear to be working, though there is no such equivalent protection of upland sites.

Nevertheless, the area's native fauna seem to be remarkably adaptable to these wholesale reconstructions of their habitat: bald eagles still soar over the West End on occasion when the thermals are working, and downtown streets and lanes are still home to skunks, raccoons and even coyotes. Large flocks of Canada geese occasionally bring traffic to a standstill on the Stanley Park Causeway as they noisily but slowly cross the road.

The Exotic Impulse

Vancouverites have always exhibited a penchant for the exotic, whether in architectural styles and materials or their choice of pets and plants. Although well-meaning, the introduction of exotic fauna and flora usually threatened or squeezed out entirely the local native species that have thrived here for so long in a previously balanced ecology. Examples abound.

Take the European starling. Please. When the first European starlings spread to the West Coast after having been released in New York's Central Park by an itinerant traveller circa 1906, little could anyone have guessed what their impact was going to be. Yet within a few short decades, the starling's singular aggressiveness, group habits and supreme adaptability have all but destroyed the urban habitat for many native bird species across the continent. More surely than anything else humans may be doing, starlings are killing Vancouver's native avian diversity.

Another bird introduced into Vancouver offers a cautionary tale from a quite different perspective. It is thought that the first pair of crested mynahs (*Acridotheres cristatellus*) escaped or were released from a visiting merchant sailor's cage, after he had acquired them on a port stop in China or Indonesia. Their numbers grew, and it looked as though Vancouver had accommodated a new species. In recent years, however, fewer and fewer of the noisy birds could be found, until in 2002 the last known pair finally died, bringing to a close this short and sad chapter of Vancouver's exotic avian history. Might there be a moral in this tale somewhere?

Vancouver's mild climate permits a wide array of plant species to survive and even thrive. Gardeners have responded enthusiastically to this happy state of affairs, planting great numbers of exotic species. Across town, for example, the so-called monkey puzzle tree (*Araucaria araucana*) is a familiar sight, but it has no business here, coming as it does from Chile. Nor do the various species of palm trees that pop up incongruously here and there, gently mocking the city's temperate latitude. Far more problematic is the spread of Scotch broom (*Cytisus scoparius*), a bush plant that has taken tenacious hold all over the region and is squeezing out native flora species and their attendant butterflies and moths.

These are just a few examples of exotic plants that have been introduced in Vancouver and that now compete for habitat with native species. Just because something will grow here does not mean that it should be allowed to do so.

As the good folks of Vancouver sit on their front porches of a summer's day, enjoying the late afternoon sunlight that warms the wood siding on

A monkey puzzle tree,
an example of the exotic.
Derek Lepper photo

their charming old homes, little do they guess that their houses may well be in the process of being eaten away. Only when there is a sudden awful eruption of the dreaded carpenter ants out of the woodwork are homeowners brought up against the inescapable reality that they are sharing this place with some very determined species and that human habits and theirs are often mutually exclusive. The carpenter ant is a prime example. While strictly speaking not an introduced exotic, this opportunistic insect has inexorably spread its range northward from its natural habitat of temperate, humid forest zones to now include southern British Columbia. Left alone long enough, nesting carpenter ants will eventually chew through the wooden structure of your house, that charming little 1920s fixer-upper you recently paid $597,000 for, leaving nothing but a pile of regurgitated sawdust. When confronted with this actual possibility, most Vancouverites quickly lose any warm fuzzy feelings they may have about all living things around them and suddenly endorse the use of chemical weapons of mass destruction.

And not just on land or in the air, but out in the water too, this taste for the exotic is having unintended consequences. Remember all those wild salmon swimming up the Fraser River every year, that mystical communing between people and fish? Well, the truth is that substantial threats exist to those wild Fraser salmon, and humans created them. Wild stocks are declining, and there is a new threat in the form of a rapidly expanding commercial salmon-farming industry, which is now introducing Atlantic salmon. The big fear is that escapees will pollute the native Pacific salmon gene pool, with potentially tragic consequences.

In addition, where young wild salmon enter the sea near fish-farm pens, there appear to be still not fully understood high levels of cross-contamination, and mortality rates are soaring. If Norway and Ireland—where fish farming has been going on for some time and the native salmon stocks are all but gone—are anything to go by, the days of Vancouver's wild salmon are likely numbered. Increasingly, at the bustling fishmongers of Granville Island Public Market, the signs over the glistening salmon read "Fresh Farmed," and fewer and fewer read "Wild." Many Vancouverites seem to have settled for this fatal compromise. You are what you eat. And apparently, according to recently released research data on farmed salmon, they are eating increasing amounts of toxins and poisonous substances in these fish.

One of the more cherished myths that Vancouverites might share with a visitor is that they can still beachcomb for food along the shorelines of the city. In fact, it is not uncommon to find oysters on the rocky shorelines of Kitsilano, Point Grey and Spanish Banks. Few locals probably realize, however, that these oysters are in fact an introduced species from Japan that has all but obliterated the native oyster.

The exotic impulse has also played out in the built environment. Vancouver's "leaky condo" scandal is an apt illustration of the city's ambivalent attitude to its natural environment. Over the past three decades, Vancouver's design and construction industries embraced the use of smooth California-style stucco as the cladding material of choice. Whole apartment buildings were coated and sealed in the cement plaster–based product synonymous with so much of Southern California's built environment. But Los Angeles is not Vancouver: or, more to the point, their climates are not the same. Stucco, when applied as part of a sealed building envelope, is a far less porous material than, say, wood siding or cedar shingles, and is much less capable of breathing in a moist climate. Although stucco on its own is not solely to blame, when used in conjunction with ever more stringent vapour

A "leaky condo" under wraps, a quintessential Vancouver viewscape.
Lance Berelowitz photo

barrier and insulation standards, the result has been the widespread failure of building envelopes.

Vancouver has suffered an epidemic of failed stucco-clad buildings: water seeping into exterior walls and trapped inside them has caused massive internal rotting of their structure. The leaky condo mess has resulted in huge legal and financial claims and a major shakeup in the local design, construction and insurance fields. It has also left a lot of ordinary homeowners with drastically diminished investments. The wholesale embrace of stucco cladding has been an object lesson in what happens when we introduce exotic or inappropriate materials or products into our environment and the environment fights back.

Dirty Little Secrets

By sea, land and air we prosper—OFFICIAL MOTTO OF THE CITY OF VANCOUVER

Sea

In recent years one of Vancouver's real success stories has been the rehabilitation of False Creek, from a stinking industrial cesspool to an attractive visual and recreational amenity. The seawater basin has gone from being surrounded by sawmills, railway yards and factories to being the locus of several marinas, parks and a manicured shoreline. Some of the city's most expensive new real estate has sprung up around its shores, offering homeowners the prospect of romantic sunsets reflecting off its sparkling surface.

But beneath that surface lies one of the city's dirty little secrets.

When Vancouver's (successful) bid was being developed to host the 2010 Olympic Winter Games, cultural organizers looked into the idea of using False Creek as a focus for the nightly public spectacles. Perhaps a water fountain in the centre of the basin, or some other animation using the water itself, as part of the show? It seemed a great idea, as the False Creek basin is in effect a giant natural amphitheatre surrounded by the city. What more compelling use of the setting could there be? But the idea was quietly abandoned when City staff pointed out that the nature and quantity of industrial pollutants that have settled to the bottom of the water basin over the past century, and their still lingering potency, made any such use of the water a dangerous risk to public health. So Vancouver's 2010 Olympic Winter Games plan now proposes to focus the nightly public spectacle on nearby B.C. Place Stadium and surrounding lands. Let sleeping dogs lie.

Land

When Vancouver is cited as the poster child of sustainable urban development—as it often is these days in North American urban planning circles—people are thinking of the downtown peninsula and the surrounding central area. Although efforts to build a more ecologically sustainable, compact urban centre are real and demonstrable, it is equally true that a large majority of Greater Vancouver's two million residents live in wasteful low-density suburban sprawl not so very different from that of most big bad North American cities. The single-family detached house on its own piece of land is a deeply held article of faith in the West. For example, most of the 390,000 residents of the City of Surrey live in a suburbia quite indistinguishable from the endless low-density sprawl surrounding so many North American cities. And Surrey is by no means alone. More than 70 per cent of the people in Greater Vancouver live in suburban settlements that are something less than the optimal compact metropolitan community of which Vancouver is held up as a shining example. And that is assuming that the entire population of the City of Vancouver is excluded from the calculation, a more than generous assumption. The reality is that outside of the central city core and a few smaller pockets of suburban nodal growth, Vancouver is squandering its usable land base almost as recklessly as the cities of the Sun Belt.

The single factor that has imposed any real limits on suburban sprawl is the Agricultural Land Reserve (ALR), instituted in the mid-1970s by a social democratic provincial government. This far-sighted policy initiative has served not only to protect much of the Lower Mainland's agricultural land base (its primary intended purpose) but also to act as a very effective urban containment barrier. However, there have been pressures on the ALR almost from its inception, with several kinds of non-agricultural uses (such as religious temples and golf courses) slipping through legal loopholes. Those pressures are mounting from real estate developers eager to spread low-density suburbs even wider. Indeed, recent amendments to the legislation augur a dangerous eroding of the ALR's inviolability. The City of Vancouver, which has no ALR-designated lands within its own boundaries, may find itself isolated on this crucial issue, as outlying municipal governments find it increasingly irresistible to chip away at the ALR. If this happens, the consequences for Vancouver's urban/environment balance could be profound.

And then there is the biggest dirty little environmental secret of them all. This is the one Vancouverites all know about but don't discuss in polite circles. Notwithstanding the litany of Vancouver's spectacular ecological attributes, the truth is that this region is fundamentally incompatible with sustainable human settlement, or at least large-scale urban settlement with a long-term predictability of survival. Vancouver sits astride a major seismic fault line in the earth's surface, and the Big One is by most accounts estimated to be imminently due.

And we are not talking about a middling or even severe earthquake. What keeps the local seismologists up at night is the very likely prospect of a catastrophic quake akin to the very worst natural disasters the world has ever seen. The Big One, when it comes, is likely to destroy a substantial portion of the metropolitan city, including major areas of urban settlement in the Fraser flood plain, such as the municipalities of Richmond (population 174,000), Delta (101,000) and large parts of Surrey. The City of Vancouver itself is largely outside of the most vulnerable area, though this is relative: it is anticipated that many buildings will crumble (especially the masonry piles in older parts of the city), that water pipes will be crushed and that the bridges linking Vancouver to the rest of Canada may well fail, leaving the city isolated.

The City has taken some measures to safeguard the most obvious infrastructure weak points: bridges have been upgraded and an emergency fire-fighting saltwater pipeline system has been installed.

Yet it is cruelly ironic that most of the City's public schools and many of its community centres, which in a triumph of optimism over pragmatism have been designated as "post-disaster assembly centres," are housed in some of the most structurally unsound buildings of all and are likely to simply pancake, burying all within. Vancouver can only hope that the Big One does not happen during school hours; not much of a strategy for survival.

Air

Vancouver's particular combination of topography, coastline, transportation patterns and urban forms "conspire to produce episodes of air pollution far worse than might be expected"[11] of a city its size. In fact, for all its professed love of the environment, Vancouver has the dubious distinction of having some of the highest air-pollution levels in North America, comparable on occasion to much larger, more industrialized centres such as Los Angeles or Toronto. This is thanks to the phenomenon of temperature inversion— a condition facilitated by the topography and prevailing winds—that traps emissions in the lower atmosphere, ironically producing those stunning red sunsets that people go into raptures over. But temperature inversion is merely the natural manifestation of air pollution. It is not the cause. Of course the real point here is that Vancouverites are apparently as addicted to their cars as any Camaro-loving Angeleno. And since Vancouver has a relatively small industrial sector, those cars are the main culprit.

It is an enduring article of faith in Vancouver that in the 1970s its enlightened citizens stopped the evil proliferation of urban freeways. This is still held out as an example of Vancouver's environmental progressiveness that sets it apart from almost all other cities in North America, which succumbed to their freeway fates. Unfortunately, the facts suggest a different, less admirable truth. According to recent data,[12] the number of cars is rising faster than the rate of population growth: by 2001 the average number of vehicles per household across the region stood at almost 1.5. This ratio is apparently still rising. And low-density single-family suburbs continue to be built on the metropolitan periphery as if there were endless land and unlimited supplies of fossil fuels.

In 1997 the City of Vancouver endorsed a wide-ranging plan[13] that attempted to readjust the transportation mix and entice people out of their cars. In 2002 City Council went even further, approving a far-reaching *Downtown Transportation Plan* that aims to rebalance the equation between cars, public transit, bicycles and pedestrians in the downtown peninsula. Cycle trips are increasing at the expense of vehicle trips, and fewer people are driving to work downtown. At least at the very centre of the metropolis, there are some positive signs.

The automobile industry is responding with new technologies. Yet even with cleaner cars, air pollution is not going to go away anytime soon. If Vancouver had fewer cars per capita, there would be less air pollution. It's as simple as that. But Vancouver's love affair with the automobile shows no signs of abating.

VANCOUVER'S APPARENTLY HAPPY COEXISTENCE with its natural environment is far more ambiguous than it would have the world (or itself) believe and is a long way from being ecologically sustainable. From exploiting environmentally fragile slopes to introducing wholly inappropriate exotic species to building on seismically unstable land, the urbanization of Vancouver has been as much an exercise in conquest as cohabitation. Far from cohabiting with nature, Vancouver stands squarely in her way.

4

The Physical Armature

Here stood Hamilton, first Land Commissioner, Canadian Pacific Railway. In the silent solitude of the primeval forest he drove a wooden stake in the earth and commenced to measure an empty land into the streets of Vancouver.—HISTORICAL PLAQUE ON HASTINGS STREET BESIDE VICTORY SQUARE

VANCOUVER'S PHYSICAL ARMATURE—its underlying infrastructure—was an act of imperial will. The untouched primordial rain forest, a Darwinian landscape of natural selection that followed the swells and dips of the land, became virtually invisible beneath the forms of urban settlement. What tools, what controlling devices, what European town-planning techniques facilitated this breakneck-speed transformation of the natural landscape?

The street-grid system forms the fundamental underlying structural armature of Vancouver's subsequent urban form. All else follows from those first measurements of the surveyor's theodolite that led to the imposition of an unstoppable grid of streets over the Burrard Peninsula humpback and its smaller outrider, the downtown peninsula.

Before the street grid, there was little in the way of human intervention, few marks on the ground, other than Native people's trails and a few small waterfront encampments.[14] It has been estimated that at the time of Captain George Vancouver's initial visit to the area in 1792, between three and five thousand Native people were living around the Burrard Peninsula, in something like five separate shoreline villages. Evidence of these pre-contact waterfront settlements has been largely obliterated, though there are still Native communities such as the Musqueam Band Reserve on the Fraser River and the Squamish Band Reserve on the northern bank of Burrard Inlet's First Narrows. An ancient midden on what was the northern bank

An artist's aerial depiction
of Vancouver in 1792, and ...
Jim McKenzie painting

... two hundred years later, the
same aerial view.
Allen Aerial Photos,
courtesy UBC Department
of Geography

of the Fraser River is still evident in today's Marpole, and Kitsilano's Vanier Park was created out of the Khatsalano Band's land.

Then in 1858 came the Royal Engineers, shock troops of the British Imperium. By 1860 they had hacked out a single isolated back route through the forest: the King's Way, a tenuous line that wound its way along a path of least resistance across the Burrard Peninsula to link the colonial capital of New Westminster on the Fraser River to Burrard Inlet. Their surveys established the main pieces of the puzzle by carving up the land into great big squared-off sections. Here would be a townsite reserve. There a military reserve. In addition to those were land parcels (called District Lots) available for entrepreneurial speculation by the first bidders. The surveyors would name, the settlers would claim and the Crown would grant. The colonial process known as pre-emption was implemented, allowing any qualified male settler to stake a claim.[15] Pre-emption frenzy followed.

Speculation in those earliest District Lots was rampant.[16] They were flipped, subdivided, resold and developed by different owners at different times. But all followed the orientation and basic pattern of rectilinear gridded streets ordained by the Royal Engineers when they established the boundaries of those first District Lots. More than a hundred years later, seemingly random, unexplainable shifts or subtle changes in the street-grid system are in fact the direct result of these earliest District Lot boundaries.

The ghosts of pre-emption remain.

A brief exploration of the salient characteristics of Vancouver's street layout begins in an unlikely location and reveals some surprising turns.

In the far northeastern sector of the future municipality, a large Government Townsite Reserve (later called Hastings Townsite), was proclaimed in 1863. The townsite was focussed on the Second Narrows and fronted onto Burrard Inlet. It was here that a town was expected to rise up, at the nearest good land access to the natural harbour of Burrard Inlet from the capital of New Westminster. However, events soon overtook this overture to city-making. The coming of the railway and the decision to extend it west as far as Coal Harbour bypassed the Government Townsite as the future centre of the city, and this remote area was to languish for many more years before being laid out and developed.

Moving westward from the Government Townsite Reserve, other District Lots were carved out of the forest along the south shore of Burrard Inlet, all, like the townsite reserve itself, oriented to the cardinal compass points. Vancouver's street grid was born.

Burrard Inlet

Stanley Park

English Bay

Kitsilano
Indian
Reserve

DL 185
(1862)

Granville
Townsite
(1870)

C.P.R.

C.P.R.

DL 541
(1885)

DL 196

DL
181

DL
182

DL
183

DL
184

Hastings St

Government
(Hastings)
Townsite
Reserve
(1863)

C I T Y   O F   V A N C O U V E R

C.P.R.

Government Reserve
DL 140
(1884)

C.P.R. Grant
DL 526 (1885)

(Kingsway)
Westminster Rd

M U N I C I P A L I T Y   O F   S O U T H   V A N C O U V E R

Musqueam
Indian
Reserve

(Granville St)
Centre St

DL 318
Eburne
(1875)

River Rd

RICHMOND

Vancouver's early land parcel pre-emptions.

Eric Leinberger. Based, by permission, on a map by Bruce Macdonald, Living History Historical Research and Consultation, Vancouver

In 1870 the colonial surveyors laid out Granville Townsite, which later came to be known as Gastown. Following the curve of the inlet's shoreline, the Granville Townsite street grid was oriented at a slight angle to the other District Lots to the east. Variant one in Vancouver's grid was established.

Beyond the Granville Townsite, moving westward onto the smaller peninsula that jutted out like an upturned thumb into the inlet, the shoreline curved up even more, and the surveyors responded by laying out District Lots at yet another, even larger, angle to the north-south line. This set up the second grid variant. Thereafter, Vancouver's downtown peninsula grid stood in singular contradistinction to the predominant street grid oriented to the cardinal compass points.

So it came to pass that three different street grids were laid out beside each other, each oriented differently from the other, within the first decade

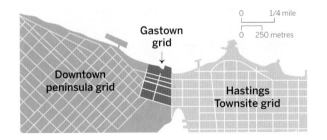

Gastown
grid

Downtown
peninsula grid

Hastings
Townsite grid

Vancouver's rotated street grids.

Eric Leinberger

Dream City

The original Gastown street grid
meets the downtown peninsula grid.

Alfred H. Siemens photo

of the city's emergence. These three grids were a primary shaper of the urban form of the city that followed. The intersection of these grids required the reconciliation of different street orientations, creating anomalous interstitial shapes that gave Vancouver its very few spatially well-defined open spaces: both Victory Square and Maple (Gassy Jack) Square occur where the grids intersect.

Another notable feature of the downtown peninsula street grid is that it is split in two by Burrard Street. This too was the result of the original District Lot surveys. Today, Burrard Street is significant in the hierarchy of downtown streets and forms the dividing line between two distinctly different grids, marking the boundary between the western and eastern halves of the downtown peninsula. The western half (District Lot 185, now the West End) was granted for development in 1862, and a street grid laid out well before the eastern half (District Lot 541) was granted to the Canadian Pacific Railway (CPR).

Thus, when Laughlan Hamilton, the CPR's first land surveyor and commonly referred to as the "father" of Vancouver, arrived to lay out the company's land parcel, he had to reconcile the already surveyed streets of District Lot 185 to the west and those of the old Granville Townsite to the east. This explains why today Burrard Street forms the dividing line between the two different downtown street-grid orientations: blocks west of the line are oriented southwest-northeast, and those on the east are southeast-northwest. As a result, most of the downtown's east-west streets do not cross Burrard Street but rather terminate there, and only every third street actually crosses Burrard Street: for example, Robson and Nelson are through streets, but Alberni and Haro are not. This had the unanticipated effect of reinforcing Burrard Street's pre-eminence as a dominant ceremonial and gateway street.

Hamilton's employer, the CPR, was understandably keen to connect the Granville Townsite's streets directly to the new Granville Street leading up from their station terminal. In order to ensure this, Hamilton aligned the first three streets (Cordova, Hastings and

Burrard Street, the dividing line between two original District Lots downtown.

Eric Leinberger

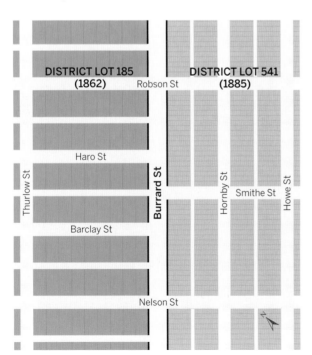

Dream City

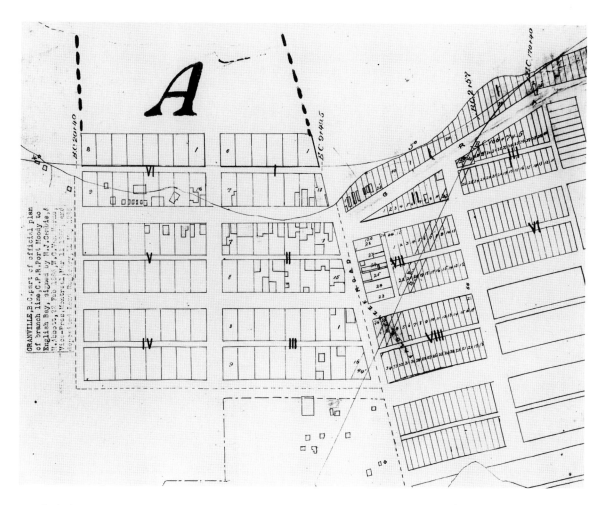

Pender) directly with the streets emerging at the western edge of the Granville Townsite. Partly because of the rotation in grids, this meant that these three streets had to be spaced more narrowly apart than the streets laid out farther south. And in order to maximize Hastings Street's commercial frontage, Hamilton rotated the mid-block lane network orientation 90 degrees to reinforce its importance. The CPR was leaving nothing to chance in developing its land grant to the optimum.

The street-grid system that subsequently developed all across Vancouver has many of the same features that these early District Lot layouts modelled.

Vancouver was surveyed and platted out using the medieval English measure known as a "chain," which is 66 feet (20 m) in length. The length and depth of blocks and individual building parcels was derived from this basic unit of measurement. The typical street block forms a rectangle approximately 4 chains or 264 feet (80.5 m) in depth on its short side; the length varies, but is most commonly 6 chains or 396 feet (120.5 m). This facilitated subdivision of the block into two parallel back-to-back rows of parcels of equal depth: 2 chains or 132 feet (40 m). A mid-block service lane 20 feet (6 m) wide was usually inserted parallel to the long side, servicing the rear of both rows. This meant that the effective depth of individual parcels, once the lane was

Part of the Canadian Pacific Railway's 1886 subdivision map, showing shifted street grids and different block orientations.
City of Vancouver Archives map P5N9

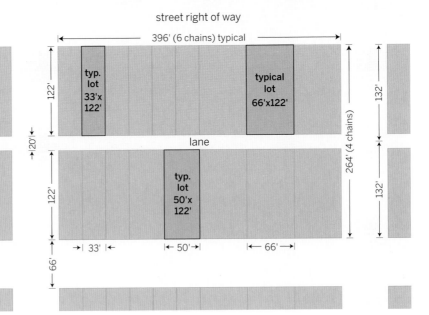

street right of way

396' (6 chains) typical

Top A typical Vancouver block diagram, based on the medieval English chain measure. Eric Leinberger

Bottom Vancouver's relentless street grid.

Eric Leinberger

122'

typ. lot 33'x 122'

typical lot 66'x122'

132'

264' (4 chains)

132'

20'

lane

122'

typ. lot 50'x 122'

132'

66'

33'

50'

66'

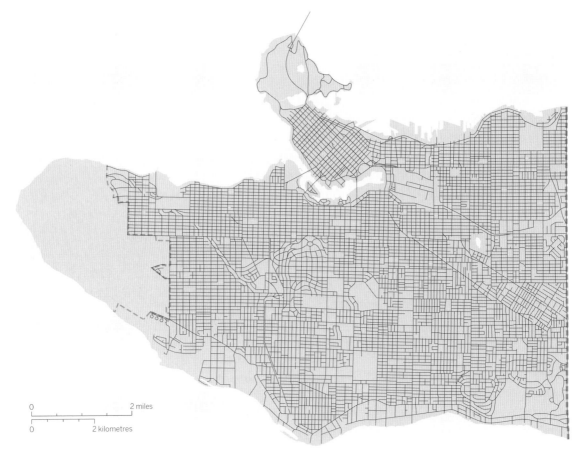

0   2 miles

0   2 kilometres

accounted for, was 122 feet (37 m). This proved to be an extremely efficient lot depth for a range of building types, from single-family detached houses to apartment buildings to high-rise towers. This dimension also neatly accommodated a double aisle of structured parking, a fortuitous circumstance that was to have great significance in the city's later urbanization.

The streets themselves were provided with a right-of-way measuring 1 chain in width. Key special streets were increased to 1½ chains, creating a simple hierarchy of street types.

And that, more or less, was it. This simple yet expedient and very efficient measuring system was responsible for almost the entire city's pattern of streets, blocks and parcels. It created the physical structure, the skeleton, on which has grown the flesh of the city.

The street grid devised by the Royal Engineers and CPR surveyors was a highly effective, if somewhat crude, way of subdividing raw land. It reflected the unsentimental military mindset of the British colonial imperative. Variations of it had worked across the breadth of the Empire, wherever the British had set up shop in new territory. What it lacked in grace or subtlety it more than made up for, in its authors' minds at least, in its promise of commercial efficiency. It had the great virtue, as they saw it, of supporting the mercantile city, one of the bases of British colonialism. And it proved to be the basic building block of real estate development in Vancouver. The grid remains resilient to this day, the structural skeleton that supports and shapes the urbanizing city.

Beyond the downtown peninsula, the typical rectangular block is usually orientated with its longer side east-west, and the shorter side north-south. This too is a result of the original District Lot surveys.

Mid-block lanes follow the dominant east-west block orientation. However, where such east-west streets intersect with major north-south arterials, the mid-block lane network is interrupted. The east-west lanes tee into lanes running parallel to and just behind the north-south arterial streets. This reinforces such streets' pre-eminence, maximizes their uninterrupted retail frontage and services their commercial uses. Thanks to this simple device, Vancouver's commercial arterials have continuous building frontage along their length, a key feature in their ongoing commercial success as retail high streets.

If Vancouver's street grid seems relentless, there are within its overarching uniformity sometimes surprising, though subtle, variations.

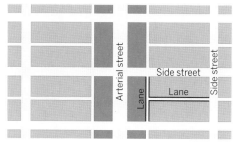

A T-junction lane typology.

Eric Leinberger

There is a wide range of different block sizes and orientations, such as the smaller blocks north of Dunsmuir Street on the downtown peninsula. Further noteworthy variations, most often in the length of blocks, are scattered throughout the city. There are clusters of longer blocks, some much longer than the typical 120.5 m (396 feet), particularly in the south in parts of Kerrisdale and most of Marpole.

And though most blocks are oriented with their longer sides east-west, there are indeed discrete, even significant sections where this pattern is reversed and the long side is oriented north-south. Again, the neighbourhood of Marpole is a prime example. Almost the entire area between Granville and Laurel streets south of 59th Avenue is oriented thus, making visible against the dominant city grain the earlier settlement of Eburne, which was laid out at the turn of the twentieth century, long before the surrounding lands were developed and Vancouver swallowed up Eburne. And many

Grid variations: the distinctive grid of the earlier Eburne settlement.
Eric Leinberger

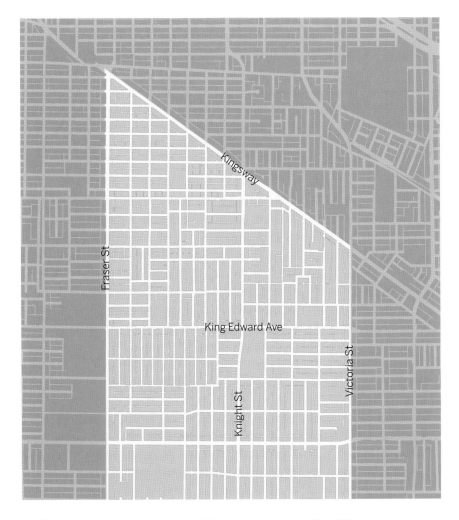

Kingsway

Fraser St

King Edward Ave

Victoria St

Knight St

Grid variations: colliding and interrupted grids.
Eric Leinberger

of the streets between Fraser and Victoria streets south of Kingsway are also oriented north-south. Here, a whole range of street morphologies and interrupted, colliding grids has resulted in great diversity, a legacy of the ad hoc speculation and uncoordinated pace of urbanization in what was then the separate—and much more anarchic—municipality of South Vancouver. From Main Street east to Victoria Drive and beyond, many smaller District Lots were independently surveyed and developed, so that a number of streets do not align. Indeed, this part of Vancouver comes closest to the more random, incomplete and diverse street patterns commonly found in older North American cities. South Vancouver remained an independent municipality right up until 1929 before finally amalgamating with Point Grey and Vancouver.

Vancouver's street grid was an abstract construct, taking little if any account of real geographic exigencies such as steep slopes or ravines, of which there were several. It would take the arrival of town-planning consultant Harland Bartholomew in 1927 to modify the grid to the landscape by introducing several judicious variations to suit the actual topography. Perhaps the most notable of these variations occurs where the street grid

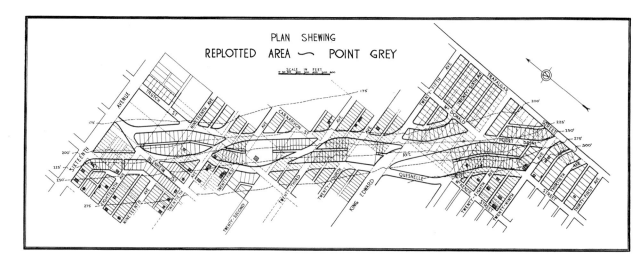

PLAN SHEWING
REPLOTTED AREA ∼ POINT GREY

confronts the Burrard Peninsula ridgeline behind Kitsilano up towards
Kerrisdale. The resulting modified road pattern follows the contours in a
complex chicane of curved roadways from 16th Avenue up to 33rd Avenue: a
kind of secret diagonal shortcut route for those in the know.

The observant reader of city maps might notice that though most
streets in Vancouver have 20-m (66-foot) wide rights-of-way, there is one
remote section where they are much wider. From Nanaimo Street east all
the way over to the municipal border with Burnaby at Boundary Road, the
north-south streets are laid out with 30-m (99-foot) wide rights-of-way,
as far south as Adanac Street. Nanaimo, Renfrew, Rupert and Boundary
Road itself all continue in their wider rights-of-way as far south as 29th
Avenue. In addition, the first five east-west streets south of Burrard Inlet are
also 30 m (99 feet) wide, as are intermittent yet regularly spaced east-west
streets farther south all the way up to 29th Avenue. This describes the shape
of the original Government (Hastings) Townsite Reserve, where it was
expected the city centre would rise, so the streets were laid out with extra
width to accommodate the anticipated traffic volumes. This area predated
the Granville Townsite, where Vancouver actually ended up growing.
Today's homeowners on the broad leafy streets overlooking the waters of
Burrard Inlet are the lucky if unintended beneficiaries of this twist of fate.
The generous outline of the Hastings Townsite no doubt registers only
subliminally for most of its latter-day inhabitants. But there it is.

And then there is the superblock bounded by Grandview Highway,
Boundary Road, 22nd Avenue and Rupert Street, in which all bets are off.

Opposite page A secret diagonal shortcut, from *A Plan for the City of Vancouver, 1929*, by Harland Bartholomew.

By permission of the Vancouver City Planning Commission

This page The Government (later Hastings) Reserve Townsite, with its 99-foot (30-m) wide streets, a stillborn downtown.

Eric Leinberger

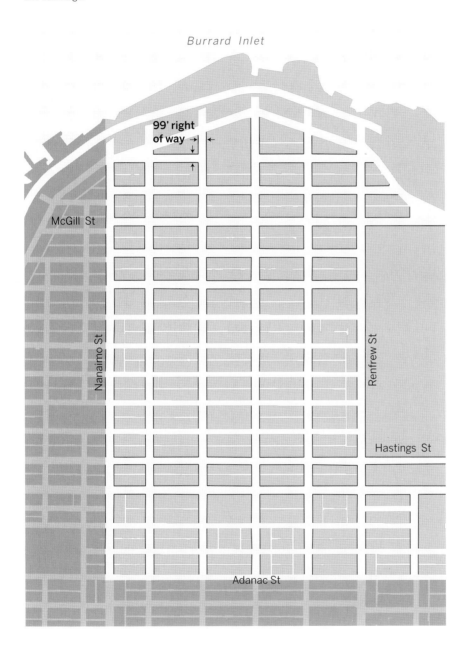

Burrard Inlet

99' right of way

McGill St

Nanaimo St

Renfrew St

Hastings St

Adanac St

One of the last portions of the Government Townsite Reserve to be released for general development, it is laid out diagonally to the city grid. At the superblock perimeter, the streets at first appear to continue the surrounding grid, but then they crank and turn into an internally consistent pattern of streets that form a series of segmented crescents. There is nothing else quite like it across the city. Finally, as the streets approach the opposite perimeter of the superblock, they straighten out again, registering like some hyperbolic infarction in the normal flatline pattern of the city grid. It's as if this section was planned in total isolation from the rest of the city. And indeed it was: Renfrew Heights was laid out as a veterans' housing subdivision after the Second World War, hence the streets named after famous battles such as Vimy, Normandy, Falaise, Anzio and Dieppe.

Another zone of aberration from the sanctity of the implacable grid is where it comes up against real three-dimensional geography and produces a site-specific response. Look what happens at the water's edge: the grid breaks down into something more parkway-like, "scenic," even sensual. South West Marine Drive, Beach Avenue, Point Grey Road and Wall Street all bend and curve in response to the adjacent shoreline, producing an altogether different experience than driving the regular straight grid streets. This special street typology was recognized recently in the City's draft *Streetscape Design Standards,* a manual that classifies streets according to their public realm role and provides design standards accordingly.

Renfrew Heights: and now for something completely different. Eric Leinberger

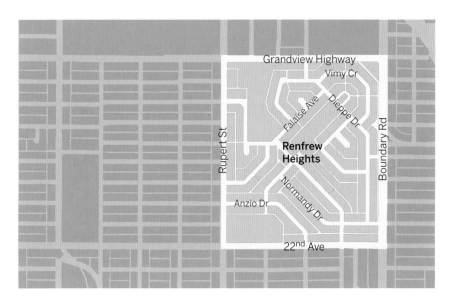

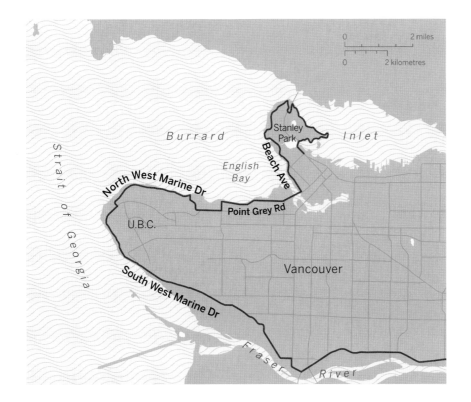

Scenic streets, where the grid meets the water's edge.
Eric Leinberger

Yet another place where the rectilinear street grid breaks down into something more dynamic, more site-specific, is where it crosses the water. The grid funnels down into a few tight straws: the bridges. The city's many bridges concentrate traffic into a singular spatial experience. There is an exhilarating sense of release as you leave the predictability of the grid and launch onto a bridge carrying you over the water. It is a bit like being shot out from a cannon. One moment you are immersed in the predictable constraints of the landlocked rectilinear grid, a stop-start form of locomotion, the next released into the air as you sail over, say, False Creek or Burrard Inlet. There is a sense of motion, of sudden freedom that—as anyone knows—you can only appreciate from a condition of constraint. It is one of the quintessential Vancouver experiences.

All in all, however, the dominant spatial experience right across the city is the grid, or variations of it. Which is not to say that, at different times in its adolescence, the city did not raise its eyes above the ground-hugging grid, did not reach for the stars, did not aspire to a more sophisticated urbanity.

5

Brushes with Destiny

Vancouver's Experience with Master-planning

We must make Plans; who looks not before, finds himself behind.
—PUBLILIUS SYRUS, 44 B.C., QUOTED IN *A PLAN FOR THE CITY OF VANCOUVER*,
1929, BY HARLAND BARTHOLOMEW

ALTHOUGH SO MUCH of Vancouver's physical layout can be traced directly
back to the earliest crude acts of pre-empting, subdividing, developing
and selling the virgin land—that is, an almost purely commercial impulse,
with financial gain at the centre of the effort—the incipient city nevertheless
had several brief brushes with attempts at producing a coherent, even
beautiful urban form: the master-plan impulse. In fact, considering how
little evidence the city evinces today of being built to a comprehensive
plan at all, a surprisingly resilient streak of the master-plan impulse runs
through its short history. Many of these initiatives were individual visions
promoted by men of passion and ambition, and most of them were never
implemented. But they reveal a little-known influence on Vancouver's
urban form, and parts of some of these plans were carried out, however
incomplete or diminished in scope.

Here then are some highlights of Vancouver's brushes with
master-planning.

The Greatest Living Authority on City Planning
In 1912, barely twenty-five years after the city's founding, a well-known British
landscape architect, Thomas Mawson, visited Vancouver. He was invited
to address the members of the Canadian Club, one of Vancouver's more elite

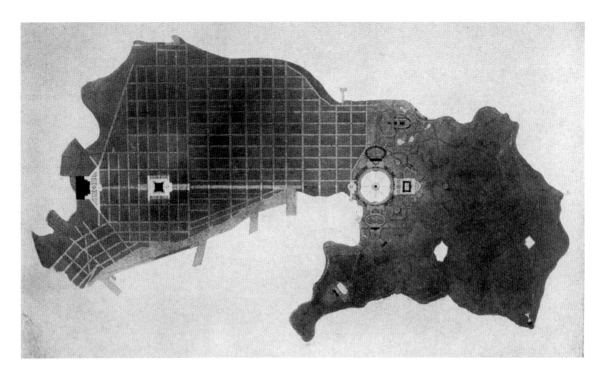

Thomas Mawson's 1913 vision of Georgia Street as Vancouver's Champs Élysée. From "Vancouver: A City of Optimists," *Town Planning Review*.

gentlemen's clubs. After being introduced to his audience as "perhaps the greatest living authority on city planning,"[17] Mawson presented a vision of grandiose proportions for the future city and suitably impressed his frontier town hosts.

Immediately noting the unusual propinquity of nature and town, Mawson proposed a dramatically integrated landscape of city and park. He sketched a grand plan that would see Georgia Street become the Champs-Élysée of Vancouver. Widened and partially pedestrianized, it would link a series of formal public spaces along its length: a large civic building and forecourt terminating its high point at the east end; a formal square carved out of four blocks in the centre of the downtown core; a large space that Mawson unselfconsciously christened "Place de la Concorde" partway down its length at the foot of the hill on Coal Harbour, and a "Grande Rond Pond"—actually Lost Lagoon redux—at the entrance to Stanley Park.

This extraordinary vision for the small mill town carved out of the Pacific Northwest rain forest clearly derived from an interpretation of civic significance far beyond what the circumstances could have reasonably suggested. With that supreme confidence in their Empire's manifest destiny that his generation exhibited, Mawson assumed Vancouver would soon take its rightful place among the great cities of the Western world, adorned with culture and the arts. Vancouver would become the Paris of the Pacific.

It was, to say the least, all a bit rich for adolescent Vancouver, yet Mawson was among the very first to recognize and articulate what has since become a central tenet of the city's public realm: that its most intense expression is not at the centre but at the periphery, near nature and specifically at the water's edge. His prediction that the Grande Rond Pond would become "the

Top Thomas Mawson's 1913
vision of the "Grande Rond
Pond" at the foot of Georgia
Street. From "Vancouver:
A City of Optimists," *Town
Planning Review.*

Bottom Thomas Mawson's
"Grande Rond Pond" plan
for Lost Lagoon. From "Vancouver: A City of Optimists,"
Town Planning Review.

great social centre of Vancouver, where rich and poor, the rough man and the spring poet, would have to rub shoulders and pass along in comfort and ease," if stripped of its Edwardian hyperbole, is as good a description of Vancouver's contemporary public life as any. Here is the proof that, from its earliest days, Vancouver's waterfront was to be the principal locus of its public life.

The City Beautiful

The City Beautiful movement was a powerful early influence on Vancouver's emergent cultured classes. Inspired by the "Great White City" designed for the 1892 Chicago World's Fair by American architect Daniel Burnham and his subsequent "Plan for Chicago," this idealistic urban planning movement heavily influenced the original 1910 plan for the new University of British Columbia's Point Grey campus, though financial realities severely diminished the campus that was eventually built.

The movement, with its neo-classical prescriptions for great formal compositions of axes, squares and public buildings, closed vistas and symmetrical arrangements, prompted a number of leading Vancouver citizens to form a local City Beautiful Association in 1912. Their principal aim was to advocate and sponsor an appropriate design for a new civic centre for their city.

The City Beautiful Association set about organizing a Vancouver civic centre design competition that produced several grand plans. The winning entry proposed an elaborately formal civic composition stretching back from the existing Victory Square on Hastings Street and encompassing the blocks bounded by Hastings, Georgia, Hamilton and Beatty streets. The plan played off the shift in street-grid angles presented by Cambie Street as it passed beside Victory Square and extended this angled portion of Cambie Street another block southwestward to intersect with Beatty Street; and it introduced a new street, mirror-angled in the opposite direction about a central axis. Where these two angled streets met, on the central axis, a formal circular public space was proposed, setting off a symmetrical composition of public buildings to include a new city hall, public library, technical college, museum, art gallery and auditorium. A series of public squares extended back along the central axis, intersecting with cross streets such as Dunsmuir and Georgia.

The plan was grandiose, formal, extravagantly self-conscious and utterly unlike anything seen before in Presbyterian Vancouver. Like Thomas

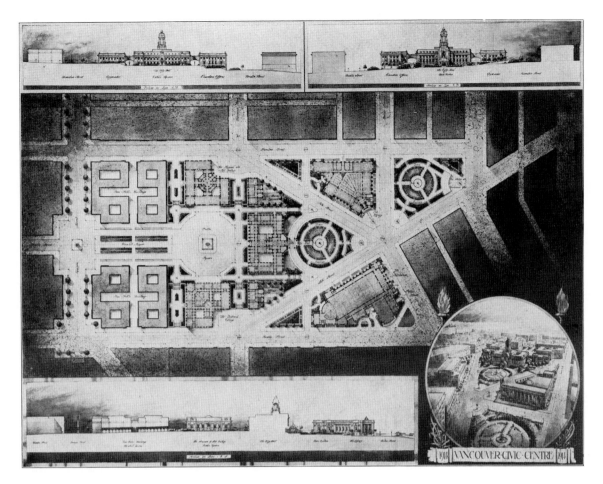

Mawson's vision, it never got off the drawing board, or at least not in its entirety. But it is interesting to note that a number of the public buildings it proposed now find themselves in this precinct of the city: the Queen Elizabeth Theatre complex, Vancouver Community College and, just across the road, the central post office and central library.

Contending with the exigencies of a remote, politically insignificant centre, Vancouver nevertheless took what it could afford from this grandiose plan, an early demonstration of the pragmatic streak that informed all subsequent episodes of city-building.

The reaction to the civic centre competition signalled a shift back to the efficiency imperative, whereby the city was planned to maximize its efficacy as a place of commerce and personal profit. Another notable British planner, Thomas Adams, was invited to Vancouver to judge the civic centre competition. He was not impressed. Rather than focussing on ceremonial public spaces, Adams argued for a comprehensive practical plan for the city, identifying "the best lines for main arterial roads, desirable railway and harbour improvements, suitable industrial areas and general provisions for convenience, amenity and proper sanitation."[18]

Hardly a vision to light the fires of the Canadian Club continentalists, but certainly a prescription more closely in line with Vancouver's reality.

The winning submission of the civic centre competition in 1913, from the Vancouver Civic Centre Report of Plans Committee, 1915. Courtesy UBC Fine Arts Library

Even more to the point, these words could very well describe the dominant mantra of planning in the intervening years since they were uttered, right up to this day.

Not long after the civic centre competition, the Vancouver City Beautiful Association became the Vancouver Planning and Beautifying Association. Its ambitions reduced, the association focussed for a while on improving Burrard Street as one of Vancouver's pre-eminent ceremonial routes and eventually faded away altogether, along with its grand plans for the city.

The 1913 civic centre competition may well have been the apogee of urban design competitions in Vancouver. Since then, design competitions have not featured prominently in Vancouver's urban planning history. Indeed, unlike many other contemporary European and American cities that have used the design competition as a powerful tool for improving the quality of their urban environments, the City of Vancouver appears to have deliberately avoided embracing this unpredictable and sometimes uncontrollable method of shaping its future in favour of a more controlled process of negotiating its urban form. Urban planners and architects have always been viewed with some degree of suspicion at City Hall.

Our Man from Missouri: The Harland Bartholomew Story
In the immediate post–First World War years, the City of Vancouver did not have the power to actually impose any planning regulations on private development. But the adjacent municipality of Point Grey had shown the way by passing Canada's first-ever zoning bylaw in 1922. And the City already had at least one example of the benefits of carefully regulated planning: the manicured suburb of Shaughnessy Heights, to which the CPR had applied contemporary principles of town planning.

It was not until 1925 that the provincial government passed legislation authorizing municipalities to establish planning advisory bodies. Thereafter, things moved quickly. Vancouver City Council appointed an advisory planning commission, made up of important business figures of the day, in 1926.

The Vancouver Town Planning Commission and its equivalent in Point Grey (then a separate municipality) quickly took up the call for a comprehensive plan to address utilitarian issues of functional efficiency, growth, commerce, traffic congestion, health and amenities. The subtext to all this was City Council's determination to maintain and enhance property values for its backers and a growing middle class. By August of that year, after inviting proposals from several Canadian and American town-planning firms, the Town Planning Commission had hired Harland Bartholomew and Associates of St. Louis, Missouri.

This decision was to prove far-reaching for Vancouver's urban form. Bartholomew had a prominent reputation, having undertaken plans for several large Midwest North American cities. He had strong ideas about what was appropriate in planning a city and was not afraid to impose these. He compared Vancouver's patterns of urban development with a set of previously established planning principles that he had tried and tested elsewhere. Detailed plans were then developed to meet these principles, covering a series of key topics that included land use, the street system, public transit, rail and water transportation, recreation and civic art.

Bartholomew presented *A Plan for the City of Vancouver* in December 1928 to the Town Planning Commission. It was an awesome and comprehensive document covering almost every conceivable aspect of planning the growth of the city for the next fifty years. It laid out detailed recommendations for land-use zoning, an arterial street and public transit network, recreation facilities and a series of scenic "Pleasure Drives." The plan addressed such diverse issues as the visual appearance of residential properties, the provision of schools and park space, local neighbourhood shops and services, the replatting of certain streets to take better account of the existing steep topography and a plan for the port. He also proposed a new civic centre and a full range of improvements to bridges, roads, monuments and sidewalks. In short, he offered Vancouver the opportunity to reinvent itself.

Bartholomew's plan was daunting. It was also somewhat formulaic, relying on principles he had developed and tested previously. If it all seemed a little too similar to plans he had prepared for other cities, none of the hard-nosed businessmen on the Town Planning Commission appeared to notice, or if they did, they said nothing.

Vancouver City Council never formally adopted the Bartholomew Plan, but it did carry out some elements of it. And—setting aside the original plans of the Canadian Pacific Railway's surveyors—this was the first (and last) time Vancouver actually followed a city-wide master plan.

Many of Bartholomew's big moves were never implemented, such as a bridge crossing False Creek that would have directly linked Robson Street and the Kingsway, or the radial street pattern he proposed for the area where Oakridge Mall stands today. Nor did his proposal for an extravagant civic centre overlooking English Bay beside the future Burrard Bridge ever get off the drawing board. But many of his ideas have become a part of the

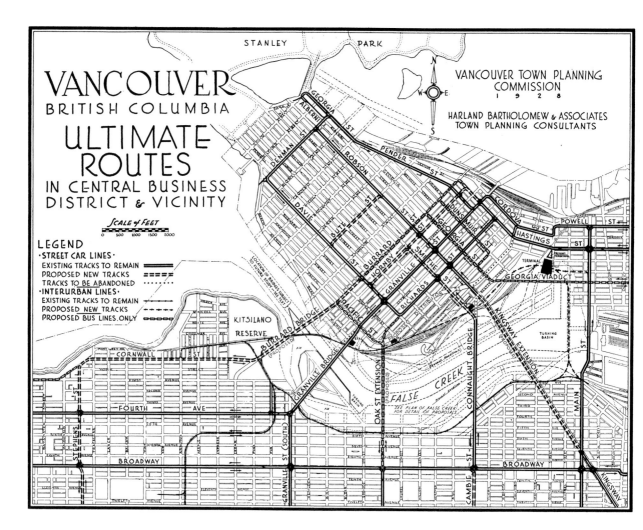

"Ultimate Routes in
Central Business District
& Vicinity" from Harland
Bartholomew's *A Plan
for the City of Vancouver,
1929*. By permission of the
Vancouver City Planning
Commission

spatial vocabulary of the city and have seen at least partial physical expression. For example, the network of crosstown arterial streets, the location of neighbourhood shops and the distribution of community recreation centres, major parks and playing fields all closely echo Bartholomew's recommendations. Indeed, his codifying of the city's land uses based on the electric streetcar routes has had a profound impact on land-use zoning and the public transit system. In addition, his concept of a network of green Pleasure Drives is largely intact, resulting in the generously landscaped parkways or central medians of King Edward Avenue, Cambie Street and Beach Avenue, to name a few. And his conception of the city's beachfront as a key component in the public commons was to find full expression decades later.

The Bartholomew Plan has left an indelible mark on the patterns and fabric of urban form in Vancouver, more so perhaps than any other single planning initiative.

City of Destiny: Gerry McGeer and Vancouver City Hall

Two-time mayor Gerry McGeer was one of Vancouver's most colourful leaders, and he had a remarkable vision for his city. In a stirring speech

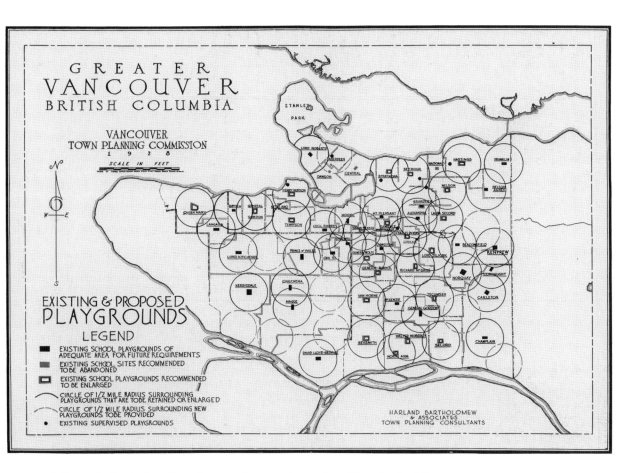

"Existing & Proposed
Playgrounds" from
Harland Bartholomew's
*A Plan for the City
of Vancouver, 1929*.
By permission of the
Vancouver City Planning
Commission

delivered after being elected mayor in 1934, he spoke of how he had "never lost the inspiration of the picture of Vancouver that came to me so many years ago. It was the enthrallment of the City of Destiny."[19] To fulfil that destiny he saw as his mission. He had always passionately advocated the building of a new city hall, commensurate with Vancouver's growing status as a leading Canadian city. The new city hall would be sited on Cambie Street, on the southern slopes of False Creek, rather than downtown, and would be complemented by other civic buildings. Cambie Street would become a ceremonial civic corridor that linked city hall northward to downtown Victory Square via a new bridge over False Creek, and southward by a grand boulevard up to the foot of Little Mountain (now Queen Elizabeth Park), where a public sports complex would be located.

McGeer got the new city hall, but not the rest of his vision.

Vancouverites had been debating the location for a new city hall for some time already. The Central School site just south of Victory Square, proposed in the City Beautiful Association's earlier civic centre competition, had been narrowly defeated in a public referendum at the same time as McGeer was first elected mayor. This was most convenient for the new mayor. Shortly after his election, McGeer appointed three "wise men" to select a location for the proposed new city hall: Chief Justice Aulay Morrison, Dr. L.S. Klinck, president of the University of British Columbia, and G.L. Thornton Sharp,

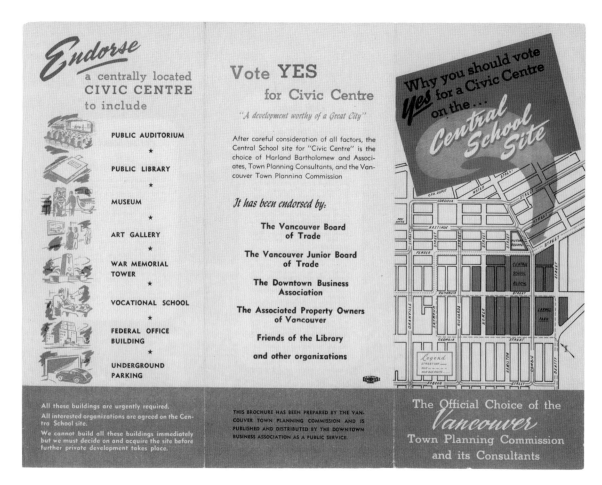

Endorse
a centrally located
CIVIC CENTRE
to include

PUBLIC AUDITORIUM

★

PUBLIC LIBRARY

★

MUSEUM

★

ART GALLERY

★

WAR MEMORIAL
TOWER

★

VOCATIONAL SCHOOL

★

FEDERAL OFFICE
BUILDING

★

UNDERGROUND
PARKING

All these buildings are urgently required.
All interested organizations are agreed on the Central School site.
We cannot build all these buildings immediately but we must decide on and acquire the site before further private development takes place.

Vote YES
for Civic Centre
"A development worthy of a Great City"

After careful consideration of all factors, the Central School site for "Civic Centre" is the choice of Harland Bartholomew and Associates, Town Planning Consultants, and the Vancouver Town Planning Commission

It has been endorsed by:

**The Vancouver Board
of Trade**

**The Vancouver Junior Board
of Trade**

**The Downtown Business
Association**

**The Associated Property Owners
of Vancouver**

Friends of the Library

and other organizations

THIS BROCHURE HAS BEEN PREPARED BY THE VANCOUVER TOWN PLANNING COMMISSION AND IS PUBLISHED AND DISTRIBUTED BY THE DOWNTOWN BUSINESS ASSOCIATION AS A PUBLIC SERVICE.

Why you should vote
Yes for a Civic Centre
on the...
Central School Site

The Official Choice of the
Vancouver
Town Planning Commission
and its Consultants

A flyer put out in 1934 by the Vancouver Town Planning Commission, urging people to vote for the proposed new civic centre.

By permission of the Vancouver City Planning Commission

one of Vancouver's most distinguished contemporary architects and chairman of the Town Planning Commission. They were directed to consider several sites, including the Central School, the King George High School grounds on Burrard Street and, McGeer's favourite, Strathcona Park on Cambie Street at West 12th Avenue.

There was never any real doubt which site they would choose. On 5 June 1935 City Council approved the panel's recommendation that the new city hall be built in Strathcona Park.

This site had a prominent elevation with panoramic views of downtown Vancouver and the North Shore mountains, and any large building on it would dominate the city skyline. Also, apparently in deference to the sensitivities of the recently amalgamated municipality of South Vancouver, this more southerly site was preferred over one downtown. Whatever the reasons, Vancouver was the first major Canadian city to locate its city hall in the suburbs rather than downtown. It still is.

Consistent with the demonstrated suspicions of previous city councils about unpredictable design competitions, McGeer's City Council chose not to hold a competition for the design of the new city hall. Instead, McGeer personally selected Fred Townley of Townley & Matheson Architects, a well-established Vancouver firm.

Mayor Gerry McGeer's
new Vancouver City Hall,
as envisaged by architect
Fred Townley.
City of Vancouver Archives
P52.6 N36.6

Townley's design was a masterpiece of art deco. Taking full advantage of its elevated site, the building crowned the slope of the former park, rising well above any other neighbouring buildings, and was visible from many parts of the city. Set on a raised podium overlooking downtown, the building rose in a series of symmetrical stepped terraces, culminating in a square central tower twelve storeys high, at the top of whose four faces were set four large neon clocks. Not content with locating its city hall in a residential suburb far from the commercial centre, Vancouver is probably the only city in the world to have bright pink neon clocks adorn its seat of municipal power; a fitting symbol perhaps of the quirky nature of local politics.

But what of the second part of McGeer's vision?

It had to wait a decade until his second term as mayor in 1946, after McGeer had pursued a varied political career, including a stint as a Member of Parliament. McGeer turned his thoughts once more to his "City of Destiny" and asked his old friend Fred Townley to draw up McGeer's vision for a larger civic precinct and formal ceremonial route. It is a remarkable drawing.

The view, from a fictional vantage point high above Little Mountain, looks north towards downtown Vancouver and shows the recently completed city hall paired with a mirror-image edifice on the other side of Cambie Street—planned as a civic centre and complete with auditorium and public

Mussolini by the sea? Mayor McGeer's grandiose vision for
Vancouver as the City of Destiny. Fred Townley Architect drawing
published in *Mayor Gerry*, by David Ricardo Williams

library. Cambie Street itself is transformed into a wide ceremonial boulevard sweeping out of the downtown peninsula, carried across False Creek on a grand new suspension bridge, and passing the city hall and its twin. At King Edward Avenue (West 25th Avenue), Cambie widens out even more, and a broad central boulevard is introduced as the route sweeps up to the base of Little Mountain. Here, the formal Cambie Street axis terminates in an Olympic-scale, circular open-air stadium and a huge outdoor swimming pool nestled into the carefully groomed slopes of the park.

This grandiose design may be read as a visual metaphor linking and balancing the urban trilogy of commercial power (the downtown business district), political power (City Hall) and individual power (the sports centre). Less charitably, the entire ensemble is eerily reminiscent of similar plans built by Benito Mussolini and of plans drawn up by Hitler's chief architect, Albert Speer. It is known that McGeer admired certain aspects of the National Socialist platform.

Cambie Street did indeed get a new bridge across False Creek, though it is a far more prosaic structure than the one envisaged by McGeer and Townley. The Cambie Street boulevard also came to pass and is today one of Vancouver's most cherished street landscapes. The city hall never did get its mirror image, though the site opposite did get redeveloped as the City Square project, which goes some way towards counterbalancing the mass of the city hall. And the Little Mountain sports complex was stillborn, though the hill was developed as one of Vancouver's most elegant urban parks. The city hall continues to dominate the view from its leafy summit.

McGeer would probably not be too impressed, but then he would not have been surprised either. Vancouver has a habit of paring down the more baroque notions for enhancing its urban form.

Greening Downtown: An Urban Design Plan
for the Georgia/Robson Corridor
After McGeer's era, a more pragmatic-minded planning ethos took over City Council and has held sway almost ever since. Master-planning was replaced with more modest, practical, smaller increments of urban change. Continuity and stability were favoured over grand gestures. Vancouver reverted to type.

One of the last gasps at trying to understand and manipulate the urban form of the city at something approaching a large scale ironically closed the circle by returning to the site of Thomas Mawson's original grand vision: Georgia Street. In 1982 the City's activist Director of Planning Ray Spaxman hired the up-and-coming Toronto urban design firm of Baird Sampson Associates. George Baird had made a national reputation for himself as a provocative and thoughtful commentator on the Canadian city and was known to Spaxman from the latter's time spent working in Toronto.

Everyone concerned seems to have recognized that Georgia Street was Vancouver's most important ceremonial street. And everyone seemed to agree that it was not performing up to par and badly needed help. Georgia Street had long suffered from the benign neglect that is pervasive in Vancouver's public realm. Where was Mawson when you needed him?

Baird's mandate was narrowly defined. Not for him any new civic centres, town squares or grand plazas. The *Greening Downtown* study was more about incremental improvements and largely cosmetic enhancements to an established street pattern. What Baird and his team did do, however,

Greening Downtown, a 1982 study by Baird Sampson Architects, for the Vancouver City Planning Department.

By permission of the Vancouver City Planning Department

was apply a rigorous urban design analysis to the centre of the city, for perhaps the first time ever.

Greening Downtown recognized a fundamental characteristic of Vancouver's urban morphology: the notion of the "double cross" pairing of key perpendicular streets. Baird pointed out that Georgia Street forms a pair with Burrard Street, the other major ceremonial street that, like Georgia Street, was laid out on an extra-wide 30-m (99-foot) right-of-way rather than the usual 20 m (66 feet). The report suggested a "strengthening and enhancement of the image of Georgia Street"[20] as a memorable gateway route into the downtown peninsula. And it advised doing this primarily through a landscape pattern, along with urban design guidelines for adjacent development and "a proposal to encourage the location of appropriate institutional uses along Georgia Street."

Greening Downtown called for intensified tree-planting along the length of Georgia Street and a "green court" urban typology for new developments exploiting the adjacent sloped grades. It made some very modest suggestions for strengthening either end of the street axis: a reconstruction of the Lost Lagoon fountain at the west end, and the placement of a "pylon" beside the Georgia Street Viaduct at the east end.

Some of the ideas of Baird et al. have been adopted in varying degrees. Several new developments in the western sector of Georgia Street have indeed delivered up creditable variants of the green court idea. The Bayshore site has been comprehensively redeveloped for two whole blocks along Georgia. And a special streetscape standard, complete with regular rows of trees, was established for the entire length, implemented gradually as development has taken place. A recent widening of the five westernmost blocks to accommodate new bicycle lanes and the reconfiguration of the street alignment into Stanley Park was accompanied by the introduction of enhanced new streetscape elements, including custom-designed street poles and lighting with granite bases. And tree-planting continues.

But other than the new central library near its eastern end, Georgia Street has not attracted the concentration of institutional facilities that Baird had recommended, nor has the eastern axis been enhanced in any way as he proposed. And the street continues in its established function as a major traffic arterial with little attraction for the pedestrian: it has yet to become Vancouver's answer to the Champs-Élysée, no doubt to the disappointment of Thomas Mawson's ghost.

Greening Downtown represents the ascendance of incremental pragmatism over sweeping vision.

VANCOUVER IS NOW past the point where the broad brushstroke approach can be imposed. It no longer looks to master planners to provide answers to its ongoing questions of civic art. It is growing up and finding that compromise and flexible accommodation with what has gone before is the true nature of change in a maturing city. Layers of urbanism are beginning to accrete.

6

The Transportation Palimpsest

TO BORROW AN APT TERM from Reyner Banham (who of course applied it to Los Angeles),[21] much of Vancouver's emergent urban form can be read as the trailing ghosts of its early transportation systems: the Transportation Palimpsest.

Vancouver's period of early growth parallels the invention of the internal combustion engine: thus, it is one of the world's few cities planned and built for the automobile virtually from the outset. This has had a profound impact on its layout and urban form. Unlike much older cities that predate the Industrial Revolution, Vancouver has no tight "old town" core where the randomly intersecting, winding pathways of animal-drawn conveyances negotiating the topography set the patterns for future road networks; its street system was essentially imposed on the landscape in one fell swoop.

Like Los Angeles, Vancouver's transportation palimpsest has several layers, which is one reason the city is so spread out. Because right from its beginning the city relied on both local and regional rail, then buses and finally cars, and never primarily on walking or animal-drawn transport, development was more evenly diffused over a large area, spreading out along with successive transportation technologies. There is no obvious transportation hierarchy with a central core of tightly intersecting routes and systems trailing off towards the periphery; rather, Vancouver is a model of transportation egalitarianism. From a transportation-infrastructure capacity perspective (that is, putting aside levels of traffic and looking at the physical network of routes), it is almost as easy (or as difficult) to move around in the suburbs as it is in the centre. This mirrors, in part, the 1996 *Livable Region Strategic Plan,* which has promoted several Regional Town Centre nodes rather than reinforcing downtown Vancouver as the only or even principal node.

First Lineaments

In the beginning was the King's Way (later Kingsway), the colonial-era trail that directly linked the first capital of British Columbia at New Westminster on the north bank of the Fraser River to the nearest safe ocean moorage on Burrard Inlet. Intended initially as a strategic back-door escape route from the capital in the event of a river-borne attack, Kingsway followed the line of least resistance across the densely forested hump of Burrard Peninsula, weaving diagonally across the peninsula up to False Creek and Burrard Inlet. It was for some time the only road (if so definitive a term may be used to describe what was by all accounts a rudimentary trail) across the peninsula.

Kingsway is still here today, slicing diagonally across the rectilinear street grid from False Creek all the way out to New Westminster. As such, it makes a dramatic counterpoint to the grid's regular north-south, east-west geometry. Where Kingsway intersects the grid, it has created a series of irregular, distinctive public spaces.

This rough-hewn and now somewhat shop-soiled yet dramatic remnant of the city's earliest transportation route scribes the first line, quite literally, of Vancouver's transportation palimpsest.

Soon after, a number of other strategic trails were hacked through the forest, radiating out from New Westminster: the North Road up to Burrard Inlet, the Douglas Road to the New Brighton landing (also on Burrard Inlet)

The original King's Way (later Kingsway) predated the orthogonal street grid.

Eric Leinberger

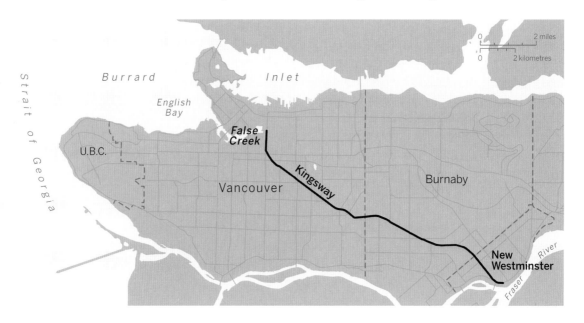

and a westerly route downriver along the north bank of the Fraser River. These too all remain today—now much straightened out and regularized of course—as the earliest lineaments in the urban road network.

Streetcar

The next layer in the transportation palimpsest was the urban electric streetcar and its closely related variant, the interurban railway between communities.

Vancouver had streetcars ten years before New York. The western city's growing street grid seemed tailor-made for these slow-moving, yet versatile, low-impact urban transporters. The electric streetcar system was based on a web of intersecting routes, rather than a linear system connecting nodes.

The city's first streetcar line opened on 28 June 1890, a mere four years after Vancouver's incorporation. The line followed Westminster Avenue (now Main Street) from 1st Avenue north to Powell Street, then branched east along Powell to Campbell Avenue, and west via Cordova Street to Granville Street. Soon it ran south on Granville as far as Pacific Avenue.

The electric streetcar caught on quickly and expanded rapidly. A year later, in 1891 it was extended south on Westminster Avenue to 9th Avenue (now Broadway), and across False Creek over the first Granville Bridge to Fairview, thus forming a large inverted U. The loop was soon closed along Broadway. This circuit helped open up Vancouver's earliest residential suburbs: Strathcona, Mount Pleasant and Fairview.

By 1898 streetcars ran into the West End and Stanley Park via Hastings and Pender streets, and further rapid expansion followed. In 1901 City Council consolidated numerous individual franchises into one city-wide system operated by the recently formed British Columbia Electric Railway Company. The following decade saw the streetcar network's greatest growth, with the line out to Mountain View Cemetery, the Kitsilano line out along West 4th Avenue and lines in North Vancouver. Many of these new routes preceded urban development and in some cases were even cut through virgin forest. To entice people to settle these areas, the B.C. Electric Railway Company offered cheap lots and one year of free streetcar service, and it worked.

More new lines soon reached as far east as Hastings Park (via Hastings Street) and Grandview (via Kingsway), south to Marpole (via Oak Street) and Kerrisdale (via Dunbar Street and 41st Avenue), and west to Point Grey (via West 10th Avenue and West 4th Avenue). Lines were extended south along Main Street, Fraser Street and Victoria Drive, connecting to the New

Westminster interurban along the Fraser River. Vancouver's suburban residential development largely followed the streetcar lines, with local shops and services opening along the key routes in Mount Pleasant, Kerrisdale, Kitsilano, Point Grey, Cedar Cottage, Collingwood and Hastings Park. By 1912, Vancouver's basic arterial retail and residential neighbourhood land-use patterns were established, largely due to the streetcar.

It is instructive to note that this pattern of land use predated by many years the introduction of land-use zoning and quickly helped establish main shopping streets, local neighbourhood retail service areas and the first residential suburbs. The streetcar network reinforced the emerging street grid and established an egalitarian spread of services and amenities throughout the growing city. The development of a number of streetcar routes into neighbourhood service arterials remains a defining characteristic of Vancouver's urban form, and these high streets have proved remarkably enduring, unlike the streetcar itself.

One of the more extraordinary historical images of Vancouver is a view of the handsome B.C. Electric Railway building erected at Hastings and Carrall streets in 1911–12 to house the increasing number of streetcars. The photo shows a streetcar emerging from (or perhaps entering) an opening in the side of the four-square, five-storey building and crossing the sidewalk, where some pedestrians wait for it to pass. Still standing to this day, the building was the hub of one of the most extensive urban transit systems in existence at the time. Seamlessly integrated into the urban fabric, as this photo so eloquently illustrates, the streetcar was an integral part of Vancouver's early public realm.

By 1914, when the First World War broke out, the system had grown to 232 streetcars. And by 1919, at the end of the conflict, a web of more than 160 km (100 miles) of track connected almost every part of the city, scribing the outline of its future growth patterns. Vancouver had come of age as a modern city.

Unknown to its many riders, this proved to be the peak of the streetcar system in Vancouver.

In 1923 the very first electric trolley bus appeared on the streets of the city, heralding the beginning of the decline of the streetcar system. As more and more buses came into service and more and more families bought newfangled automobiles, streetcar ridership began to fall. It continued to do so steadily over the next several years, despite renewed investment in bigger and more comfortable streetcars. The private automobile was

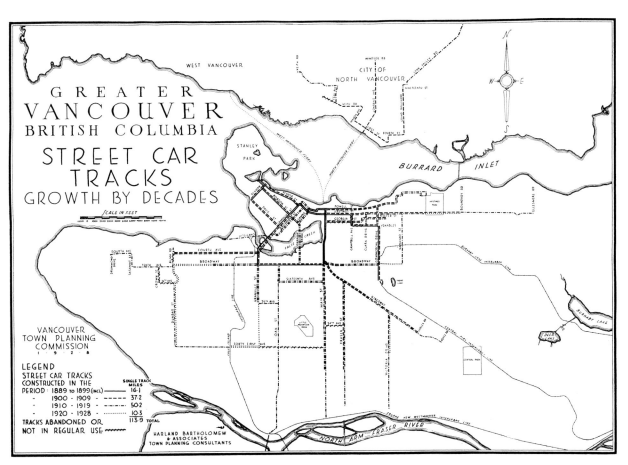

Top Vancouver's streetcar track growth from Harland Bartholomew's *A Plan for the City of Vancouver, 1929.* By permission of the Vancouver City Planning Commission

Bottom The B.C. Electric Railway building.
Vancouver Public Library 22735A

beginning to exert its irresistible, fatal attraction. Only war slowed down its increasing predominance. By the end of the Second World War, Vancouver's streetcar system was more than fifty years old and in need of significant upgrades. At the same time, trolley buses were becoming widely available, and at a fraction of the cost of a fixed-rail system. The B.C. Electric Company faced a choice: streetcar or trolley bus, either of which would still use its electricity. After test-driving a trolley bus borrowed from Seattle, the company's directors chose the latter, moving from rails to rubber. It was a fateful decision.

In April 1955 the last streetcar trundled down Hastings Street East, ending sixty-five years of streetcar service in Vancouver. In its stead, Vancouver now has one of the largest urban trolley bus systems in the world, built almost route for route on the electric streetcar palimpsest.

The streetcar may be gone, but its legacy and profound influence on Vancouver's urban patterns remains.

Interurban Railway

Vancouver introduced North America's first true interurban railway service connecting regional communities. This service was a corollary to the urban streetcar and was run by the same company, the British Columbia Electric Railway. Although the interurban used the same gauge tracks as the electric streetcars, it had larger, more ornate cars for the comfort of passengers on the longer routes and was the earliest intimation of Vancouver's ambition to become the centre of a regional metropolis.

In 1891, barely five years after the incipient city had been proclaimed on the shores of Burrard Inlet, the first interurban, officially dubbed the Central Park Line, began service between Vancouver and New Westminster. This heralded a shift in the balance of power between the older capital of New Westminster and the upstart new city of Vancouver, a trend that was to accelerate in the coming years.

By 1902 a second interurban—the Lulu Island Line—was operating southward to the fishing village and canneries of Steveston, running along Canadian Pacific Railway tracks (now the Arbutus railway corridor through Kerrisdale and Marpole), with passenger stations in Shaughnessy/Kitsilano and Eburne (now Marpole). In 1909 a spur line branched off from the Lulu Island Line at Eburne and ran along the north bank of the Fraser River all the way upriver to New Westminster. By 1911 yet another interurban, the Burnaby Lake Line, was extended eastward from Commercial Drive

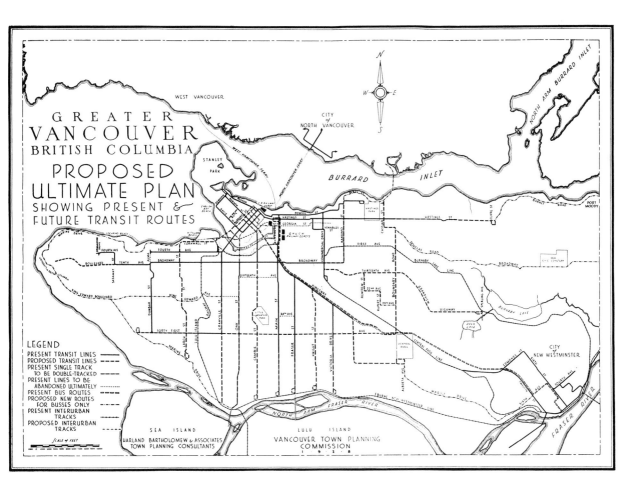

through Burnaby and on to New Westminster. This gave the suburban community of Burnaby access to no less than three interurban lines.

Together, the interurban routes and the streetcar lines gave early Vancouver a comprehensive and startlingly sophisticated urban transit system that set the stage for, and facilitated, much of the city's subsequent growth. In many ways, this era was the apogee of efficient urban transit in the city, providing as it did convenient access to regular service from almost every area.

In the post–Second World War years, as the regional road system and private car ownership expanded exponentially, the interurban railway, like the streetcar, was increasingly supplanted by the efficient, economical bus and the private automobile. One by one, the interurban lines were abandoned: the old Burnaby Lake Line right-of-way eventually was used by the Trans-Canada Highway, and the Eburne/New Westminster line reverted back to strictly freight use. The last interurban railway service was finally terminated in September 1958.

The old interurban stations have long since disappeared, though an obscure little railway shed—its purpose apparently forgotten—still stood until recently at the bottom of Milton Street in deepest South Vancouver, alongside the old Fraser spur track on the Eburne Mill site: just perhaps a remnant of this early transportation network.

The "Ultimate Plan" of existing and public transit routes from Harland Bartholomew's *A Plan for the City of Vancouver, 1929*. By permission of the Vancouver City Planning Commission

SkyTrain

For several decades after the demise of Vancouver's last interurban, there was no equivalent to the regional transit service that it had provided. Finally, by the time Vancouver's date with Expo 86 approached (a world's fair whose theme was transportation), it had become glaringly obvious that the baby had indeed been thrown out with the bathwater and that the city needed a new regional public transit system. What emerged was SkyTrain, an automated, advanced light rail system touted as the latest in rapid transit. SkyTrain was promoted by the provincial government and its designers as the high-tech answer to Vancouver's increasing regional traffic congestion, air pollution and suburban sprawl. It was going to get people out of their cars and into trains that would move them effortlessly and quickly on elevated rail lines, watched over from an operations centre computer screen, with no unionized drivers or ticket collectors to threaten inconvenient job action. And, because SkyTrain would traverse municipal boundaries, it would become an agent in shaping regional urban growth: the line and its stations would be strategically located to support the Regional Town Centre concept of the *Livable Region Strategic Plan*.

To some degree, it did both of these things.

The first section of SkyTrain opened in 1986 to coincide with Expo 86. The Expo Line ran from downtown Vancouver out along the old Central Park interurban route through Burnaby's Metrotown (one of the *Livable Region Strategic Plan*'s designated Regional Town Centres) and on to downtown New Westminster (another Regional Town Centre). Echoes of the interurban indeed. *Plus ça change, plus c'est la même chose.*

A second phase extended the Expo Line across the Fraser River and into the hinterlands of suburban Surrey to terminate at Whalley Town Centre, yet another designated Regional Town Centre. Only in 2003 did Whalley get an edifice remotely appropriate to its ambitious new name of Surrey Central. The architecturally impressive Surrey Central City project[22]—part office tower, part shopping mall makeover—rises incongruously out of its amorphous suburban context, a harbinger perhaps of future urbanization.

Then, in 2001, just about in time for a critical provincial election that the New Democratic Party government of the day was desperate to win (but didn't), the ribbon was cut on a second SkyTrain line. This, the so-called Millennium Line, ran from New Westminster into Burnaby and back to Vancouver, completing a loop that connects the Expo Line to the Expo Line.

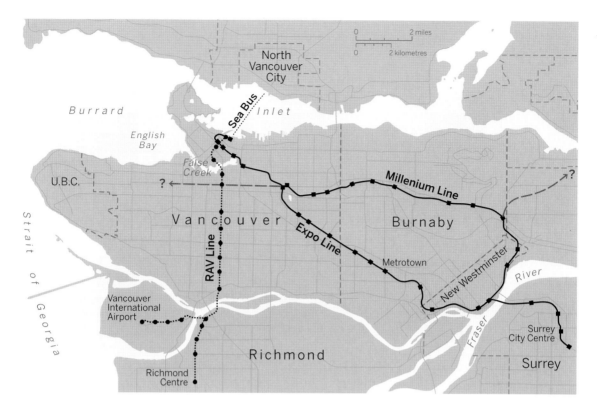

The SkyTrain Expo and
Millenium Lines and the
proposed Richmond-
Airport-Vancouver
(RAV) Line follow in the
interurban's footsteps.
Eric Leinberger

This line, too, roughly follows part of an old interurban, the Burnaby Lake Line, thus helping to re-create the original interurban network.

Out of twenty stations on the entire Expo Line, nine—fewer than half—are located within the City of Vancouver. Of the twelve stations on the Millennium Line, only three are within the City of Vancouver, including the interchange station adjacent to the existing Broadway/Commercial Drive Expo Line station. Put another way, twenty of the thirty-two SkyTrain stations are in neighbouring municipalities. This is clearly a system focussed primarily on the region and not on the centre.

Today, most of the gleaming new Millennium Line stations stand in splendid isolation, surrounded by low-density suburban sprawl, still awaiting the urban response intimated in their futuristic design. But will it happen?

In the latest chapter of Vancouver's unfinished quest to get back to the future of an interurban regional transit network, TransLink, the regional transportation authority, in December 2004, after several votes back and forth, finally approved proceeding with the controversial proposed Richmond-Airport-Vancouver Rapid Transit Line, more commonly known by its acronym RAV. While not following the exact original interurban route (which used the Arbutus corridor), the eighteen-station, 20-km (65-mile) RAV Line essentially will replicate the service the interurban once provided, connecting Vancouver and Richmond, though it will not actually go as far south as Steveston. Instead, it will provide a high-speed spur connection to Vancouver International Airport, which has, over the past decade, spectacularly reinvented itself as a major global gateway.

But the RAV Line initiative was (and remains) controversial because, among other reasons, many people are afraid that its high capital costs could bleed dry the rest of the regional and, most importantly, the local, public transit system. Most worrisome for some of its fiercest critics is what this focus might do to Vancouver's aging trolley bus system, now requiring the same kind of investment upgrades that its predecessor, the streetcar, faced after the Second World War. The fear of course is that high-profile, high-cost RAV-type lines will spell the demise of the trolley bus, just as definitively as the bus replaced the streetcar.

On the other hand, and this is what brings a gleam to the eyes of Vancouver businessmen and transit managers, the RAV Line will take the original interurban concept up to a new level of integration, linking it directly with national and global transportation systems. The old interurban will have come back with a vengeance, now conjugated with the global web of international air travel.

Freeway

Unlike most North American cities, Vancouver has never developed a comprehensive regional freeway network. One reason is simply the level of need. Since Vancouver was not a major manufacturing region and since the port transshipment system was based initially on railways, freeways were not a requirement back when other cities were being garlanded with elevated flyovers. To this day, much of the shipping freight—especially raw materials such as sulphur, grain and coal—is handled by trains servicing the ports of Vancouver and Roberts Bank, though less exclusively than before. As a result, freeway infrastructure was mostly limited to expanding and upgrading the Trans-Canada Highway. Highway 99, the principal route from Vancouver to the United States border at Blaine, Washington, was also upgraded to freeway standard, but only from Richmond southward.

Another reason for this paucity of freeways is, or at least was until recently, low population density and a relatively low absolute population level (though low densities did not stop Los Angeles from embracing freeways).

In addition, there remained the residue of a comprehensive urban streetcar system, replaced over time by North America's most extensive urban trolley bus system. These lumbering, yet low-impact, slow-moving leviathans of the road seemed to symbiotically match Vancouver's slower pace. And they cost much less than freeways.

Moreover, Vancouver's geographic remoteness from the national centres of political and economic power meant that it always got the short end of the federal infrastructure investment stick. And—unlike their American counterparts—Canadian cities have a limited capacity to raise funds or borrow money, being the subservient political creatures of provincial governments, making it even less likely that the City of Vancouver would invest in freeways.

Yet another reason was the absence of the military imperative. Unlike so many cities in the United States, on which were foisted a federal freeway network ostensibly for military transportation, often against the wishes of the local populace, Vancouver was not considered a strategic military base by the Canadian government. Victoria (on Vancouver Island) is Canada's Pacific naval headquarters, Comox (also on Vancouver Island) its western air force base, and Edmonton (in Alberta), well over 1000 km (620 miles) distant from Vancouver, its main western army base. Vancouver, Canada's third-largest city, has virtually no military presence, and has not had for a long time.

And then there was local popular opinion. In what has become a central tenet in Vancouver's urban mythology, the people defeated a major freeway proposal in the late 1960s. In common with many cities, Vancouver had experienced a slump in the early '60s, with spreading urban decay around the central business core. Alarmed, the City hired American planners and economists to advise on how to turn things around. Among other suggestions, the consultants recommended an urban freeway system to maintain the City's regional dominance and enhance truck access to the central port. It would also provide direct access to a third crossing being mooted for Burrard Inlet. The proposed freeway route would run right through Gastown and Strathcona, ripping apart the urban fabric of those historic areas. The enraged local populace, led by a new class of political activist, would have none of it, and made its views loudly known.

Meanwhile, City Council had instructed its own Engineering Department to replace the aging Georgia Viaduct. The City's engineering consultant proposed that the new viaduct should connect to the proposed freeway system, and then go on to the Trans-Canada Highway. The proposed connector would follow Carrall Street, severing Chinatown in two. When council decided to proceed with the consultant's advice and build the Georgia Viaduct and Carrall Street connector, it faced unprecedented opposition from a broad coalition of interest groups.

In early 1968 City Council blinked. The Georgia and Dunsmuir viaducts went ahead (and are still resented by many locals), but council backed off

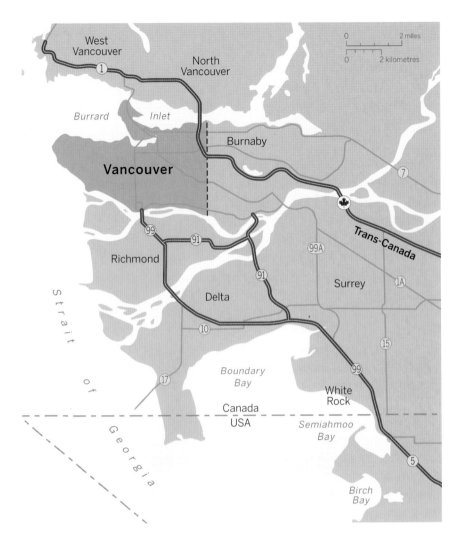

No freeways, thank you: Greater Vancouver's limited freeway system.

Eric Leinberger

on the Carrall Street connector, effectively abandoning all efforts at planning an urban freeway system.

The people had won. It was an exhilarating experience of popular empowerment, and it led directly to a new political party, TEAM (The Electors' Action Movement), coming to power in the 1972 civic election. With the freeway defeated at the municipal level, senior levels of government quickly reallocated moneys that had been designated for the third crossing, and instead Vancouver got the SeaBus ferry service across Burrard Inlet.

Today, Vancouver notably remains one of the only major North American cities with virtually no freeways within its municipal boundaries (the Trans-Canada Highway barely crosses into City of Vancouver territory along its easternmost boundary, before crossing back out over Burrard Inlet to the North Shore).

The consequences of these circumstances are significant, particularly in the downtown peninsula, where Vancouver has never been cut off from its waterfront by elevated freeways as have other cities. As the waterfront railways and industries moved out, the city was able to extend the downtown street grid and urban fabric right down to the water's edge. Both the Coal Harbour and Concord Pacific neighbourhoods have benefited directly from this strategy. Strathcona, Gastown and Chinatown remain largely intact in their historical urban form, remnants of the city that once was. Rescued and now protected as pedestrian-friendly, finely scaled precincts, they provide case studies in a form of tight street-oriented urbanism that would otherwise be all but absent from Vancouver. The city's arterial road system, once the basis of the streetcar network, continues to accommodate a public transportation system that, in turn, supports several neighbourhood commercial high streets.

These strategies, modest perhaps in comparison with those of European cities, should not be underestimated in a North American context, where so many cities have struggled mightily to get back to the basics of sound traditional urbanism. Through a fortuitous combination of late blooming, blind luck, foresighted vision and benign neglect, Vancouver finds itself a model of balanced post-industrial urban transportation.

In its virtual non-presence, the freeway layer of Vancouver's transportation palimpsest is experienced more as a negative presence that makes manifest what might have so easily been lost.

Bicycle

No review of Vancouver's transportation palimpsest can ignore the recent efforts at re-engineering the city's infrastructure to accommodate the bicycle as a serious transportation option. As former city councillor and cycling advocate Gordon Price points out in his electronic newsletter,[23] the City of Vancouver has completed more than 180 km (110 miles) of bikeways on public streets over the past decade. Additional significant bicycle routes are planned, not least as part of the implementation of the City's far-reaching *Downtown Transportation Plan.*

Vancouver now has a comprehensive, and growing, recreational and commuter bike-route network across the City. Bikeways, with their associated traffic calming and distinctive signage, are becoming a familiar sight. Streets are being redesignated, redesigned and restriped to rebalance the privileging of the automobile and give over more space to the bicycle. According to Price, cycling trips have grown by more than 30 to 40 per cent in Vancouver over the past three years, more than any other transportation mode.

And it is not just the City of Vancouver that has embraced the bicycle as an alternative to the automobile. Several other regional municipalities now have active bike-route programs, and a major new regional project, the $14-million Central Valley Greenway, funded by several different governments and the private sector, will connect a number of Vancouver municipalities along a proposed 25-km (15-mile) bike route.

The bicycle, for most of Vancouver's history consigned to the margins of transportation options, has arrived, and is making its presence felt. In much the same way as Vancouver's streetcar helped set the scale and grain of the city's urban fabric, the bicycle is helping to effect a redesign of the public realm, a resizing and reshaping of streets and public spaces into a more condensed, layered context: yet another diagram in the transportation palimpsest.

Ferry

In a city virtually surrounded by water, and whose constituent parts are indeed separated by water, waterborne transportation was always going to be part of the transportation palimpsest. And so it has.

The earliest urban settlements clung to the shores of Burrard Inlet, both north and south. And from the beginning, water transportation was a convenient and integral means of moving about the area. What started as ad hoc steamboat ferries soon developed into a comprehensive system, connecting several points along the North Shore of Burrard Inlet with Vancouver's growing downtown. For many years prior to the construction of bridges across the inlet, the ferries were the only way for people to commute between its shores and were instrumental in opening up the North Shore communities to development. By the early 1910s, steamboat ferries carried passengers back and forth across Burrard Inlet to several North Shore landing points, including Dundarave and Ambleside (in what was to become West Vancouver), and Lonsdale in North Vancouver.

In addition, the Union Steamship Company connected Vancouver to the hinterland with an extensive passenger and freight service up the coast and over to Vancouver Island. By the 1920s the company's fleet of distinctive steamships also offered Vancouverites summertime day excursions to beaches and resorts up Indian Arm and Howe Sound. This service was very popular. The Union Steamship fleet was part of a true regional transportation system.

By 1927, when Vancouver's Town Planning Commission retained the services of Harland Bartholomew to prepare a comprehensive plan for the city,[24] ferry service was well established, serving North Vancouver from a

Early steamship ferries
in Vancouver. Vancouver
Public Library 2908

wharf near the foot of Main Street, and West Vancouver from the CPR wharf
at the foot of Granville Street. A separate service, labelled the "P.G.E. Car
Ferry" in Bartholomew's plan, departed from yet another wharf between the
foot of Bute and Thurlow streets, from where car ferry service to Vancouver
Island also embarked.

The ever-thorough Bartholomew, despite his obvious predilection for
the benefits of the car, recognized that "the demand for rapid and high-
class ferries … will rapidly increase." He called for a new combined local and
coastal ferry pier to be constructed downtown, either at the foot of Granville
Street on the CPR's Pier D or farther east at the foot of Gore Avenue. This
vision for an integrated downtown ferry terminal—such as exists at Circular
Quay in Sydney—never did come to pass. As with the streetcar and the
interurban, the automobile would soon spell its demise.

The first bridge over Burrard Inlet was built at the Second Narrows in
1925. The Lions Gate Bridge over the First Narrows followed in 1937. With
their advent, and the increasing use of cars and buses, ferry service across
Burrard Inlet began to decline and ended in 1958. The Union Steamship
Company went out of business as well in the 1950s, its summer day trips
now a fond memory.

Over the years several ferry operators have come and gone, including
local service to Port Moody at the head of Burrard Inlet and high-speed
passenger service to Nanaimo and Victoria on Vancouver Island, bringing
each within an hour's commute of downtown Vancouver. None of these
services has lasted very long. Recent suggestions by TransLink for a more

comprehensive commuter passenger ferry service around Burrard Inlet remain just that.[25] Two small privately run water taxi services, Aquabus and False Creek Ferries, operate mini-ferries around the False Creek basin.

The CPR's Pier D was demolished, though its remnant stump became the terminal for the SeaBus ferry service, the only part still left of a much atrophied urban ferry system. The integrated, comprehensive public ferry system that might be expected of a city so intimately shaped by water still awaits its reincarnation.

Airplane

There is another, less obvious, layer to the transportation palimpsest: small commuter aircraft. Whether you are lying on a beach in Stanley Park or at home in your Kitsilano backyard, you can hear the drone of low flying propeller-powered aircraft punctuating the sounds of the city, year round.

This fleet of small planes—in effect commuter air-buses—provides daily scheduled and on-demand charter connections to outlying communities such as Abbotsford, Bowen Island, Delta, Langley, Pitt Meadows, the Sunshine Coast and the southern Gulf Islands, as well as to the nearby towns and cities of Bellingham, Chilliwack, Nanaimo and Victoria.

This local air travel network, using both land-based and water-based planes, is in effect an extension of the local and regional arterial road network. Taking full advantage of the abundant water in the region, float-plane landing areas on both river and sea often provide the most direct access to

A float plane landing in the water near downtown Vancouver.

Lance Berelowitz photo

Dream City

many local communities and extend urban lifestyles into otherwise isolated rural locales. The small float plane effectively extends the metropolitan sway over a far larger region than solely land-based transportation. In this lies the beginnings of a virtual metropolis, wherein the more obvious geographical interconnectivity of a traditional metropolis is replaced by a more diffuse, discrete model of urbanism.

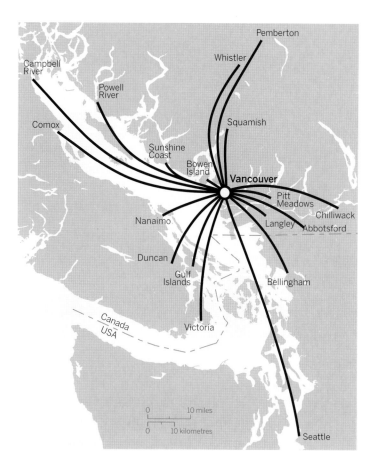

Vancouver's commuter air routes.

Eric Leinberger

A quite unintended yet profound experience of the dramatic transition from urban to rural derives from using this air transportation system, in a way no freeway commute could ever convey. Anyone returning by float plane to Vancouver on the flight from, say, a business trip over to Sechelt or Campbell River or up to Squamish, cannot fail to be struck by the city's abrupt, absolute, geographic finality. By this I mean that extraordinary moment when, as your plane rounds the last ridge of coastal mountains and Vancouver hoves suddenly into view ahead, the utter contrast between its sharply delineated urban forms on the flat land in front of you and the uninterrupted alpine hinterland stretching back behind you is starkly revealed. There is the overwhelming sense of Vancouver being the last possible outpost of urbanity before the heaving wilderness escarpment takes over forever from hereon north.

Of course it is an optical illusion, not least because it presumes a Westerner's view of civilization (as if no aboriginal settlements farther up the coast count), but also because there are, indeed, other outposts, however few, of so-called civilization farther north.

But it is a poetic measure of the possibilities of the unique multi-modal regional transportation system that Vancouver enjoys.

7

The Road Not Taken

ALTHOUGH IT IS WESTERN Canada's largest urban centre and the de facto capital of British Columbia, Vancouver is in fact not a capital city. Nor has it ever been. Indeed, it was passed over twice as the provincial capital, with profound consequences for the urban form of the future city.

When the British government proclaimed the Crown Colony of British Columbia in August 1858, it dispatched Colonel R.C. Moody and a regiment of Royal Engineers to select a site for the new colony's capital.[26] Sailing up the Fraser River, Moody chose "the first high ground on the north side after entering the river" as the site, and it was named New Westminster. The New Westminster Capital Plan, laid out by Moody's Royal Engineers in 1862, was remarkably formal, even elegant: an Enlightenment-inspired Eurocentric world view imposed onto the forest wilderness.

Colonel Moody, a man whose family name suggests a certain temperament perhaps conducive to flights of romantic planning fancy, wasted no time in bestowing New Westminster with an embellished street-grid layout that included a series of squares, crescents, terraces and public gardens. The design was laid out symmetrically on either side of a central sequence of formal public spaces that progressed at right angles up from the Fraser River. Starting at the riverfront with the Quay Side wharf and Lytton Square, it moved up through Victoria Gardens, the Government Offices Gardens and a central parade ground to St. George's Square, from whence a broad ceremonial street continued the axis away from the river. Flanking blocks presented a sophisticated rhythm of alternating dimensions and orientation, either moving up or across the slope. A secondary series of outlying squares and crescents rounded out the plan.

Much of Moody's plan succumbed to subsequent land assemblies, speculative contingencies and a vigorous local working-class aversion to symbols of imperial elitism, and most of the original public spaces have long since been covered over with buildings, but fragments of New Westminster's

The Royal Engineers'
original plan for the
colonial capital of
New Westminster.
Eric Leinberger. Based
on the New Westminster
Capital Plan, c. 1859,
drawn by J.R. Launders
under the direction of
Captain Parsons, by
order of Colonel R.C.
Moody. Courtesy New
Westminster Library

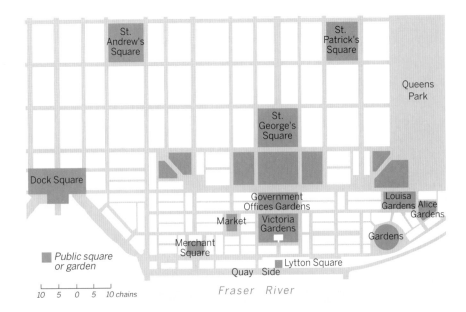

formal layout can still be discerned. As a result, though it soon withered to a smaller satellite in the constellation of bedroom communities surrounding the rapidly growing City of Vancouver, New Westminster continues to evince a whiff of the royal, the oversized urban gesture, in its contemporary physical incarnation.

In 1866, when the colony of Vancouver Island was joined to the mainland colony of British Columbia as one administrative entity, New Westminster enjoyed a brief interlude as the capital of the united colony. It did not last long. Two years later, much to New Westminster's chagrin, the capital reverted to Victoria at the southern end of the island. It has remained there ever since, relegating Vancouver to a strangely split personality: not formally the centre of political power but practically speaking the centre of British Columbia in virtually every other way. Even so, Vancouver, by its very size, exerts a disproportionate influence over provincial political power (five of the last six premiers resided in Greater Vancouver, and two of them were former mayors of Vancouver).

Meanwhile, over in Victoria, urban planning attention had focussed on developing an appropriate legislative precinct in the heart of the city, fronting onto the Inner Harbour. Among other things, this resulted in the present legislature complex of buildings and public open spaces, a spacious, decorously English colonial ensemble of urban planning that incorporates the formal waterfront edge around the Inner Harbour and the grand Empress Hotel. Whatever else its limitations may be as a city, there is no mistaking central Victoria as a capital. It has the self-conscious *gravitas* of all urban centres that have been conceived as a representation of political power.

Why does this little bit of obscure local history matter to the story of Vancouver's emerging urban form? Because New Westminster and Victoria both received special urban planning attention as befitted capitals, whereas Vancouver did not.

The urban planning consequences of being a capital continue for Victoria, as the Provincial Capital Commission is responsible for reinforcing and shaping its image. An equivalent influence over its evolving urban form is noticeably absent in Vancouver. For example, Vancouver has no major civic square or central public open space that is comparable to the Legislative Assembly grounds. Further, compare New Westminster's original street layout to Vancouver's more utilitarian—and egalitarian—street grid: no formalism, little hierarchy, few symbolic public spaces (with the exception perhaps of Victory Square).

There is almost no historical—or ongoing—provincial government physical presence in Vancouver such as Victoria's legislature buildings, lieutenant-governor's residence, provincial museum, numerous government agency head offices and so on. Consequently, there is little senior government influence in the shaping of the city and concomitantly little government investment in civic improvements or the public realm.

It is instructive to compare this state of affairs in Vancouver with, say, Montreal, Glasgow, Sydney or Barcelona, all cities central to a national project. Whereas in cities such as these, senior levels of government invest heavily in the public realm, civic symbols and government edifices, government is largely a missing constituency in the making of Vancouver. Vancouver lacks a certain *gravitas,* a sense of self-importance. Symbols of civic power are few and far between, the grand urban gesture largely absent.

This circumstance—the lack of any appreciable senior government presence in Vancouver—has in fact pitted the city against the provincial government more often than not, to the detriment of Vancouver. Competing senior governments have not duelled it out in the streets with the typical results of more investment, more public buildings, more symbolism, a more charged public realm.

The problem has been compounded by Vancouver's geographic remoteness from the centres of national political and economic power (Ottawa and

Looking east on Columbia
Street, New Westminster,
British Columbia's one-
time capital, in 1911.

Courtesy New Westminster
Library 2404

Toronto respectively). There is little presence of the government of Canada
in the city (Canada Place and Granville Island excepted). The situation is
even further exacerbated by the relative powerlessness of Canadian cities, which are creatures of their provincial governments and, as such, rely
almost exclusively on them to determine the scope of their powers, particularly in matters of taxation and raising capital. This strikingly hierarchical,
condescending power structure has severely limited local governments,
Vancouver's included, from playing a more activist role in shaping their
cities. Consequently, decisions are taken about major urban infrastructure
investment based on provincial or national rather than local political calcu-
lations. So when Vancouver is offered an Expo 86 world's fair or federal support for a 2010 Olympic Winter Games bid, it is unlikely to pass them up,
however disinclined it might be, as attached to these strings is money that is
just too good to say no to.[27]

The end result: Vancouver historically has operated on a notably parochial ethos, with typically anaemic government budgets for cultural and
civic facilities, the public realm, festivals and the arts, in comparison with
capital cities. Vancouver's residents have correspondingly modest expectations

regarding the quality and level of investment in their public realm and cultural amenities, versus any expectation that it is the capital of a province or state (Sydney), an autonomous region (Barcelona) or a nation (Berlin).

As we are about to find out, for such investments are on the rise with recent urban growth, Vancouver has come to rely largely on the contributions of the private development sector through the City's discretionary rezoning process, in which planning staff negotiate a range of public amenities with a developer, in return for supporting the proposed development.

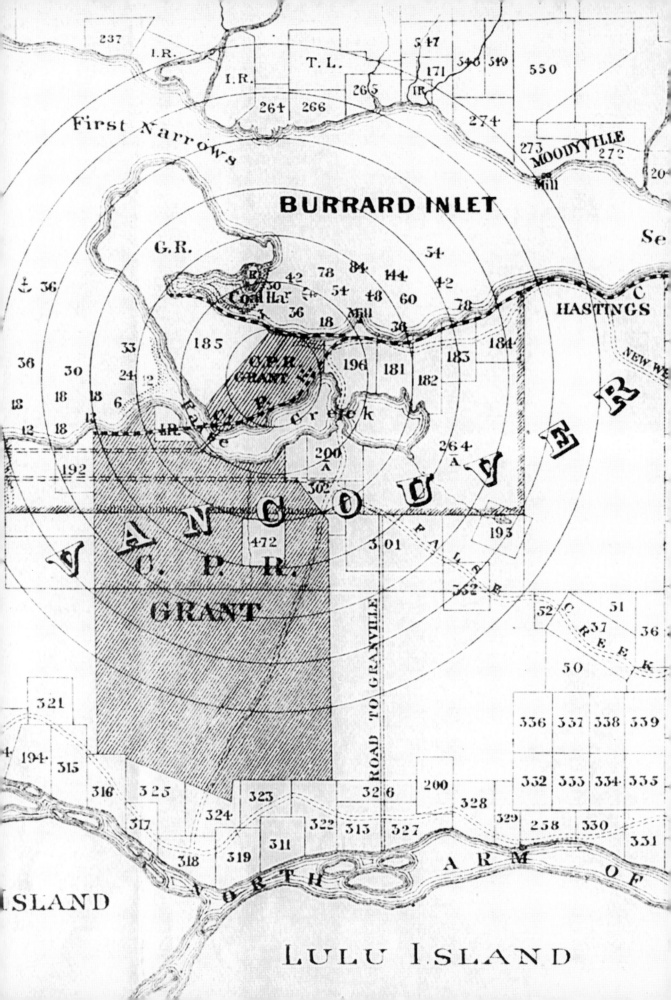

8

For Sale

The (Abridged) Story of Vancouver's Development Community

IN *CITY OF GLASS,* his personal paean to Vancouver, hometown author Douglas Coupland points out that a reliable measure of a neighbourhood's health is the number of "For Sale" signs on front lawns.[28] Too few signs and things are bad, but too many and things are *really* bad. There are few subjects that exercise Vancouverites more than property value fluctuations and the attendant windfall profits or losses, and this is the topic of almost every conversation sooner or later. Real estate is Vancouver's true passion, its real blood sport. Vancouver is a culture of speculation.

This culture has its roots in the city's earliest days. Indeed, its very founding was based on the speculative land development that both anticipated and attended the arrival of the transcontinental railway line on the Pacific Coast.

Of course these early realtors ignored the inconvenient possibility that others already using the land might have prior claims to it or other ideas about what to use it for. Native land rights or interests were simply not considered. From its earliest days, the history of Vancouver has been one of unscrupulous and profitable subdivision and sale of land. There is nothing subtle about this history, and the developer impulse continues to this day as a prime agent in the city's transformation. The story of Vancouver's earliest developers, and its current big players, is central to deciphering the city's emergent urban form.

The Canadian Pacific Railway: Vancouver's First Developer

To get things going, in 1885, Vancouver's first developer, the Canadian Pacific Railway, received a huge land grant from the Crown in return for

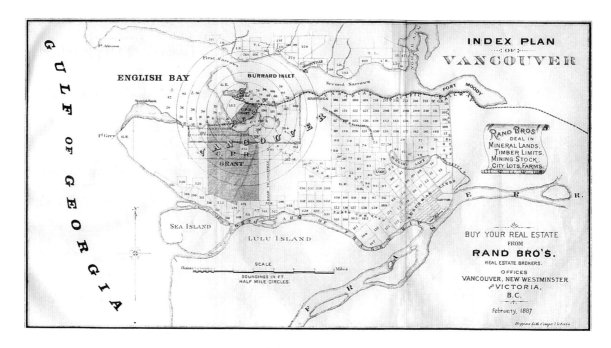

agreeing to extend the rail line westward from the original terminus at the head of Burrard Inlet as far as the Granville Townsite (later downtown Vancouver). The grant consisted of two land blocks, an enormous one of 2347 ha (5,800 acres) and a smaller one of 194 ha (480 acres). This grant—which covered a sizable chunk of the future city—and the CPR's active involvement in bringing the land to market, set the tone for a future of speculative real estate development that remains at the core of Vancouver's culture.

The very earliest maps and bird's-eye views of Vancouver, commissioned by the CPR, illustrate an over-optimistic representation of the built street layout and number of buildings constructed, anticipating the future as a kind of advertisement to encourage settlers to purchase land. The best known of these maps is the 1890 bird's-eye view produced for the *Vancouver Daily and Weekly World,* in which much of the downtown peninsula and even parts of the south shore of False Creek are shown as already built, well in advance of reality. A direct line runs from this classic example of early real estate marketing to today's glossy coloured renderings of yet-to-be-built condominium towers splashed across the pages of the local newspapers, siren calls to the consumer.

The CPR did not stop there. Shortly after establishing the railway terminus at the northern foot of the street it named Granville, the company

Opposite page "Buy your real estate from Rand Bros.,"
Vancouver in 1887. City of Vancouver Archives FC3847.22 V2 P52

Overleaf A bird's-eye view used to market real estate in
Vancouver in 1890. City of Vancouver Archives map P18 N20

began surveying and laying out the streets of the future city, in anticipation of the growth that was quick to follow.

Raising its sights beyond the downtown peninsula, the CPR extended Granville Street across False Creek via the first Granville Bridge (erected in 1889) and, shifting the street alignment due south through the middle of its main land grant, eventually pushed it through the surrounding forest all the way south to the Fraser River. This pioneering route (originally called Centre Street) was the spine, the organizing element, around which the city's urban structure grew. The CPR's surveyors rapidly established a simple rectilinear grid of numbered east-west avenues and named north-south streets on either side of Granville Street. The grid blocks were oriented east-west to maximize access from Granville Street, which, in turn, connected directly to the Canadian Pacific Railway station, a study in land development efficiency that was replicated across Canada in countless railway towns. The CPR land grant thus accessed was opened up for sale and development in carefully timed phases, thereby limiting and controlling the supply and maintaining its value, an important lesson not lost on future big developers.

One of the earliest of these phases was also one of the most successful for the railway company.

Shaughnessy Heights

The CPR planned, developed and marketed the Shaughnessy Heights subdivision as an exclusive enclave for the wealthy elite of the growing city. Straddling the high ground on either side of Granville Street to the south of False Creek, the area covered some 100 ha (250 acres) of the company's enormous land grant. Occupying the ridge of the Burrard Peninsula, with sweeping views to the north, Shaughnessy Heights was laid out with curving boulevards and crescents that followed the natural contours of the land.

Shaughnessy Heights is one of the earliest examples of residential master-planning in Canada. Under the direction of CPR General Superintendent Richard Marpole, it was laid out by Danish engineer

The softening of the rigid street grid in Shaughnessy Heights.
Eric Leinberger

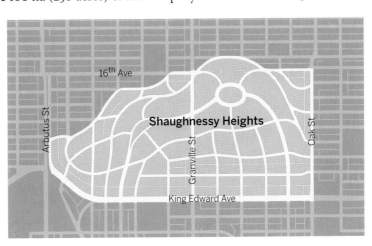

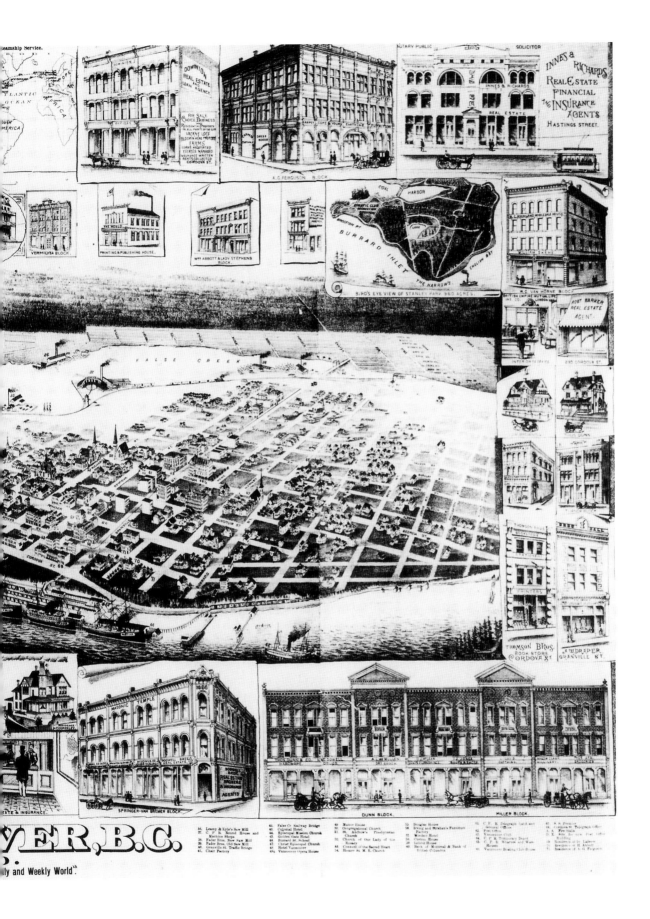

Shaughnessy Heights, Vancouver's first enclave for the wealthy elite, developed by the Canadian Pacific Railway.

Derek Lepper photo

L.E. Davick and Montreal landscape architect Frederick Todd, who were influenced by the town planning style popularized by the famed American landscape architect Frederick Law Olmsted. Its curvilinear street plan is in notable contrast to the rectangular street grid that otherwise covers the city: a rare Canadian example of the Garden City and City Beautiful town planning movements that were then *de rigueur* in Britain and the United States respectively.

The entire Shaughnessy subdivision—curving wide roads, sidewalks, custom street lighting, landscaped boulevards, medians and open green spaces—was carefully laid out before the houses were built, thus establishing the tone and quality. With restrictive covenants built into the title deeds and high minimum house prices ($6,000 in 1909!), this master-planned neighbourhood immediately became—and remains to this day—one of Vancouver's most exclusive and expensive single-family residential enclaves. Shaughnessy Heights is a classic early illustration of how speculative development lies at the heart of Vancouver's urban growth.

The Canadian Pacific Railway also played a very significant role in the development of Vancouver's downtown peninsula, especially along the waterfront edges of the company's lands. From its very beginning, the role of the CPR as a speculative agent for growth has been central to the city's urban development. It still is today.

Coal Harbour

Marathon Developments was the name of the real estate development/disposal arm of the Canadian Pacific Railway. In Vancouver, Marathon was responsible for the wholesale redevelopment and marketing of a huge swath of railway lands stretching from Burrard Street to Cardero Street on the Coal Harbour waterfront along Burrard Inlet.

The transformation of the Coal Harbour working waterfront began with the redevelopment of the CPR's Pier B-C into the Canada Place pavilion for Expo 86. Canada Place provided a first intimation of what was to come.

As port-related transportation technology changed and new container terminals were developed farther east along Burrard Inlet and south of Vancouver on the Strait of Georgia, the CPR reassessed its trackage and marshalling needs in Coal Harbour. The railway-freight ferry terminal serving Vancouver Island was removed (the passenger ferry terminal had already closed). Coal Harbour was recognized as having much higher value as waterfront urban land, close to the central business district and amenities, and ripe for high-density residential development. By the early 1990s the railway company had pulled up all its remaining tracks west of Burrard Street.

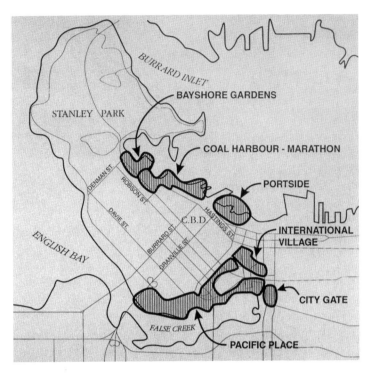

Development precincts in Vancouver's central area since Expo 86 (with Concord Pacific Place referred to as Pacific Place). Courtesy City of Vancouver

Marathon embarked on a major development plan for the 32-ha (80-acre) site—17 ha (41 acres) of land and 15 ha (39 acres) of water—that became one of the city's prime waterfront residential areas. Over a period of several years, Marathon engaged in a megaproject process with the City's Planning Department, coming up with a three-phase master plan for the entire site. The first, most westerly phase is complete, as is much of the second, which occupies the central portion of the lands. The third, most easterly phase will accommodate a substantially expanded Vancouver Convention Centre.

When completed, Marathon's Coal Harbour project will include about twenty-two hundred residential units housing more than thirty-eight hundred residents, plus a mix of hotel, office, retail and services, and the expanded convention centre. A civic arts centre containing a 1,500-seat performance hall and a 350-seat studio theatre was part of the original package negotiated by City planning staff, but to better accommodate the convention centre

expansion, this arts centre will be relocated. Coal Harbour also includes a
major new 3-ha (8-acre) waterfront park (Harbour Green), a community
centre, an elementary school, two daycare centres and a 250-berth marina
complete with waterfront restaurant. The total development of all three
phases will be some 436 630 m² (4.7 million square feet).

Coal Harbour is an audacious plan. A key urban design move was to
open up and maintain water views at the ends of all the north-south streets.
Optimizing public views of landmarks such as the Marine Building was
also incorporated into the plan, as were private views from adjacent upland
properties. To a large extent, building locations were predetermined by such
view corridors, as well as by the technical and cost limitations of building
too far out into the water.

The shape and form of the new shoreline were cued off the existing one
and scalloped to create a series of focal points along the length of the site.
The usual Vancouver waterfront walkway/bikeway is well integrated here,
entrenching the ever-present impulse to look out at the setting rather than
in towards the city.

References to the site's historical role as the western terminus of the
trans-Canada railway line and as a working waterfront are built into the
design, in the form of public art and landscape gestures, though these are
probably lost on today's users. An attempt has been made to create a diverse
urban waterfront, with park spaces, marina activity, a restaurant perched

Opposite page Marathon Development's original Coal Harbour
master plan, prior to the convention centre expansion proposal.
Courtesy Marathon Developments Ltd.

This page Coal Harbour residential towers, community centre and
redeveloped public waterfront. George Vaitkunas photo

over the water and one block of waterfront commercial frontage. However,
most of the streets do not extend to the water's edge, and the dominant
experience is still very much as passive park space.

To its credit, the City insisted on a demographic mix. Non-market
housing, affordable rental housing, high-end condominiums and hotel uses
are all part of the new neighbourhood profile. One result is broadly equi-
table access for all, a rare achievement for a high-value urban waterfront.
However, pretty as it is, there is no escaping the sense of serious gentrification of what was a working waterfront.

canada place way

cordova

hastings

pender

thurlow

burrard

hornby

The revised plan for the east end of Coal Harbour, showing the proposed new convention centre and the extension of Canada Place Way. Courtesy Downs-Archambault Architects

The eastern end of Coal Harbour, dubbed Burrard Landing, is the third and final phase. Here are rising a couple of commercial/residential towers (the Shaw Tower was completed near the end of 2004), to be followed by the expansion of the Vancouver Convention and Exhibition Centre. This $565-million facility will add some 33 500 m² (360,000 square feet) of exhibition/conference space to the existing centre at Canada Place, which has served this function since its construction for Expo 86, as well as more meeting rooms, a ballroom and administration facilities. The expanded convention centre will connect directly to the adjacent Canada Place. A major waterfront public plaza will be part of the convention centre, something downtown Vancouver has always sorely lacked. The seawall from Stanley Park along Burrard Inlet finally will stretch as far as Canada Place.

This final phase of Coal Harbour will complete the creation of an entirely new elevated ground plane and new streets, reaching out with a viaduct structure over the natural escarpment and the former railway yards below to extend the downtown street grid. A new city is, quite literally, being built here. And finally, the foot of Burrard Street, one of Vancouver's major ceremonial streets, will get the terminus it has long deserved, crossing the future westward expansion of Canada Place Way to become a waterfront promontory overlooking Burrard Inlet.

Marathon has now sold off its last land holdings in Coal Harbour to independent developers whose high-rise residential projects are rapidly, and utterly, transforming this northern edge of the downtown peninsula, including the very shoreline itself.

With the 2001 reorganization of Canadian Pacific Limited, Marathon became a subsidiary of Fairmont Hotels and Resorts, and was renamed Fairmont Developments. When Coal Harbour is finished, the reinvention of downtown Vancouver's urban waterfront will be substantially complete, even to the point of effacement of the very company that started it all some 120 years ago.

AN EXTENSION to the Coal Harbour lands, Bayshore Gardens, though not actually owned or developed by Marathon, was created in parallel. The Bayshore lands were acquired by the Aoki Corporation of Japan as part of the portfolio that company inherited when it bought the Westin Hotel chain, an outpost of which has long resided on the Coal Harbour waterfront. The 6.5 ha (16 acres) of land have been developed as a kind of bland expansion of the original "resort" hotel, itself one of the more archaic hostelries in town with its 1960s-era Hawaii resort/Hollywood movie ambience, recently refreshed with a multimillion-dollar makeover.

Bayshore Gardens has several distressingly similar, unremarkable residential towers[29] (which, when completed, will house some eighteen hundred well-heeled residents), arrayed around a series of formal gardens and a small public green space that forms the roof of a central public parkade.

An aerial view of the Bayshore Gardens development, 2002.
Courtesy Vancouver Park Board

The bits of land surrounding the hotel have been rearranged to accommodate the obligatory waterfront promenade, and a hotly contested waterfront restaurant has opened on the small concrete platform in the water beside the marina. Yet for all this, Bayshore Gardens does not really feel like an organic extension of the city but rather retains something of the air of a separate resort. For such a dramatic, strategically located urban site, the whole ensemble feels slightly frumpy and buttoned-down. It is the art of the enclave, determined to snuff out the first signs of messy individualism.

COAL HARBOUR CONSTITUTES a radical reinvention of Vancouver's urban waterfront from working port to master-planned waterfront community. As such, it is a significant contributor to Vancouver's emerging new lifestyle myth. And though it is a particularly pronounced form of gentrification, the more than fifty-five hundred new residents will also add greatly to the downtown population, reinforcing Vancouver's growing reputation as a livable city.

An aerial view of Coal Harbour, 2002. Courtesy Vancouver Park Board

Dream City

The Expo Lands: Concord Pacific Place

Another prime example of developers acting on opportunities arising from the railway's retrenchment from the downtown peninsula is the north shore of False Creek. Here, the CPR had extensive trackage, sidings, a roundhouse and railcar repair shops. As these became increasingly obsolescent in the 1970s and early '80s, the area was pegged as the site for the Expo 86 world's fair and transformed into a gigantic theme park. After Expo 86, the provincial government, which had effectively acquired the land as the underwriter of the world's fair, sold it to Hong Kong developer Li Ka-shing's company, Concord Pacific.

The Concord Pacific lands cover some 67 ha (166 acres) of waterfront stretching along the north shore of False Creek from Granville Bridge eastward to Quebec Street. This huge area, equivalent to more than ten city blocks in length, defines the southeastern edge of Vancouver's downtown peninsula, from Pender Street south to Beach Avenue. Once the contaminated soil was remediated by the provincial government and the land sold to Concord Pacific, it was rezoned to permit a comprehensive, mixed-use, high-density development. A portion of the original lands, the inland area to the north of Dunsmuir Viaduct and Expo Boulevard that lies adjacent to Chinatown, was spun off to become International Village, a separate development entity.

Initial concepts for the Concord Pacific lands played on using the waters of False Creek itself as a major organizing element and conceived of the project as a "resort in the city," but ultimately a more organic, straightforward extension of the city fabric and street pattern was settled on.

The resulting master plan had several urban design strategies, reflecting a set of organizing principles that were agreed to with City Planning Department staff. Key among these was the creation of a series of local neighbourhoods along False Creek, each focussed on a bay and separated by a large public park. Another was the decision—obvious in hindsight but a radical influence on the emerging urban form—to simply extend the existing downtown street grid across Pacific Boulevard towards the water. As with Coal Harbour, this simple yet powerful notion repudiated eighty years of urban planning in which the dominant model was a city cut off from its waterfront by an impregnable layer of industry and railways. The development of Concord Pacific Place reaffirmed the principle that public streets are the primary ordering device of city-building, accommodating incremental development, providing robust flexibility and helping to integrate new development with the surrounding built fabric.

The Concord Pacific Place master plan. Courtesy Concord Pacific

The creation of several distinct precincts has helped with the phasing of development and also helps to break down the deadening effect of a community master-planned by a single hand. By employing a diversity of designers and creating distinctive design guidelines for each of the precincts, there is a variety—though perhaps not enough—of built forms and public spaces.

Concord Pacific Place also explored new ideas for high-density, high-rise residential living. Vancouver's well-established rule of a 24-m (80-foot) minimum distance between high-rise residential towers was first tested here. In addition, strategies such as staggered tower locations, streetwall housing podiums and the use of outdoor podium rooftops for family play space were all explored to achieve a high level of private amenity.

**Concord Pacific Place
as seen from False Creek.**

Derek Lepper photo

One of the most laudable achievements of Concord Pacific Place, from the public perspective, is the remarkable range and scope of civic amenities that were extracted from the developer through the rezoning process. Some 17 ha (42 acres) of public park space have been created, in addition to semi-private open space. A continuous, uninterrupted 10.5-m (35-foot) wide waterfront walkway/bikeway seamlessly links the parks and streetends, and substantially completes the public waterfront loop around False Creek. New policies ensured that 25 per cent of the housing would be designed for families. The required 20 per cent of non-market residential units are carefully spread throughout the development rather than being ghettoized in one precinct. Two elementary schools, several daycare centres, a full-service community centre (the Roundhouse, which adapted the historic CPR railcar roundhouse and repair shops), multi-purpose meeting rooms and a sports field house complete the impressive civic amenities package. A public art program also is being implemented within each phase of development. This range of facilities and the local retail uses fronting Pacific Boulevard all contribute to the sense not of a single-use enclave but rather a complete urban community.

Impressive as these features are, perhaps the most remarkable aspect of Concord Pacific Place is what it has done to reinvigorate downtown Vancouver as a compact, vibrant, mixed-use community. When completed, Concord Pacific Place will have added some fifteen thousand new residents to downtown, and this, combined with many more thousands moving into the other areas undergoing redevelopment on the downtown peninsula, is responsible for Vancouver's becoming a North American model of inner-city revitalization. The City's "Living First" strategy for downtown densification is working. There is the sustainable development advantage as well that comes from bringing people and their workplaces closer together: more and more Vancouverites are walking, cycling or using public transit on the downtown peninsula. And public safety has also improved with many more "eyes on the street." Concord Pacific Place is making a major contribution to the emergence in Vancouver of a new urban paradigm.

Yaletown Edge: A Case Study in Urban Repair
The first phase of Concord Pacific's development was the area known as Yaletown Edge, completed in the mid-1990s. Adjoining the historical Yaletown warehouse district, Yaletown Edge straddles three blocks along the upland side of Pacific Boulevard, whose broad sweep of asphalt girdles the former Expo lands, cutting off the site from the placid waters of False Creek. Indeed, this significant traffic artery has been a major challenge to the concept of knitting the city fabric back to the waterfront. It is far from a satisfying urban promenade. However, it is a measure of the success of Concord Pacific Place that, in the intervening years, with both sides of the street now developed, Pacific Boulevard has slowly taken on more of an urban characteristic and feels less like the arterial it really is. A recent City initiative to redesign the boulevard itself will hopefully complete this transformation.

The initial credit for the transformation of Pacific Boulevard must go to the rigorous approach taken along the three blocks of Yaletown Edge to create a streetwall built form. In fact, this first phase was seen as both a harbinger of things to come on the rest of the Expo lands and as a major litmus test for the acceptance of a gutsy approach to urban street definition, an approach for which Vancouverites had seemed to have largely lost their taste in previous decades. Here, though, a concerted effort was made to establish a significant amount of built form to help define and contain the street. With retail at grade and three to six floors of residential above, Yaletown Edge set the stage for the incremental urbanization of Pacific Boulevard.

However, because of the overscale width of Pacific Boulevard, there are still valid questions as to whether the height of the streetwall, let alone the permitted uses of the ground plane, will be sufficient to tame the beast.

If an urban approach to streetwall built form is one of the most positive attributes of Yaletown Edge, it is by no means the only one. This assemblage of some eight residential towers, a major streetwall and a public park—designed by a number of firms—has several other virtues.

The new development nuzzles up against the formally powerful hundred-year-old Yaletown warehouse district, with its stepped cross-section loading docks that brilliantly exploit the natural slope of the land. For the most part, this is four- to six-storey brick warehouse territory, and the new buildings carefully respond and relate to this context, in both form and materials. Generally, new elements are stepped to align with adjacent existing cornice heights and are clad in similar red brick. However, this sensitive contextualism is achieved without resorting to slavish replication, and there is no mistaking the new for old. This distinction is as it should be, in a city that is frequently presented with "Heritage" as a style.

Another noteworthy design gesture is the way in which the orientation of the new towers south of Davie and Drake streets reinforce the dominant city street grid, even while the lower elements of these buildings align in response to Pacific Boulevard, thus reconciling the two different street grids. Both Mainland and Hamilton streets are axially terminated with carefully placed towers, picking up on an almost abandoned Vancouver tradition of terminated axes such as the Marine Building on Hastings Street, St. Paul's Hospital on Helmcken and the old Canadian Pacific Railway station on Seymour—all completed long before the current cult of the view rendered them apostate.

If there is one quibble with Yaletown Edge, it might be to question the height and breadth of some of the tower forms in terms of responding to the low-level warehouse context of Yaletown. From certain viewpoints, Yaletown appears dangerously overwhelmed. However, this has more to do with high land costs than design judgment, and it is difficult to imagine economical alternatives. It is also worth noting that this scale/form problem is not confined to Yaletown Edge; indeed, some of the surrounding new projects are even larger, with a correspondingly bigger impact.

With a development of this scale, there is always the danger of giantism: the dead hand of megaproject architecture. Happily, this problem was avoided by assigning different parcels to different architects and by varying

The Yaletown Edge
along Pacific Boulevard.
Derek Lepper photo

the treatment of individual buildings within a broadly recognizable family of materials and palette of colours. This approach provides the impression of a more incremental, heterogeneous urbanity and also softens the impact of so large a development on so unique a context.

One minor, if expensive, gesture of compensation to this community context was the creation of a small landscaped public square at the intersection of Davie and Mainland streets. This space, designed in part as a buffer between new development and old, consists of a landscaped zone behind a curved low wall—apparently intended (with questionable accuracy) to evoke the original False Creek shoreline hereabouts—fronting a hard-paved plaza. Holding the street corner and announcing the public elevator access to an underground public parkade is a small "historical fragment" structure that reflects the surrounding industrial architectural heritage, a folly in the tradition of English country gardens. Although a piece of whimsy, this red-brick and heavy timber–framed pavilion is certainly superior to the postmodern elevator shelters in other downtown mini-parks.

However, the real concern with this square is a more practical one: its degree of usability. For most of the day, it is shadowed by the wall of new buildings to the east and south, a major drawback. This site-planning flaw curtails the square's function, particularly as a lunchtime retreat for local workers, and especially in the shoulder seasons when the sun angle is lower.

It is ironic that this square, focussed as it is on the pedestrian in repose, is named after Bill Curtis, the late old-school city engineer who more than anyone of his era was responsible for pushing Pacific Boulevard as a high-speed bypass through this area.

One other found opportunity presented by the Yaletown Edge site has remained unexploited. Cutting diagonally through all three blocks and roughly parallel to but predating Pacific Boulevard by a century is the CPR's original False Creek spur line, long since abandoned and now only traced by the angles of those older warehouse buildings abutting it and a utilitarian service lane. Of such fragments is the story of this young city told, and it is regrettable that the current development, for all its other virtues, largely ignored this layer of the site's history. The rail line right-of-way could easily have been responded to in the design of the park at least and possibly in the buildings as well.

Along with the rest of Concord Pacific Place and other downtown megaprojects, Yaletown Edge incorporates the City's current requirement of 20 per cent affordable housing. A non-market seniors' residence occupies the middle of three towers of the central block, and there is a stand-alone seniors and family non-market housing block at the most northerly edge of the project. It is commendable that, from the outside at least, market and non-market architecture are virtually indistinguishable.

Finally, the thoughtful if rugged care with which the architecture of the building skins has been applied extends too into the public realm with the streetscape treatment, which was seen as integral to this project. A significant effort was put into sidewalk design, materials and landscaping, and much of it is of high quality. The streetscape has been a key element in helping to unite this side of Pacific Boulevard with the subsequent development on the opposite side.

With its still evolving mix of high-tech start-ups, advertising agencies, furniture stores, fashion designers, artist studios, pool halls and restaurants, and now both upscale and subsidized residents, Yaletown Edge is perhaps the closest Vancouver comes to the dynamic potential of a district such as Manhattan's SoHo. Although it brought a wave of gentrification to this previously all but forgotten part of town, there is no doubt that the first phase of Concord Pacific Place has regenerated this precinct and helped to repair the city's downtown edge. It also set a high standard for subsequent development.

MUCH OF Concord Pacific Place has been built according to plan. Pacific Boulevard is now lined with new buildings on both sides. The Beach Avenue neighbourhood to the west is rapidly rising out of the ground to complete the ensemble as far west as Granville Bridge. Concord Pacific's last remaining development sites lie to the east of Cambie Bridge. They are not far behind.

If there is a major criticism of Concord Pacific Place, it may be that it is a victim of its own success. So much new development has happened so fast and under single ownership that it seems almost too pat, too pristine, somehow untouchable. Many of the residential buildings have a sameness of architectural style and material whose aggregate effect is the very opposite of urban diversity. And too many of the new streets and spaces still have that squeaky clean sense of control that is emblematic of the master-planned ethos, untroubled by the layered complexity that comes from a negotiated urbanism. All great city neighbourhoods reflect the colourful diversity of human endeavour and adaptation to individual creativity over time. This aspect of interaction with the built form of the city has yet to take hold in Concord Pacific Place. New as it is, it still lacks the messy vitality of organically evolving urban neighbourhoods. This is instant urbanism. Concord Pacific Place represents a blink of the eye in city-making terms. But in the grand scheme of city-building, Vancouver is barely at the beginning, a much overlooked and underestimated factor in urban design.

But setting aside this criticism, Concord Pacific Place unquestionably is a big part of the extraordinary phenomenon of Vancouver's urban renaissance. With its mix of high-density residential housing, parks, shops and rich range of community amenities, this part of the downtown peninsula—like Coal Harbour—has been utterly transformed in the past ten years. The waterfront has been completely rehabilitated, providing public access to long stretches of hitherto inaccessible shoreline. And by all accounts, Concord Pacific cannot build housing units fast enough: sales have been consistently strong and continue to drive the real estate market. The company's initial land cost has long since been recouped by its condominium sales revenue. And Vancouver has received a new neighbourhood in the process. The achievement stands as a powerful refutation of the inevitability of decline of the North American inner city.

Neighbourhood Densification: The Suburban Players

Although Marathon and Concord Pacific have had greatest influence on the city's downtown skyline, several other major developers are active, among them Aoki Corporation, Bosa Development, Concert Properties, Delta Group, Grand Adex, Onni/Amacon and Polygon. Some of these players have focussed on the downtown stage, and others on the surrounding suburban areas.

Concert Properties has been involved in two of the largest suburban neighbourhood developments. Originally called the Vancouver Land Corporation, the company started life as an entity created jointly by the provincial government, the City of Vancouver and several trade union pension funds to deliver affordable housing in what had always been a tough market for this sector. Three name changes later (from Vancouver Land Corporation to Greystone Properties to Concert), the company has been responsible for creating more than five thousand residential units across Vancouver, many in the affordable category. Most of these units are clustered in a couple of major developments that have contributed to the sensitive intensification of otherwise low-density, single-family areas: Arbutus Walk and Collingwood Village.

Arbutus Walk

Arbutus Walk in the inner-city suburb of Kitsilano is a pivotal example of the comprehensive redevelopment of obsolete industrial lands (the former Carling O'Keefe Brewery) into a medium-density residential precinct set in an established, predominantly single-family area, with minimal negative impact. In fact, it has if anything improved its neighbourhood.

From the outset, homeowners in the surrounding area were determined to ensure that the character of their mostly single-family neighbourhood was not overwhelmed or overrun with traffic. At the same time, the landowner and developer quite naturally wanted to optimize their return on investment while still creating a desirable and marketable new higher density residential project. City planning staff were also very concerned about establishing an appropriate level of density and contextual fit, as well as pioneering several new approaches to neighbourhood planning, such as a new street system and new street design standards, the introduction of an urban greenway and innovative public open spaces. Recalling the site's industrial heritage was also an important aspect of the architectural and public realm design.

Arbutus Walk covers almost 10 ha (25 acres) of land encompassing four standard city blocks between Connaught Park to the west, Arbutus Street to the east, and 10th and 12th avenues to the north and south. An important urban design principle of locating higher densities beside the most significant amenity (in this case, the existing local park with its community centre and ice rink) is admirably demonstrated: several four- to eight-storey buildings range back from the park edge, maximizing the benefits of this space for the largest number of residents. The surrounding area has a mix of single-family and multi-family residences.

Arbutus Walk houses some 2,100 new residents in 1,450 units, at an average density of 210 people per ha (85 people per acre). A mix of street-oriented townhouses and apartment buildings has been achieved with no structure higher than eight storeys, while leaving 0.8 ha (2 acres) for a central park and a generous pedestrian greenway. Approximately 145 non-market housing units (10 per cent of the total number) are seamlessly integrated into what is otherwise primarily market housing. A seniors' assisted-housing project rounds out the residential mix.

An innovative street layout is notable in several respects. The strategy of closing off 11th Avenue through the site has resulted in an east-west greenway that traverses the heart of the project, linking Arbutus Street to Connaught Park. In addition, the new internal streets have been designed to much tighter standards, reducing their widths and intersection turning radii to provide an enhanced pedestrian environment. The streets are further distinguished through the selective use of a rich palette of materials that extends the pedestrian realm across intersections and at mid-block crossings. Traffic calming devices are integrated throughout.

The two new east-west streets read more as narrow lanes, while providing streetfront addresses to Arbutus Walk townhouses as well as other residential buildings beyond the project site to the north. This taming of the street and blurring of pedestrian and automobile use suggests creative strategies for adapting the many existing mid-block lanes that are one of Vancouver's most underappreciated legacies.

The Arbutus Walk master plan, with Connaught Park and the community centre to the west. Courtesy Durante Kreuk Ltd.

The design of individual buildings was parcelled out to a number of different architects, thus avoiding the sterile hand of a megaproject. The results, while varying in success, are generally pleasing to the eye and provide diversity and a strong sense of local identity. Although the awkwardly historicist recreation of the former brewery building facade and entryway is perhaps the least satisfying of these architectural commissions, at its best Arbutus Walk boasts some of the most handsome multi-family residential architecture in the city.

One of the most remarkable results of the Arbutus Walk development is how it has spurred the adjacent three-block length of Arbutus Street (between Broadway and 12th Avenue) into becoming a viable, pedestrian-oriented neighbourhood high street, where none existed before. If this perhaps seems a slight achievement, consider how difficult it has been across North America in recent decades to build traditional, fine-grained, street-oriented retail projects that reinforce the public realm in the face of dominant alternatives such as shopping malls, big-box retailers, strip malls and so on. But it has happened on Arbutus Street.

Here, Vancouver's C-2 zone form of mixed-use development—with three floors of housing over one of shops fronting directly onto the street—has paid off handsomely. With new developments now emerging on both sides of the street, including properties both within and beyond Arbutus Walk, the street has been transformed. Well proportioned and with attention to detail in the public realm, Arbutus Street is fast becoming the focus of neighbourhood public life, with many new shops and services. It may not be avant-garde cutting-edge design, but as solid urbanism, it works.

Arbutus Walk admirably demonstrates many strategies for successfully intensifying a residential neighbourhood without detracting from its pre-existing character and qualities. Indeed, a strong case can be made that this neighbourhood has been improved and enhanced with the Arbutus Walk development.

Collingwood Village

Collingwood Village is a textbook demonstration of the coordination of land use and transportation planning, to the benefit of both. As the result of a new rapid transit station being located in an older industrial pocket surrounded by single-family suburban housing, a major upzoning to higher density housing and commercial uses around the station has taken place. Located next to Vancouver's Joyce SkyTrain rapid transit station, which

Top The view west along the Arbutus Walk greenway.

Bottom An emerging new neighbourhood high street along Arbutus Street.

Derek Lepper photos

The Collingwood Village master plan. Courtesy Durante Kreuk Ltd.

opened in 1986, Collingwood Village is a major contributor to the otherwise limited success of transit-oriented densification within the city.

Collingwood Village is also an exemplar of community-based planning, in which area residents received substantial improvements in local amenities and services as the result of a co-operative planning process with the developer and the City.

About 11 ha (27 acres) of land was assembled by the developer and comprehensively rezoned in 1993. In addition to a total potential of twenty-eight hundred housing units—most of which have been completed—to accommodate approximately five thousand people, there is a significant basket of community amenities: a neighbourhood house, a community gymnasium, a daycare and an elementary school. In addition, 3 ha (7.5 acres) are dedicated to three separate neighbourhood parks programmed for active uses, accommodating sports facilities such as tennis courts and a baseball diamond.

Another significant innovation is the provision and endowment of a community police station by the developer, a first in Vancouver and possibly in Canada. This addressed a key concern of local residents, and by all accounts the result has been a significant drop in crime.

The police station anchors the north end of a short stretch of streetfront retail along Joyce Street near the SkyTrain station, a kiss-and-ride area and a bus loop. Although the crucial corner site at Joyce Street and Vanness Avenue was not part of the original plan, it too has now been redeveloped with residential and commercial uses and, together with some other retail shops across the street, contributes to what is a critical mass of commercial activity around the SkyTrain station.

The housing mix is innovative as well: a combination of affordable market housing and rental, with 20 per cent designed for families with children. A significant number of the housing units are ground-oriented, reflecting this target market. The housing is a mixture of three building types: up to four-storey townhouses and garden apartments, six-storey mid-rise apartments, and several high-rise towers to a maximum of twenty-six storeys. The high-rise towers are on the northern edge of the site to minimize overshadowing and overlooking of the existing single-family houses to the south.

The new housing is buffered from the elevated SkyTrain route that runs along the northern edge of the site by means of landscaping, modest setbacks and acoustic treatment of north-facing units.

A new street grid has been extended across the site, linking back to the surrounding street grid. A central formal street traverses the site east-west from Joyce Street in the west. Development parcels are arranged along this central spine, with short cross streets teeing into it, creating a fine-grained block system.

Buildings have been generally oriented to the adjacent street grid, and they reinforce the street and public open space pattern, particularly along the central spine. However, two towers—to be built in the last, most easterly, phase—will be rotated approximately 45 degrees from this orientation, a decision that is questionable because they do not reinforce the street and public open space pattern. It also remains to be seen how effective and compelling the architectural closure of the eastern end of the central axis will be: the illustrative drawing suggests a very modest architectural element only four storeys in height. A more robust termination of this main axis would be an improvement.

The central street was intended as a major pedestrian axis, but this has not been fully exploited: the double row of street trees called for in the zoning guidelines has for the most part not materialized and the sidewalk treatments are, well, pedestrian. More impressive are several north-south, mid-block pedestrian routes that connect across the site into the surrounding neighbourhood. These pathways should significantly enhance the public realm and pedestrian environment. The overall effect is one of a humanly scaled, very comfortable residential environment in which pedestrians are accommodated.

A significant factor in the success of Collingwood Village as a viable residential neighbourhood is the well-conceived phasing plan. The project is being developed over four phases, and the first three are now complete. With each phase, the amount of proximate industrial use has shrunk, and maintaining an appropriate temporary interface between residential and industrial uses has contributed to achieving residential livability.

When fully complete, Collingwood Village will offer a well-considered mix of housing types for a range of residents and incomes, arranged within a sensible urban street grid, sensitively sited and well connected to the surrounding urban fabric, and with convenient access to the regional rapid transit system. Generous community amenities and recreational facilities belie the fact that this project is in a lower income part of the city that has hitherto had little planning attention. Collingwood Village raises the bar substantially on planning for transitional suburban neighbourhoods in Vancouver.

WHILE NEITHER Arbutus Walk nor Collingwood Village represents a radical reinterpretation of traditional street-oriented urbanism and may even be said to represent a profoundly Northern European bias towards an urban design of bourgeois *politesse,* of peace, order and good governance, they nevertheless are good examples of the type and should be acknowledged as such. Whether this is a relevant strategy for rapidly diversifying Vancouver at the beginning of the twenty-first century is another question entirely.

The British Properties

This brief review of some key players in the story of Vancouver's development community would be egregiously incomplete without at least a passing reference to one of its more colourful constituents.

British Pacific Properties is the land company of the famous Irish Guinness family and a group of West Coast British investors. In the 1920s the Guinness family, sensing a huge real estate bonanza in the then isolated, almost exclusively residential North Shore community of West Vancouver, acquired a large portion of the lands stretching up the slopes of Hollyburn Mountain (commonly referred to as Cypress Mountain). They hired the famous New York–based Olmsted Brothers landscape firm (successors to Frederick Law Olmsted of Central Park fame), to master-plan the layout.

Opposite page Collingwood Village. Derek Lepper photo

This page The future British Properties (then called Capilano Estates) and Lions Gate Bridge, shown hand-drawn on a contemporaneous aerial photo. City of Vancouver Archives Out P625, RCAF photo

The entrance to the British Properties in West Vancouver.

Derek Lepper photo

With its gently curving, quiet streets focussed on the exclusive British Properties Golf Club, this was meant to be high-end territory. Over several decades, and continuing into the present, the company has brought carefully phased subdivision parcels to market, in the process creating one of the most exclusive residential areas in the region: the British Properties.

The key to unlocking the potential of this then inaccessible real estate was the company's foresighted yet audaciously self-serving construction of the Lions Gate Bridge over Burrard Inlet. This Depression-era feat of entrepreneurial engineering, long baulked at by the federal government, finally linked Vancouver to the North Shore, thus assuring the status of West Vancouver (and the British Properties) as a desirable and highly valuable bedroom community.

Ever growing, the British Properties today climbs the slopes of Holly-burn Mountain right up to the 365-m (1,200-foot) contour limit for development. Its sprawling luxury homes boast uninterrupted views over the city, to the southern Gulf Islands and to Vancouver Island. This is the closest equivalent Vancouver has to Los Angeles's exclusive hillside communities of Bel Air and Beverly Hills. And, as with that city, the British Properties illustrates one of the fundamental axioms of real estate development in

Vancouver: that financial and topographical contours correspond almost exactly. The higher the ground, the higher the income.

The irony is that what was intended to be an exclusive enclave for Vancouver's Anglo-Celtic elite has, in recent years, become the home base of an increasing number of expatriate ethnic communities, including a number of the late Shah of Iran's closest friends.

AS THESE FEW EXAMPLES illustrate, large areas of Vancouver have been created or transformed by major speculative developments. It follows, then, that land developers hold a central place in the pantheon of Vancouver's civic and business leadership. And developers are quick to remind their interlocutors, justifiably, that it is they who have delivered most of the newer public amenities that Vancouver now enjoys. Developers are a major force in the urban evolution of the new Vancouver, far more so than individual property owners or indeed perhaps the City itself. The local chapter of the Urban Development Institute is a powerful force in the business community. Perhaps inevitably, the development community has also extended its influence into the political sphere, with strong ties to the current provincial government of Premier Gordon Campbell, himself a former employee of Marathon Developments.

Although it is a force that cannot be underestimated, and one that has contributed mightily to Vancouver's emergence as a model of urbanism, the development community also represents a particular vision of the city's future. It is not one that all Vancouverites share. What many of these projects represent in a very real, tangible way, is the future of the city. As might be expected coming from the development industry, by and large it is not a vision of radical creativity or messy heterogeneity. Rather, it reflects the conservative, conformist tendencies of an industry that markets a soothing image of the city as a place of placid consumption in a setting of languid, unruffled splendour. It is always a glorious sunset in the promotional brochures. The developers have colonized our future, and, as in their photographed sunsets, it is always rosy.

9

A Sense of Place
Characteristics of Vancouver's Public Realm

VANCOUVER HAS a strong sense of place, perhaps as a result of the city's dramatic physical setting, located as it is on a peninsula between mountains, sea and river. Taken together, these powerful natural features give Vancouver much of its distinctiveness and contribute strongly to its physical identity. But these are natural factors. Vancouverites are not responsible for them, protective and sentimental as they may get about them. They were here long before the city was built, and they tell only part of the story.

The city's constructed public realm—that is, the network of streets, formal spaces and buildings that make up the venue of collective urban life—is also an essential contributor to defining this sense of place. And it does not always improve upon the natural setting. Take away its setting, and Vancouver might qualify as one of the more banal architectural constructs of any Canadian city. Until very recently, many of its buildings and particularly its public spaces often have not seemed equal to its setting. Or, to put it the other way, perhaps its natural blessings have made Vancouverites lazy, smug about their environment, even as they ignore it in their city-making. It has been suggested that Vancouver gets away with mediocre public architecture precisely because it has such an overcompensating natural setting.

Nevertheless, there are some notable urban characteristics that contribute to Vancouver's unique sense of place, though it is not always easy to identify these or to differentiate what is constructed from what is natural. But differentiate them we must in order to begin to understand the peculiar nature of this place.

A Waterfront Edge
Vancouver's physical setting, edged by water, has resulted in a significant portion of the city's public realm being located along the waterfront. From the city's beginnings, this was always the case, though on a far smaller scale

historically. Most of it was inaccessible to the public, but the accessible waterfront was from the outset constructed as a space of civic leisure. Many old photographs offer evidence of an intensive community life on the waterfront, with infrastructure to support it: piers, bandstands, bath houses, pavilions and promenades graced the Edwardian waterfront of early Vancouver. English Bay was the principal locus of the waterfront as a zone of leisure, and later Kitsilano Beach as well.

With the decline in waterfront industrial uses in recent years, public access has been significantly expanded and enhanced. A growing proportion of Vancouver's constructed public realm is now waterfront-related: formal seawall walkways and bikeways, lookouts and piers, beachfront parks (Vanier, Kitsilano, David Lam, Jericho Beach, among others), numerous smaller pocket parks overlooking the water, and several streetend access points. In many ways, these elements are a substitute for the more traditional centrifugal public spaces of older cities.

Another unique feature of the waterfront's influence on Vancouver's constructed public realm is how the orthogonal street grid is interrupted and distorted where it intersects with the waterfront. Streets either

Opposite page An urban waterfront: English Bay, c. 1910.

Vancouver City Archives L9N 467

This page An early gracious public waterfront:

the Alexandra Park bandstand, promenade and pier.

Vancouver Public Library 6608

terminate abruptly, as if they might plunge into the water, or they turn and inflect upon themselves, bending to the shoreline to create serendipitous, irregular, sinuous public spaces. The result is several distinctive curvilinear scenic routes along the city's waterfront. More than just streets, these routes are used as places of leisure or at least non-linear movement. Harland Bartholomew recognized this characteristic explicitly in his 1929 plan, in which he identified a network of "Pleasure Drives" across the city. Some still even have the signs identifying them as "Scenic Routes," erected on street lamp poles in an earlier, more innocent time when such gestures were not too self-conscious.

The packs of cyclists who sweep along the curves of South West Marine Drive, or the family taking their gawking out-of-town visitors for a slow meandering drive along Beach Avenue, or the couple languidly walking their dog along the uplands of Wall Street, are all participating in this

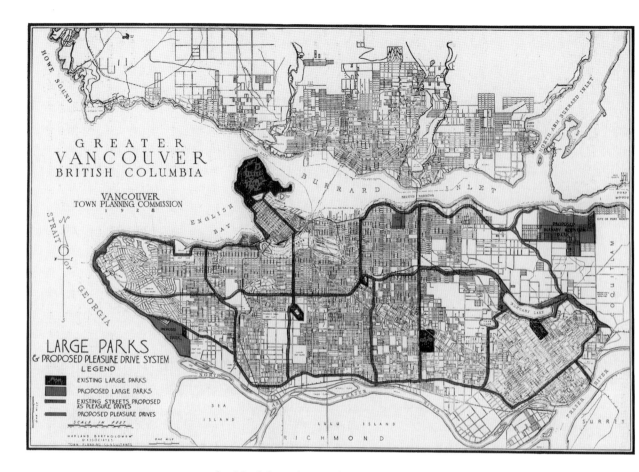

"Proposed Pleasure Drive
System" from Harland
Bartholomew's *A Plan for the
City of Vancouver, 1929*.

By permission of the
Vancouver City Planning
Commission

aspect of public life in the city by the sea, however dimly they may be aware it. Some people even have the good fortune to commute to work by such routes, though for them of course there is perhaps not much succour in this knowledge.

The Missing Centre

The corollary to the waterfront edge condition is that Vancouver really has very few of the more traditional public open spaces at the centre. It lacks the obvious centralizing grand space analogous to Old World cities such as, say, Prague's Wenceslas Square, London's Trafalgar Square or Venice's Piazza San Marco. Even New World cities such as Philadelphia, New York and San Francisco have such spaces, dating back to their origins, whose names act as a kind of shorthand, instantly identifying the city: think Penn Square, Washington Square, Union Square.

What central spaces Vancouver does possess have for various reasons very limited functions in this sense, and in any event they have been effectively overshadowed by the more compelling waterfront edge.

Consider Arthur Erickson's 1970s-era Robson Square complex,[30] which though a formally distinctive, even heroic piece of architecture, aptly symbolizes the point. Robson Square is an unlikely cohabitation of modernism and neo-classicism that helps neither and that fails to engage the surrounding streets. Like a curtain-wall tower lying on its side, the complex straddles three city blocks, bridging over one street and burrowing under another.

Robson Square was carved out of three blocks in downtown Vancouver to become a hybrid of law courts, art gallery, terraced landscape and urban space. But this is a square in name only. There is no primary, substantial open space that is recognizable as a public square in the conventional sense of the word, but rather a diffuse series of interconnected platforms and token tableaux of nature in a labyrinthine sprawl. The closest thing to a square was an ice-rink-cum-plaza (now disused) underneath Robson Street and formerly serviced by a subterranean food fair reminiscent of the ubiquitous suburban shopping mall.[31] The remaining open spaces are heavily planted in a kind of miniaturized recapitulation of surrounding nature, with landscaped mounds, mini-forests, winding paths and hidden spaces.

In the process of creating Robson Square, the old provincial court house was converted into the Vancouver Art Gallery. But most significant was what happened to the public square that fronts onto Georgia Street to the north of the former court house. This formal open space once gave access to the court house's main entry and had served for many years as the city's central square. Although it always had some limitations as a place for public rituals, being spatially weak at its corners and bounded on three sides by busy and wide streets, it nevertheless did have a sense of *gravitas,* a suitably civic function (the court house) as its focus and some fine facades surrounding it.

A remarkable historical photograph of the space at its height of public use shows Vancouver society out in full force to welcome a visit by Canada's new governor general (HRH the Duke of Connaught) in 1912: the court house and surrounding buildings, including the old Hotel Vancouver, are decked out in flags, bunting and swags, people crowd at every opening, and the space itself is filled with officials, soldiers, cadets and citizens in their best finery. The photo illustrates how this space once functioned as the city's main public square. This kind of public assembly is almost inconceivable in this space today, given its subsequent disconnection from the buildings—particularly the court house—that surround it.

As part of the Robson Square conversion, the main entrance to the court house on the north side was permanently closed in favour of a new one facing Robson Street to the south, thereby radically distorting the square's public function and downgrading it to a kind of backyard. The grand steps up to the former court house now lead to nowhere.

The old court house square has been further degraded by the addition over time of several physical elements that have reduced its effectiveness as a place of assembly: a large central fountain, heavy landscaping and planting beds, fencing, railings and so on. Around 1967 the space was officially renamed Centennial Plaza—to commemorate Canada's centenary—a name virtually (and tellingly) unrecognized by Vancouverites today. This largely forgotten public space—by whatever name it goes—now has the air of an orphan, surrounded by wide busy streets, isolated from the life of the city around it and disconnected from the buildings that front onto it. It is a space waiting to be reclaimed in the public consciousness.

And despite its orphaned state, the old court house square to the north is still sometimes preferred for major public gatherings. When Vancouver still officially celebrated New Year's Eve downtown (it has been several years since the City has done so), the space attracted thousands for the year-end midnight countdown, with crowds spilling out onto the surrounding closed roadways. It was exciting, even metropolitan. This not-quite-square almost seemed to work as a focus for public life, in a way that Robson Square never will.

One other space that functions in this more traditional centralizing sense, Victory Square, is discussed in a later chapter.

The Implacable Grid

Overlaid on Vancouver's physical setting is the implacable street grid laid out by the Royal Engineers and the Canadian Pacific Railway's surveyors. Almost the entire network of the city's public streets follows one or another variation of the cardinal grid. The grid is a mechanistic, brutally efficient, universalizing form of subjugating the landscape.

Vancouver's street layout and design is an overarching grid of rectangular street blocks aligned (nominally) on the cardinal compass points. In most parts of the City the dominant (that is, longer) block direction is east-west, with the north-south blocks being shorter: thus, most property frontage faces either north or south. However, this grid orientation is sometimes reversed: then, the dominant block direction is north-south, with the east-west blocks being shorter, and most property frontage facing either east or west. And while there is no readily apparent logic to where the grid orientation changes or why, it is usually a reflection of the different timing of urbanization of various pre-empted land parcels.

Another factor responsible for variations in the street grid, both in its orientation and alignments, as well as in block proportions and dimensions, is the early development of Vancouver as a number of separate municipalities.

Vancouver's street grid is further characterized by a system of mid-block lanes that reinforce the grid and parallel the dominant east-west block direction. However, where east-west streets intersect with major north-south streets—such as Dunbar, Granville, Cambie, Main, Fraser, Commercial, Victoria, Renfrew and Rupert—the east-west lanes usually do not cut through

Top The public space in front of the old provincial court house, crowded for the 1912 visit of HRH the Duke of Connaught.
City of Vancouver Archives Duke of Conn P25

Bottom The old provincial court house square, renamed Centennial Plaza, as it is today, a half-forgotten orphan.
Derek Lepper photo

but tee into a north-south lane system that parallels and supports the major north-south streets. This "T" lane configuration[32] is a unique characteristic of Vancouver's street grid. It reinforces the built form continuity of the primary north-south arterials, key components of the city's public realm.

There are a few notable exceptions to the street grid, the most obvious being Kingsway, which predated the grid and linked New Westminster to Burrard Inlet. Kingsway's diagonal alignment, cutting across a large portion of the city, presents a striking counterpoint to the regular street grid. A small area of streets in the wedge between Kingsway and East 29th Avenue inexplicably follows the diagonal Kingsway alignment, running against the grain of the dominant grid. And of course there are the incongruous curves of Shaughnessy Heights where the regular street grid morphs into a constellation of wavy-line boulevards. And the post–Second World War Fraserview and Champlain Heights subdivisions in southeast Vancouver display their era's predilection for curving suburban street patterns.

Vancouver's rectilinear street grid, however, contains approximately 70 per cent of the total public space within the City. And "single-family" residential streets (that is, streets running through residential neighbourhoods of single detached houses) represent approximately 70 per cent of the total streets in Vancouver. These tree-lined neighbourhood streets, often

Opposite page The post–Second World War subdivision of
Fraserview with its curving streets, in southeast Vancouver.

Vancouver Public Library 9642

This page The ubiquitous tree-lined neighbourhood street,
a quintessential characteristic of Vancouver's public realm.

Lance Berelowitz photo

with grass boulevards and parallel parking on one or both sides, are a
quintessential characteristic of Vancouver's public realm.

A map of Vancouver's street grid reveals several key streets that stand
out as significant both historically and functionally:

- Georgia Street and Burrard Street: With their wider than normal
  rights-of-way of 30 m (99 feet) instead of 20 m (66 feet) and their direct
  connections to bridges, both function as major gateway routes into
  the centre and as pre-eminent ceremonial routes; also, Burrard Street
  defines a significant change in the street grid and block orientation.
- Broadway: The dominant east-west, cross-town spine, and the single
  longest continuous east-west street, it stretches from Boundary Road in
  the east to the University of British Columbia in the west.
- Several other historically significant gateway routes into Vancouver
  include Hastings Street, Granville Street and Kingsway.
- Other key cross-town routes include Main Street, Cambie Street and
  Marine Drive.

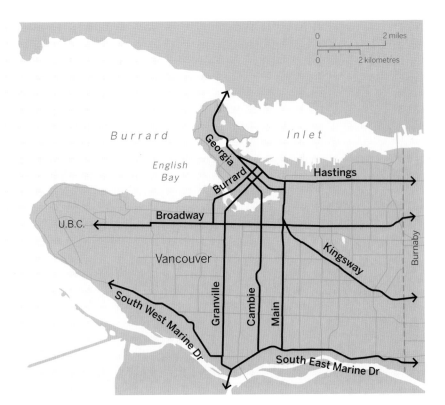

Vancouver's most significant streets.

Eric Leinberger

Sections of these special streets have been recognized as significant through approved special streetscape treatment (for example, downtown Georgia Street). For much of their length, however, many of them do not yet have a consistent quality of streetscape commensurate with their importance. They represent the key links and the city-wide, high-level network of routes by which people create their mental maps of the city. They are the locus of much of the city's public life and most of its commerce.

In a further elaboration of the street grid as a defining characteristic of Vancouver's public realm, the downtown peninsula represents a concentration of those special streets, a more intensive use of the street system, and an increase in the number and diversity of special public spaces.

Shifting Grids and Reflections

Vancouver spreads over a series of geographically distinct peninsulas and promontories, separated by water. As a result of this complex physical geography, another defining aspect of Vancouver's sense of place is that striking views of the city are presented from different vantage points. The city is constantly reflecting on itself in a kind of narcissistic self-display. In addition, and fortifying this appearance of a stage-set city, water and mountain backdrops often terminate the axial views down numerous streets.

Reinforcing the city's sense of place is the fact that the entire downtown is itself located on a small peninsula to the north of the much larger Point Grey peninsula that the rest of the city occupies, separated from the latter by English Bay and False Creek. The downtown peninsula is surrounded by

water on almost all sides, adding to its perception as an island. This physical separation clearly defines the geographic limits of the centre and sets it apart from the rest of the city.

In addition, the downtown peninsula street grid is rotated approximately 46 degrees from the dominant grid, thus intensifying its difference and presenting a unique visual aspect, with two frontages of most buildings being simultaneously visible from parts of the city outside the downtown peninsula. When combined with the reflections of downtown buildings in the water at their feet, these conditions further add to Vancouver's sense of place, its collective visual mnemonic.

Bridges

Where there is water there are bridges, and Vancouver has lots of both. The city's bridges are another defining characteristic of its public realm. In addition to being the city's key physical links, the bridges act as important places of transition, thresholds as well as public promenades. They are also deeply embedded in the collective consciousness of the city, in people's mental maps.

Vancouver, a city constantly reflecting upon itself.
Lance Berelowitz photo

Vancouverites have a store of meaning, images and historic significance associated with many of their bridges:

- Lions Gate Bridge: Gateway to the North Shore, guarded by cast-concrete lions, sculptured portal to Burrard Inlet and the harbour, narrow point of endless constriction, entryway to Stanley Park, object of ineffable beauty, metaphor for land speculation,[33] Gracie's necklace.[34]
- Second Narrows Bridge: Also known as the Ironworkers Memorial Bridge (for the twenty-five men who died in four accidents during its construction), though almost no one calls it that except history buffs and certain local radio traffic reporters. This is the *other* bridge to the North Shore, utilitarian, functional, fast (relatively speaking) and largely out of sight.
- Burrard Bridge: The painted lady, the grand dame of them all, guarding the entrance to False Creek and wearing its art deco styling elegantly, with its playful light towers at each end, its powerful tapered piers, and its curious central overhead structures, mysterious and inaccessible, which span the bridge deck.
- Granville Bridge: High-speed gateway to downtown Vancouver and its first quasi-freeway, with six broad lanes, soaring off-ramps and cloverleaf interchanges at each end.
- Arthur Laing Bridge: Gateway to the airport, escape route to the sun from Vancouver's endless dreary winter.
- Oak Street Bridge: Perhaps Vancouver's longest bridge; its southern end promises the open road, the forbidden freeway, the leaving of urbanity behind and the United States border just down the road. From here on south, it's freeway all the way to Tijuana.

Traversing Vancouver's bridges is a rite of passage, each with its own features. The crossing is always eventful, whether it's a high-speed rush high above the water or an agonizing communal crawl across the tightrope. Negotiating the city's bridges signals a kind of transition from one sense of place to another within this most geographic of cities: you are either in downtown, or in the suburbs, or on the North Shore. The bridges make these transitions absolute; there is no gradual blurring. You are never in any doubt. And with this certainty comes different expectations as to the urban experience. There is no mistaking West Vancouver for the West End.

Residents have their personal favourite bridge routes around which they carefully construct their daily lives, arguing passionately about the

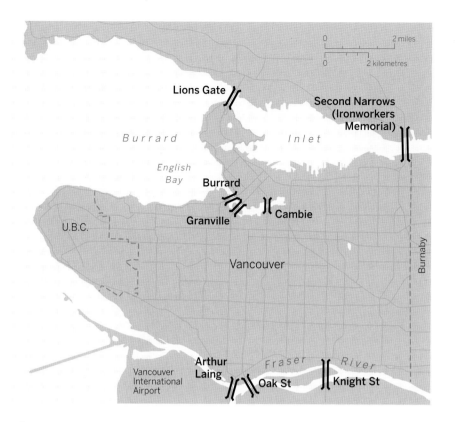

Vancouver's bridges are central to the city's sense of place. Eric Leinberger

relative merits of, say, crossing Burrard Inlet via Lions Gate versus the Second Narrows (locals don't add the word "bridge"), like Parisians with their deeply held parochial loyalties to certain streets and *quartiers*, their preferred *pâtisseries* and cafés.

Each bridge has its coalition of fans and protectors. So, when a few years ago the provincial government proposed replacing the dangerously narrow, substandard and aging three-lane Lions Gate Bridge with a wider and safer new one, complete with dedicated transit lanes, the uproar was immediate, loud and sustained. When the dust had settled, Vancouver got to keep its old Depression-era bridge, and some $100 million later, the lanes are smoother and a little bit wider, but there are still only three.

Vancouverites can be very sentimental about their bridges. They cling to idealized mythologies about them, conflate them into phenomena beyond mere public infrastructure. Listen to Generation X celebrity and writer Douglas Coupland go on about his favourite, Lions Gate Bridge:

> I want you to imagine you are driving north, across Lions Gate Bridge, and the sky is steely grey and the sugar-dusted mountains loom blackly in the distance. Imagine what lies beyond those mountains—realize that there are only more mountains—mountains until the North Pole, mountains until the end of the world, mountains taller than a thousand me's, mountains taller than a thousand you's.
>
> Here is where civilization ends; here is where time ends and where eternity begins. Here is what Lions Gate Bridge is: one last grand gesture

of beauty, of charm, and of grace before we enter the hinterlands, before
the air becomes too brittle and too cold to breathe, before we enter that
place where life becomes harsh, where we must become animals in
order to survive.[35]

Whew! This is no longer a mere bridge but more like a portal to the
netherworld. Such is the power of place.

Neighbourhood Open Spaces

Another defining characteristic of Vancouver's public realm is the significant
number of small neighbourhood parks that are scattered all over the city.
They range in size and scale from a single block simply left undeveloped to
multi-block land assemblies. They are typically surrounded by houses. In
the city's first hundred years of existence, these smaller spaces were significant nodes of neighbourhood life, such as informal meetings and gatherings, sports events, even concerts. Some have commercial uses associated
with them (usually a corner grocery store). The example shown opposite is
Oppenheimer Park in Strathcona, which served as a place of assembly and
protest for Vancouver's working classes.

Many of these small local neighbourhood parks were called for in the
famous 1929 *Plan for Vancouver* by Harland Bartholomew. According to that

Opposite page Lions Gate Bridge at its opening in 1937.

Vancouver Public Library 3036

plan, each 2.5 km² (1 square mile) of residential area was targeted to include four 0.4-ha (1-acre) play parks, one 2.4-ha (3-acre) elementary school playground, up to 2.4 ha (6 acres) of recreation fields and a large neighbourhood park of up to 12 ha (30 acres) in size. Many of the larger park spaces did not get built, but most of the smaller ones did.

Usually laid out with small playgrounds and undeveloped grass fields, these small open spaces will play an increasingly important role in the public realm as the city matures and is further intensified. Over time, they will likely take on more urban attributes, including more hard surfaces and structures. And they are beginning to be surrounded by higher density buildings and a mix of uses. They will, in time, turn into the equivalent of the European urban neighbourhood square. They are one of Vancouver's greatest assets: a network of small public open spaces right across the city.

Top A meeting of the unemployed in Oppenheimer Park, 1938. Vancouver Public Library 6674

Bottom One of a network of small neighbourhood parks.
Lance Berelowitz photo

Granite

A distinctive materiality is often a significant feature of a city's physical identity, its *genius loci*. Think of Jerusalem, built almost entirely of the soft pink stone quarried from the hills on which it stands, or of monumental Third Republic Paris, uniformly clad in its Île-de-France limestone. Such cities are inseparable from their physical materiality. If Sydney is rightly described as a sandstone city, then it might just as correctly be said that Vancouver is a city of granite. The distinctive local "salt and pepper" flecked grey-black granite is found almost everywhere there are rock outcrops. Indeed, one of the world's largest single granite outcrops is located not far north of Vancouver up Howe Sound: hiking the Stawamus Chief is a favourite local activity.

So it is no surprise that another defining characteristic of Vancouver's public realm has been the widespread use of dressed granite stone. This local granite was quarried from Texada and Fox islands up the Sunshine Coast, and barged down to Vancouver.

Historically, dressed granite was widely used for Vancouver's street curbs, especially for intersection radii curves, where its superior strength and durability prevented it from being crushed by the wheels of turning vehicles. These robust granite curbs have easily survived the hundred or so years of use since they were first installed, and still today, you can observe many of them all over the city, though the Engineering Department has an ongoing program of replacing them with poured concrete curbs. Whatever the reasons for this, these old granite curbs, if allowed to remain, will outlast their concrete replacements.

Another widespread use of granite in Vancouver's earlier days was for street paving: rectangular cobble setts laid in a bond pattern. Today, almost all such stone paving has either been removed or covered over by asphalt. But here and there, in obscure corners of the city, the observant urbanist will discover remnants of this paving material that once carpeted the public realm. One or two short stretches of granite-paved streets remain (Hamilton Street along the west side of Victory Square, for example), and occasionally where patches of the now ubiquitous asphalt have worn off to expose the cobblestone layer below.

Granite was widely used for retaining walls, raised planting borders, steps, balustrades, pillars, gateways, bollards and other components of the traditional urban streetscape. It was also popular for cladding public buildings and the most expensive homes of Vancouver's elite.

The local granite can been seen all over the city wherever the public landscape has been modified or required restraining, most notably in retaining walls on sloping topography. Prime examples include the extensive stonework along the Stanley Park seawall, and indeed dressed or rough-split granite is used along most other parts of the city's waterfront walkway network.

Over the years, the local quarries were scaled back significantly as more economic sources of stone (often in mainland China) became available and

the age-old stonemason skills died off. Although its public use has declined in recent years, granite, with its unique textures, colour, durability and strength, still contributes towards distinguishing Vancouver's particular sense of place. Private developments use granite extensively for retaining walls, garden walls, entry gateposts, and even as building cladding.

The City of Vancouver has belatedly begun to recognize this distinguishing feature: several streetscape policies and design guidelines now call for the use of granite in private developments. To date, however, the City has not adopted these guidelines for public works. But that may be changing. In 2003 the City completed a major retrofit of several blocks of Georgia Street and the Stanley Park Causeway. As part of this project, all the new lamp poles have been mounted on custom-designed tapered granite bases,[36] and granite is widely used in the new roadworks and retaining walls as the road enters the park. A case of back to the future?

THESE THEN—the city's waterfront edge, its bridges, its shifting street grids, its "missing" centre, its widespread scattering of small parks and its use of granite—constitute some of the more notable features of Vancouver's enduring sense of place.

Granite, Vancouver's traditional material for civic works.
Lance Berelowitz photo

10

Urbanists at Large in the Garden City

The Search for an Urban Tradition

These fragments I have shored against my ruins.—T.S. ELIOT, THE WASTE LAND

IF VANCOUVER HAS a distinctive sense of place, in large part derived from the intimate intersection of the natural and the built, are there also elements of a tradition of urbanism based on this sense of place? And, if so, is that tradition still informing contemporary urban design in the city? Or has it succumbed to the amnesia of global influences and transient design fashion?

That West Coast equals anti-urban is almost axiomatic in the conventional wisdom of recent architectural criticism. The clichés about Los Angeles, for example—"suburbs in search of a city," "a city built on transport"—were nevertheless founded in facts both incontrovertible and obvious. But are they equally applicable to Vancouver?

When first confronted with Vancouver, it's easy to accept these "truths" about the West Coast and report a region mired in suburbia, a populace infatuated with the pursuit of private gratification and a public life more pleasure craft– than piazza-oriented: all, incidentally, reinforcing the myths so fondly cherished by central Canadians of Vancouver. And it is no accident that Vancouver has long been acknowledged to have the largest opus of quality custom residential architecture in the country: here the individual rules.

But on looking beyond the obvious, there is evidence at odds with received opinion, evidence of a suspiciously urban character lurking in unlikely quarters, suggesting that in an earlier era the city had a clear, if nascent, urban vocabulary, and further suggesting that perhaps only recently did that

Vancouver's earliest
buildings defined the
street edge and reinforced
the grid. This photo was
taken looking out from
the first Hotel Vancouver.
City of Vancouver Archives.
L9N476 Neelands Bros.

urbanism lose some of its potency. Early Vancouver offers a plethora of possibilities and references for those now engaged in the ongoing business of
city-making. And there are signs that the references are being heeded again.

Where to begin the search for an urban tradition?

One way is to look at archival photographs of the city. An extraordinary
fact of Vancouver's history is that because it is so recent, all of it has passed
before the eye of the camera. There is an excellent photographic record
of the city's historic evolution from its very founding onward. Vibrant,
immediate and intensely urban images abound. Even in the earliest photos,
the ordering power of the street grid is apparent, clearly articulating future
development. As the city grew, streets defined by the superimposed grid

were reinforced over time by buildings in a densification of the downtown core. In archival images of the downtown streets, buildings define the street edge clearly, reinforcing the grid and announcing the corner with the placement of the more important buildings. Photos of the harbour, with its urban bustle, recall images of early Manhattan and, before that, of London's long-gone Adelphi Terrace or that "part Durand part Piranesi"[37] extravaganza, the waterfront promenade of Algiers. More recent were the notable boat shed "row houses" lined up in Coal Harbour, a kind of city on the sea and, with the waterfront's recent gentrification, now mostly gone. The late Italian rationalist architect Aldo Rossi would have loved them for their simple, clean restatement of the primal architectural forms of shelter.

Consider this image of early downtown Vancouver, with its strong streetwall, streetfront shops, streetcar and public clock—a picture of surprisingly sophisticated urbanism. With strong build-to lines and an innocence

Downtown Vancouver, c. 1910: a surprisingly sophisticated urbanism. Vancouver Public Library 6645

of floor space ratio computations, many of these buildings, despite their relatively low height, gave a more urban sense to the public space between them—the street—than their thirty-storey reflective-glass successors.

The space between buildings was regarded as a positive rather than a negative void; facadism, even in its one-storey frontier town guise, addressed the street as much as the building. It is curious and perhaps telling that even today, Vancouver's most urbane, lively streets, such as Denman and Robson, are essentially one-storey streets.

Early photos also indicate that public space was defined by rules both well established and simultaneously moulded to the city's particular social and climatic conditions. For example, in rainy Vancouver, the great urban rooms of the old Canadian Pacific Railway station on Cordova Street and its Canadian National Railways counterpart east of Main Street remain, in their current incarnations, among the most appropriate, usable spaces in the city.

These two public structures were complemented by other monumental building types, neighbourhood focal points that rose above the surrounding fabric of residential housing. The city's earlier neighbourhood fire stations, for example, with their elongated "chimneys" and bright red oversized front doors, resembled bloated versions of the neighbouring houses. Or consider

Opposite page Frontier town facadism addressed the street as much as the buildings. Vancouver Public Library 6729

This page B.C. Place, a pre-coital incarnation of the Goodyear airship condom? Derek Lepper photo

the monumentality of the city's earlier brick-clad school buildings, many of which still stand today (though they may not stand up for long in a major earthquake, but that is another story).

The early yet extensive network of small neighbourhood parks (read village greens), those pleasant yet vital urban spaces, often no more than a street block simply left open—prefigure urban squares such as Léon Krier proposed in his Paris La Villette project.[38] As Vancouver urbanizes and densifies, these green patches will inevitably become neighbourhood squares, in much the same way as jousting fields and market gardens became Paris's Place des Vosges or London's Covent Garden. Even Vancouver's rows of early wooden houses, with their simple, repetitive typology, clearly articulated front facades, porches and stairs, gave the streets a sense of urbanity and continuity much as the urban-villa type does in, say, London or Greenwich Village.

These early building types, then, form a by no means exhaustive list of Vancouver's nascent urban legacy—what might be called anonymous urbanism. The evidence is still there, scattered about across the city.

And so to proceed to the more recent past which, for the lonely urbanist in the crowd, is somewhat bleaker than the early evidence.

Frankie may have gone to Hollywood[39] to seek his Pleasure Dome, but he may just as well have found it right here in Vancouver, both metaphorically and literally. For what else is that bloated white dirigible squatting at the edge of downtown but a pre-coital incarnation of Madelon Vriesendorp's Goodyear airship[40] condom? I am referring to the air-pumped, fabric-roofed B.C. Place Stadium, erected in 1983 as Vancouver's panacea for the power of the crowd. B.C. Place is unfortunately neither an appropriate response to its site nor an elegant example of the stadium building type, and it sticks out, quite literally, like a bandaged sore thumb. It is a non-urban form, though, to be fair to the architects, at the time it was built the surrounding area was still largely an open wasteland. The best hope Vancouver has (short of its inevitable demolition at some future date) is that over time it will be increasingly hemmed

in and swallowed up by encroaching development. There are accelerating signs of this happening already in the immediate vicinity.

And you need not have gone to Hollywood either to find the populist movie image of the instant, painless "modern" city. Indeed, you need not have looked further than Expo 86, the world's fair where, adrift in a sea of adoring consumers, you could spot the occasional urbanist, an interloper bemused by the eye-glazing display of gypsum-board fakery posing as the "new" technology come to redeem our post-industrial city lives. But this was 1986, not 1966, and as design critic Mark Potter so eloquently pointed out at the time, the crisis of futurism was never so manifest, nor perhaps so malign, as the Expo 86 site's "Helvetic model of good taste."[41] Looking at and beyond the Expo site, at the swath of land that awaited its future benediction as Concord Pacific Place, you could have been forgiven for being no more sanguine about the prospects for urbanism there. The early post-Expo proposals did not bode well. The first plans for North Park, as the proposed initial phase of development in the northern sector was named, illustrated that a strong sense of urbanism was not high on the designers' list of priorities. The existing adjacent city street grid was largely ignored; streets curved and bent in a parody of suburban tract developments, partly to avoid the Georgia and Dunsmuir viaducts and the SkyTrain support structure, and partly to create a larger park space. Proposed building densities and their disposition expressed a suburban rather than a central city sensibility. The wavy-line school of urban design seemed to hold sway.

However, after much debate and iteration, a more urban plan did eventually emerge, one that attempted to better knit the site back into the fabric of the surrounding city. A key piece of this plan was a public stairway connection between Beatty Street at the top of the escarpment and the vacated Expo lands below. The Keefer Steps, as this piece of public space came to be known, was an important investment in the public realm. And the first phase of what came to be known as International Village extended Abbott Street southward, narrowing the gap between Chinatown and the Expo lands, though to this day only part of the master plan has been implemented, the remaining development still awaiting improved market conditions and amelioration of the persistent social stresses of the nearby Downtown Eastside.

Vancouver's architectural community is justifiably proud of its modern West Coast design identity. This was the city of experimentation, of the new. For some period of time, it forswore any European influences as inappropriate for the rain-forest city. During the 1970s and 1980s and even into the 1990s, the mere mention of European urban models was sometimes enough to earn derisive dismissal, especially in academic circles. The irony was that some of the very things that made Vancouver special and desirable were those very ideas and urban forms initially brought from the Old World. Precious view corridors exist because the streets are straight. The urban scale and charm of Gastown and Chinatown derive from the dense coherency of streets lined with buildings built right to the property lines. Some of the city's most cherished heritage buildings (the Sylvia Hotel, the Manhattan Apartments, the Hotel Europe, among others) are built to densities well above what might be considered for those sites today. And yet it's precisely buildings such as these that help make up the city's urban identity.

The apparent demise of street-making is illustrated, for example, by a fundamental lesson that early city builders understood well but that appears to have been forgotten or discarded during this era. I refer to the case of the missing corner.

Historically, urban corner sites commanded a critical, superior position and were invariably developed first, often with a primary function that defined the pattern of development while leaving room for "a thousand architects"[42] to build between them over time. A short drive up Main Street from 8th Avenue to 16th quickly illustrates the point. The principal public and commercial buildings occupy the corner sites, with more modest infill buildings in between. The venerable Lee Building at the prime intersection of Main and Broadway exemplifies this strategy.

More recently, however, the standard solution to commercial corner sites, based on automotive consumer convenience more than urban design niceties, ignored the traditional practice: parking lots now often occupy what once was the prized piece, with the new building wrapping around the empty corner in an inverted L. The resulting weakening of the intersection and street echoes the North American suburban sprawl of parking lot–swathed supermarkets and strip malls. The missing corner building type can be seen at intersections all across the city. The corner, as a vital part of the urban vocabulary, seemed to be in danger of disappearing.

This makes it all the more ironic that a new phenomenon, which has nothing to do with urban design and everything to do with land speculation, offers a golden opportunity to reverse this troubling trend. Dozens of corner gas stations across the city have been closed down by the large oil companies in recent years. Vancouver's ever-increasing land values, combined with a captive auto-driver market, make it profitable for the oil companies to reduce the number of gas outlets and to sell off these prime corner sites. The sites sit vacant for three or four years, awaiting their decontamination certification, and then they are redeveloped. A new wave of corner buildings is coming on-stream. The missing corner may be about to be rediscovered.

These, then, along with a seeming preoccupation with curving roads, a soft-edged greening of the urban waterfront, ubiquitous potted-plant mini-plazas and a pastoral vision of public space, constituted some of the major components defining the parameters of much of the urban design debate in Vancouver during the 1970s and 1980s.

In this apparent desert of anti-urbanism, it came as something of a relief to discover the interventions of those few architects of that era who, drawing on a different sensibility and alive to the urban vocabulary that Vancouver does possess, produced work that both acknowledged and transcended this vocabulary. A generation of designers such as Alan Parker, Peter Cardew, Richard Henriquez, Norman Hotson and Joost Bakker, Roger Hughes and Nigel Baldwin, and Xavier Bellprat, have each contributed to what French theorist Antoine Grumbach called the "Theatre of Memory"[43] or what Aldo Rossi referred to as *"la fabbrica della città."*[44]

Alan Parker, who was the author of several unrealized planning studies and has since left Vancouver, nevertheless contributed two quintessentially urban insertions that pointed the way for future developments. He worked on the site planning and urban design of two of the city's first SkyTrain rapid transit stations. In the case of the Waterfront Station (1986), Parker grafted the building onto the rear facade of the old (1912) Canadian Pacific Railway station, an architectural collage that both retained and broke through the older building. The addition now serves as a transportation nexus, connecting the SeaBus ferry terminal, West Coast Express train service and SkyTrain station to the old railway concourse, now revamped as a grand vestibule to the city. The result is a dense layering of interconnected urban spaces.

Something of this urban layering occurs in a vertical form in the Burrard SkyTrain station (1986), on which Parker collaborated with Don Vaughan and Peter Cardew. Here, an indoor/outdoor sunken urban room skilfully uses an awkwardly shaped land parcel left over from road realignments and connects the street surface to the lower level of underground routes and malls. The scheme is somewhat reminiscent of the exquisite if diminutively scaled early urban works of Mitchell/Giurgola Architects, such as their subway concourse entrance (1971) and Liberty Bell Pavilion (1975), both in Philadelphia. It is perhaps no coincidence that both these architects and Parker studied under modern master Louis Kahn.

A third Parker project, the curved Expo 86 Canada Gate at the bottom of Granville Street, which wrapped around and screened the brutalist base of the Granville Square tower in a virtuoso display of *bricoleur*[45] collagism, was unfortunately dismantled at the end of the world fair's, to be replaced eventually by yet another sterile reflective-glass corporate tower. Linked to the neighbouring Sinclair Centre redevelopment, it could have formed part of a pedestrian connection between the city and the still-to-be-redeveloped central waterfront.

Richard Henriquez's Sinclair Centre[46] (1986), which cleverly appropriated the mid-block lanes as pedestrian routes, remains somewhat isolated, its putative pedestrian connections that brilliantly bind the four renovated heritage buildings stopping at the edges of the block. Despite this frustration of possibilities, the Sinclair Centre remains Vancouver's most clearly articulated recent response to a highly urban, contextually sensitive brief. That this brief was in fact largely the architects' authorship indicates the rigour with which an urbanist ideology has always been pursued in the Henriquez office.

Indeed, going back to an even earlier era when wholesale redevelopment was the mantra of the day in Vancouver, Henriquez's apostasy of that dogma is revealed in his 1975 Gaslight Square infill project on Gastown's historic Water Street. Maintaining the adjacent streetscape, the new facade, with its repeated bays and brick cladding, acknowledges the rhythms of its older neighbours while remaining resolutely modern, allowing the building behind to step down to an enclosed courtyard. To one side of the courtyard, a stepped incision allows the public almost the only opportunity along this stretch of Water Street to look out over the railway tracks to Burrard Inlet and the North Shore beyond.

Henriquez's ongoing preoccupation with facadism, memory and urban monumentality informs all his work, whether it be the discreet street-making of the Oak Street Fire Hall in deepest south Vancouver or the West End's more obviously mnemonic Sylvia condominium tower (1987), with its blatant references to its much-loved adjacent hotel progenitor. Rather than the politically more acceptable lower envelope built form that city bureaucrats preferred at the time, the tall slim configuration of the Sylvia tower contributes to the visual densification that lends the West End such a powerful

urban imagery from across the waters of English Bay, while simultaneously blocking fewer views than an envelope scheme might have done.

This is not to say all urban housing must be tall. On the contrary, some of Vancouver's most successful inner-city housing was built on the Fairview Slopes leading down to False Creek, at net densities not much lower than the Sylvia tower. Peter Cardew's crisply calibrated row of narrow attached townhouses at 682–698 Millbank Street (1975) along the False Creek South waterfront, for example, was a prototypical contemporary interpretation of that old workhorse of urban housing, the row house. Sadly, this exquisite little project has seldom been emulated since, and never bested. Row housing remains an endangered species in Vancouver.

Roger Hughes and Nigel Baldwin's Governor General's Award–winning Sixth Estate (1982) residential project, to choose another example farther up the hill in Fairview Slopes, with its continuous "city wall" to busy 6th Avenue, forms a bulwark to the many other housing projects that threaten to tumble down the slope behind it. In the Sixth Estate, a clear hierarchy of streets was created: 6th Avenue, the primary vehicular route; a pedestrian route, the internal street through the scheme that separates the retained commercial buildings on 6th Avenue and the new housing above it; and an integration of the existing lane to the rear through a series of cross-routes and facadal elements. This positive response to the "service" lane, elevating it in an enrichment and densification of the public realm through use of the existing street grid, provided a valuable lesson to other architects in the city.

Similarly, Hughes and Baldwin's Pacific Heights Housing Co-operative (1983–85), on Pacific Avenue near the foot of Burrard Bridge, reinforced and intensified the existing street pattern with the insertion of an internal *ruelle* (or alley), which, in this case, separates the restored old detached houses on Pacific Avenue from the new housing block behind. This hierarchical scheme produced a dense, layered block within the relatively modest permitted density parameters, with old and new elements engaged in a rich dialectic of memory and monument.

Another architect who was involved in designing housing co-operatives, and whose work recalls a somewhat more enigmatic "memory" refracted through distance and local exigencies, was Xavier Bellprat. Trained under Aldo Rossi in Switzerland, Bellprat brought a European sensibility to Vancouver, and in doing so arrived at some interesting results. One is the admirably insistent street-making, the boldly urban massing, of his Broadview Housing Co-operative on Broadway (1983), with its almost wilful quoting of forms. Acknowledging the nature of Broadway as a major artery, the co-op, with its innovative (for Canada) mixed-use program, is an urban monument to the collective set in a suburban sea of extraordinarily ordinary Vancouver Specials and single-family homes. In another suburban housing scheme, Bellprat's David Wetherow Housing Co-operative (1985), the theme of public front versus private rear was continued and developed. The formalized regularity of the streetfront facades recalls the collective, while the more variegated rear elevations celebrate the individual. Even in somewhat diluted form (the federal government's Canada Mortgage and Housing Corporation funding agency apparently balked at the first three versions of the design), this project produced a sense of density, community and place that augured well for the future filling out of the Vancouver grid.

Finally, a sense of place, too, is what perhaps most characterizes the early work of Hotson Bakker Architects, particularly their seminal work on the master plan for Granville Island (1979) and the transition from factories to public market that marked this urban renaissance. With its bold adaptation of obsolete industrial buildings, finely scaled sense of density, deliberate mix of uses and immediacy to the water, Granville Island has a

Granville Island, with its finely scaled sense of density and mix of uses.
Lance Berelowitz photo

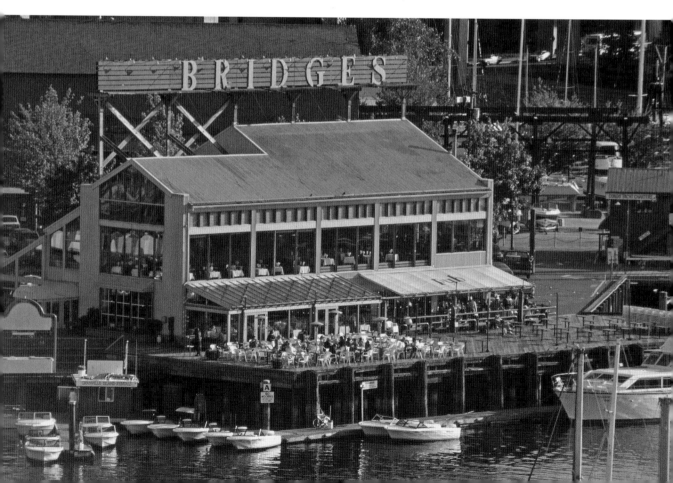

place deep in the heart of Vancouver, perhaps is the heart of Vancouver, beating a rhythm that vaguely resonates in scattered locations about the city.

For, of course, along with all these examples, further "shored fragments" of anonymous urbanism can be found by the careful observer.

Looking back over this assemblage of somewhat tenuous threads from the recent past, and with some serendipity in assimilating the historical precedents still extant, it is tempting to ask if we might not have begun to construct a theory of urbanism pertinent to future development in Vancouver. Perhaps.

In the last decade or so, as new architects came into play, it seemed that the work of the earlier handful described above (in this highest architect-per-capita city in Canada), who produced truly urban work, might have represented the leading edge of a growing body of influence. Indeed, since then, Vancouver has seen the emergence of a particular kind of urbanism, one that builds on this earlier work and—more importantly—has assimilated some basic tenets of sound urban design. Vancouver exhibits if not cutting edge then at least a well-mannered form of urbanism, with the increasing acceptance of such things as the street as the prime venue of public life and the importance of appropriate built form to frame and support it. There has been a significant increase in street-oriented urban housing. Streetfront townhouses have emerged as a viable and growing new part of the housing mix. And there is the emergence in places such as Coal Harbour and Concord Pacific of balanced new neighbourhoods, with a certain rigour to the street pattern and a growing mix of uses.

The city, still embryonic even twenty years ago, is beginning to fill in.

Although advances have certainly been made in many aspects, areas remain to be challenged. The city's streets are still far too wide, or at least far too much of the space is designed for vehicles over pedestrians. And the downtown lanes have yet to be capitalized on as the valuable extension of the public realm that they could become. Vancouver still has a dated approach to land-use zoning, in which uses are over-rigidly separated. And perhaps most glaringly, it has not yet fully embraced the complex, messy diversity of true urbanism that real cities offer. That is going to take time, something that is on this young city's side. But Vancouver is indubitably more urban now than it was even twenty years ago. And the trend is increasing, with the torch about to be passed to a new generation of urbanists. The search for an urban tradition, which might thus inform a dynamic future, continues.

MOST ENVIABLE PA**N**O**RA**MIC

views

Skyline
SKYLINE VIEWING CENTRE

FRO
PAC
ENG
FAL
AND
CITY

11

Edge City

IN HOLLYWOOD CIRCLES, it is referred to as the money shot: the one moment in the movie that costs the most and is the hardest to pull off, but is the best bet to bring in the punters. Vancouver's money shot is a carefully framed view of the Coast Mountains looming over the sunset-coloured waters of Burrard Inlet or English Bay, the middle distance occupied by Stanley Park's groomed greensward, with well dressed strollers taking the evening air along the seawall in the foreground. That is the million-dollar view marketed—if not actually always delivered—by every new housing development.

More than any prevailing theories of urban design or town planning, certainly more than the physical expressions of power of any absolute leader (of which Vancouver has been blessedly bereft) that so often informed the design of older cities, and more even than the deeply rooted culture of land speculation that is central to Vancouver's short history—more than all these possible influences on the city's urban form, there is the View.

Embedded in this cult of the view is an entire construct of urban values that is barely articulated yet powerfully informs the making of the city, and in particular its public spaces.

"Sous les pavés, la plage ..."[47]
In Vancouver, the beach is not far beneath the paving. Indeed, the famous 1968 rallying cry of the student protesters in Paris, as they lifted the paving cobbles to reveal the sand below, finds a deep echo in the collective psyche of Vancouver, one that continues as a powerful impulse in the city. It is the psyche of a city as adolescent, who does not want to grow up, who is not yet ready to acknowledge what she has become ...

The complex symbolic relationship between the quintessentially urban and the profoundly natural as represented in that Parisian battle cry had its counterpart in the West Coast's back-to-nature movement, though,

Top **"*Sous les pavés, la plage* …": graffiti from the May 1968 demonstrations in Paris.** From *La France de '68*, by Alain Delale and Gilles Ragache. A. Bugat photo

Bottom **Lifting the cobblestones of Paris to reveal the sand below.** From *La France de '68*, by Alain Delale and Gilles Ragache. Jean Pottier photo

Billboard for a new
Vancouver development:
selling the view.
Lance Berelowitz photo

Vancouver, it was more a case of staying *in* nature than getting back *to* it. This is a young city, and for many of its residents, it is actually an excuse for the place, a necessary inconvenience on the natural landscape; it is a means to an end that has little to do with urban living but a great deal to do with the private pursuit of nature and leisure. And this, of course, is the opposite of what is conventionally understood as the basis of a public domain.

Gertrude Stein's famous remark, "There is no there there," might well have been said of Vancouver, if she had known of the place. It aptly summarizes the dilemma of this city. Born as it was of a set of accidental imperatives and nurtured more as an ideal or a state of mind rather than an economic entity, Vancouver is the ultimate vanishing trick. At a distance, the city appears as a nascent Manhattan, rising sheer out of the surrounding sea: tall, dense, complex and urban. But the more you look at it and the closer you get, the less of a city it is.

The combination of an overwhelming topography that lends itself to, even demands, contemplation; a benign climate that requires very little shelter, which is the more usual first demand of built urban form; and the soft materiality of a city built primarily of wood, forms an urban ethos peculiar to Vancouver. This is a soft, predominantly low-density city that is open to the environment and revels in its stunning natural setting. It is easy to describe Vancouver as anti-urban, but it may be more apposite to define it as a particular type of urbanism in which the city acts as a sort of mirror or a vast display case for the aesthetic consumption of nature. In this context, it is interesting to note the changed role of the voyeur in society as he has moved off the boulevards of the Old World onto the freeways of the New: Charles Baudelaire's Parisian public *flaneur*[48] has been transmogrified via Raymond Chandler's Los Angeles private eye[49] into the near mystic voyeur of nature in Vancouver. In this metamorphosis from the street-oriented and centripetal urban model to the outward-looking Centrifugal City, activity intensifies towards the edges. The centre is stilled.

This distortion of public space, where people are supplanted by nature as the primary actor in the public domain, is very much in evidence in what is supposedly Vancouver's central public space: Robson Square. This confusing, multi-levelled public space is treated as a miniaturized wilderness and presented as a public labyrinth, complete with arbour, waterfall and hillock. In a city surrounded by nature writ large, these seem misconceived elements that recall the old saying, "If Mohammed won't go to the mountain, the mountain must come to Mohammed." Under the overbearing metaphor of building and urban space as natural landscape, it is difficult to actually see where Robson Square itself is. The square encompasses, in a miniaturized form, the idealized image of Vancouver as a city of nature; it is a Lilliputian representation of the natural idyll. As an iteration of the Pacific landscape, Robson Square is a measure of the myth of the city, but as a public space it largely fails.

Robson Square's architect, Arthur Erickson, whose contribution to Vancouver's impressive modernist residential architectural heritage cannot be underestimated, is the classic "object" architect, whose most imaginative work (the North Shore custom houses, Simon Fraser University, the Museum of Anthropology, etc.) shows best in pristine landscaped settings uncluttered by urban contextualism, unfettered by the need to fit in. That Erickson has been so much admired and emulated throughout his illustrious career reveals more about his admirers than about the architect. And the fact that so many of the city's design practitioners have passed through his office is no source of succour to the urbanist. After Robson Square, a plethora of other architects' projects sprouted across the city, many of them—with their potted trees, meandering streams, rolling hillocks and weak street frontages—representative of an anti-urban ethos.

Preoccupied with the experience of nature, Vancouverites have reduced their public spaces to serving private experience: the public *flaneur* becomes the private voyeur. Of course the transformation of public person from performer to consumer of spectacle (in this case of nature) has had a profound effect on the forms of public culture. This effect is best epitomized in Vancouver in what may be called the Cult of the View. The Cult of the View, in turn, has been a powerful imperative in the creation of a distinct typology of public spaces in the city: Public Platforms for contemplation of the Natural Tableau.

Before considering specific cases of this in Vancouver, it is worthwhile recalling the wealth of historical precedent. From Camillo Sitte's description of the Piazzetta San Marco with its "splendid view across the Grand Canal toward San Giorgio Maggiore"[50] to Frederick Gibberd's "open fourth wall,"[51] the public space that draws the landscape into the city is well documented. Gibberd cites Michelangelo's Piazza del Campidoglio in Rome as the classic example.

In *The Design of Cities,* Edmund Bacon points out numerous Italian examples of this enduring phenomenon, and indeed this urban type abounds in the hill towns of Italy in which the quintessentially urban is tied into a wider geographical whole. Similarly, Colin Rowe's atemporal, catholic collection of favourite stimulants in *Collage City* includes, under the category of "splendid public terraces," Florence's Piazzale Michelangelo and Vicenza's Piazzale Monte Berico, which he compares to the terraced promenades of London's Adelphi, Baden-Baden's Friedrichspark and Algiers's waterfront.

And while thinking of port cities, an attenuated version of the platform type becomes evident: the Promenade. Examples of the waterfront promenade could include lesser known but perhaps more directly comparable examples such as the Sea Point promenade in Cape Town, the heroic hard-edge seawall encompassing the old town of Syracuse in Sicily and of course Venice's Riva degli Schiavoni.

From all of this, it is clear that far from being unique to Vancouver, the platform type of public space that draws countryside and town together is a well-established part of the urban vocabulary. What remains different about Vancouver, certainly in the Canadian context and perhaps even in the global one, is the extent to which the surrounding natural landscape, as opposed to the built city, is the source of inspiration in the creation of urban form. There is a strong, almost "moral" sensibility that unsullied nature is superior to human artifact and that the urban construct is an intrusion on, and not a complement to, the landscape.

There is something oppositional about this sensibility when stated in such a binary way: the city as Experience versus the land's Innocence. And this is directly reflected in the polarization of local politics. You are either a preserver of the sacred ways or a builder of the new way. It is difficult to carve out any middle ground, politically as much as in the design of public spaces.

The formal equivalent of this polarization may be interpreted as the opposition of static and dynamic public spaces. The static platform has an overriding quality of passivity and contemplation while the dynamic platform serves spontaneous collective acts. In the case of the static platform, nothing much public, let alone revolutionary, is going to happen; with nature as the principal actor, there is little to fear from the public now rendered as passive spectator.

If public space is where homogeneity breaks down, where civic rights and rituals are exercised, then what Richard Sennett[52] calls a Public Geography—that is, a coming together of a Crowd in a Public Space—has but a tenuous foothold in Vancouver. The city is endowed with a number of platform spaces in which the public is rendered passive. Indeed, this is the dominant typology, and there are many examples ranging from larger central spaces such as CRAB Park overlooking Burrard Inlet to the pocket platforms along suburban Point Grey's northern shore.

A sequence of view platforms punctuates the Burrard Inlet edge of the downtown peninsula, where the focus is as firmly on the natural tableau as in the previous suburban examples. Here, the surfaces are harder, but nature is still venerated. In these platforms, bridges, arcades and lookouts, the focus is clearly on the distant, not the immediate.

This sequence culminates at the foot of Thurlow Street in the aptly named Portal Park,[53] which formerly overlooked Burrard Inlet. Portal Park is a classic example of the platform type. It faces outward, turning its back to the city, which in turn does not address the space. There is no public activity save for the contemplation of nature. The View function is reinforced by the formal Lookout at the former escarpment. Just in case you miss the point, a large and rather crude pavilion shelters an inlaid map representing Vancouver's so-called "neighbours" around the Pacific Rim. It is surely significant that the only built structure in the space does not offer any public activity but rather enshrines the Distant. Here, you are definitely at the Edge.

These static platforms reflect the centrifugal nature of public space in a city in which activity constantly tends towards the edges. Nothing happens in these spaces; they simply exist. Public life requires collective activity,

Portal Park, enshrining the Distant: it was at the edge of the downtown escarpment until Marathon's Coal Harbour development created a new ground plane.
Lance Berelowitz photo

but these are platforms for private consumption. The tourists pointing their cameras here at the panoramic view beyond are really focussing on their homes across the Pacific.

Ironically, Portal Park now has lost its unconstrained panoramic view from the edge: with the rapid filling out of Marathon's Coal Harbour development in front of it, the natural escarpment edge has all but disappeared, as the new ground plane has been extended out over the former railway yards below. A new manicured waterfront park, Harbour Green, will take its place. The aestheticization of public space continues.

The other kind of platform space, the dynamic space, is more rare in Vancouver, though it does exist. The dynamic platform has an overriding quality of active space where public life may take hold. The natural tableau is just as spectacular, but in this variant it is a backdrop against which such daily rituals or urban interaction as may remain in the North American city are acted out. Perhaps the best Vancouver example of this type is the small square beside the Granville Island Public Market, overlooking the waters of False Creek.[54] The setting and views are dramatic, but there is a multiplicity of public activity, by no means confined to consumption of the natural tableau. Nature is displaced, in this case by food!

The bath house at English Bay is another example. The bath house itself forms an active built edge to Beach Avenue, providing both an extension and enrichment of the beachfront promenade activity below it and a platform to beyond. With its rooftop terrace and stepped cross-section, the bath-house structure forms a happy connection between the city and the sea, supporting a range of urban uses that connect the active and the passive.

Which brings us to the Promenade. The linear promenade is a version of the dynamic platform in its most stretched, idealized form. This formal distortion of public space is reflected in a parallel distortion in public activity. The linear promenade has now become the *sine qua non* of all waterfront development in Vancouver. No developer can now contemplate a new waterfront project without its automatic inclusion. The waterfront walkway has become a sacred cow in this city, and its citizens ardent worshippers. Everything happens at the edges of Centrifugal City.

The most heroic exemplar of this type, the apotheosis of public space as linear viewing platform, is surely the Stanley Park seawall. Begun in the 1930s, it took master stonemason James Cunningham thirty years to complete: 10 km (6 miles) long and some 3 m (10 feet) wide, it may qualify as the narrowest and longest public space of any city in the world. It is probably fair to say that here, girdling the western perimeter of the downtown peninsula, Vancouverites come closest to enacting the rites of the *passeggiata,* that quintessentially urban form of public passage. But an interesting paradox arises when the most active public life of a city happens not at its centre but at its edges. In the case of the Stanley Park seawall, a rich lexicon of public forms can be discerned, albeit in ways distorted from the more conventional sense of urban public space.

At English Bay beach, where the grid of city streets melts into the park, the seawall appropriates the role of the typical street sidewalk, beginning the displacement of the public street life from the city. Following the curves of the shoreline westward, the seawall forms a distinct edge to the land, a sinuous delineation in granite of the public domain, much as would a medieval street.

All along its length, a set of public space typologies is revealed: the Intersection, the Terraced Connection, the Grand Stair and the Lay-by. A series of nodes, such as where routes intersect service facilities, form the major foci for civic activities. Here, the civic architecture is enhanced, much as it would be in a piazza. All the while, the natural tableau is never far away; but as you move farther out, the city itself begins to enter the natural backdrop, engaging and indeed even usurping it at points. There is drama in the detail and clarity in the sweep, which are admirable conditions of any cityscape.

The rigour of the route is implacable, in some places carving through the rock face like a Roman road, in others turning a corner to reveal another exemplar of heroic civic engineering, such as the Lions Gate Bridge.

Opposite page The English Bay Bath House forms an active built edge.

This page The Stanley Park seawall carving its way through rock.

Lance Berelowitz photos

Two views of the Stanley
Park seawall: a set of public
space typologies is revealed.
Lance Berelowitz photos

The mythology of the rain forest is clearly acknowledged in certain places, such as in the case of a creeper-clad archway into the green underworld, an entrance to the park's interior that is reminiscent of the baroque Italian villas of Bomarzo or Lante.

Swinging around from the depths of the forest, the simple yet powerful forms of the seawall become increasingly stylized as it approaches the city again, until, nearing Georgia Street, it disappears completely beneath the manicured recapitulation of nature in the city. The public promenade has come full circle, its strength waning again as it is repossessed by the city, in perfect expression of the paradox of a city whose most active public life is at its edges.

The quest, then, should be for a combination of the obvious virtues of natural setting with the equally obvious ones of urbanism. It ought to be possible to live at the doorstep of nature, yet participate in an active collective public life. Vancouver, it seems to me, has just this opportunity, and if so developed, could be one of the most rewarding urban experiences anywhere.

The conjunction of natural topography and formalized city could result in powerful public spaces that are part of the natural context while enhancing the urban context. The Stanley Park seawall gives a clue as to the power of the possibilities. It ought to be possible to bring the seawall back to town.

There is an area that presents just such an opportunity, in which the Cult of the View might meet the Culture of Congestion.[55] It is an opportunity that, I venture to suggest, would have long since been developed in any European city. The site consists of a sequence of spaces along the northern edge of the downtown peninsula, between Howe and Richards streets.

More through serendipity than any grand vision, a series of interconnected interior spaces and public platforms can be experienced or almost experienced.

The sequence of public spaces begins at the Sinclair Centre,[56] a city block comprising four discrete old buildings knitted together by enclosing the mid-block alleys between them. Passing through a covered public

From the Sinclair Centre to The Landing, a sequence of interconnected public spaces.

Lance Berelowitz drawing

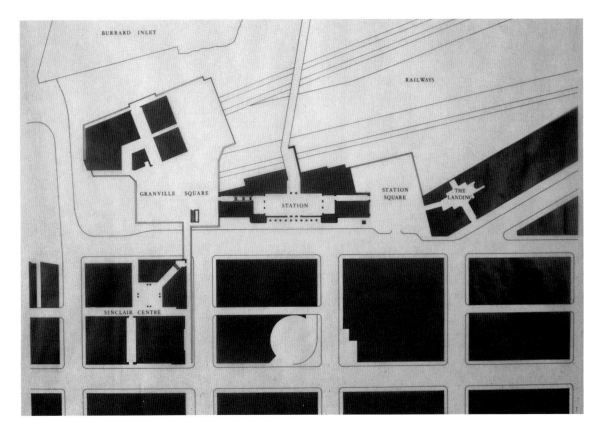

court (an urban room) carved out of the middle of the block, you move out onto a pedestrian bridge that crosses over to the public platform of Granville Square. Originally built over the railway tracks as a podium for the Vancouver Port Authority office tower, Granville Square recently underwent a major facelift. Once a rather tired-looking space, it now sports a fresh new collection of seating walls, raised planters and trees, and, though it is somewhat disconnected from the rest of the city, it nevertheless forms a strong, hard-edged platform to Burrard Inlet. The square occupies an impressive position at the foot of Granville Street, the city's major shopping and entertainment thoroughfare, and forms a vital connection between the city and the adjacent former Canadian Pacific Railway station. The CPR station[57] has an upper-level entry from Granville Square that begins a major axis of movement through this renovated building. Inside, the station has been very successfully adapted to serve as an important transportation nexus connecting buses, the SkyTrain rapid transit system, the West Coast Express commuter train service and the SeaBus ferry across Burrard Inlet. Its hall is also one of the finest urban rooms in the city.

Walking eastward through the great hall of the CPR station, you approach a putative public platform that might optimistically be called Station Square. It is in fact the roof of a parking structure that bridges out over the natural escarpment below. Currently a surface parking lot, this stunningly underused public platform overlooking Burrard Inlet and the entire North Shore now provides a spectacular view for a bunch of parked automobiles, whose owners pay dearly for this dubious privilege.

This sequence of public spaces ends with the old warehouse building that forms the east side of Station Square, reincarnated in 1988 as The Landing mixed-use development[58] and which, until recent renovations closed it in, had a double-height public atrium at its centre. This internal public space is accessible from the square only through double-fronting retail shops, but it would be simple to re-create it and provide a better connection to the square, thereby further intensifying this chain of spaces.

As for Station Square itself, it also has a direct relationship to Cordova Street, which passes behind it to the south. It is a true square in the sense of being a space carved out of the fabric of the city, as opposed to an open block surrounded by streets. And what a public space this could be, with a little imagination and some capital. However, the civic and economic mechanisms must still be found to bring this piece of the urban fabric to its full potential as a major public space. It would not take much. The space

Station Square, a putative public space.

Lance Berelowitz photo

has well defined edges to the west and east, with older buildings (including the CPR station) fronting right onto it, providing the possibility of active uses such as cafés and restaurants. With the parked cars removed and the handsome heritage buildings flanking it opened up to the square, it could become the most cogent and dynamic public platform in the city. A low wall with lookout points along the edge, a unified design for the space that combines access, surface treatment, street furniture and pedestrian lighting, and perhaps the relocation of the adjacent war memorial statue to provide a focal point, would result in a rich public domain animated by people, traffic and trains. Without aping the contrived historicism of adjacent Gastown's so-called beautification, the task here is simply to complete the square. Perhaps here, finally, you could imagine a true Public Geography.

And what of the natural tableau? Looking out from Station Square, Vancouver's essence is richly revealed. The ever-changing waterfront, the containers of goods that enter the country here, the trainloads of grain just arrived from the Prairies, are all evident. Beyond is the bustle of the port with its freighters, ferries, seaplanes, cranes and tugboats. Across Burrard Inlet on the North Shore are the grain silos holding Canada's ransom. And beyond, above the traffic and the commerce of the city, rises the majestic panorama of nature, a fitting backdrop to an active scene, neither dominating nor demeaned, but balanced with the city.

On the North Shore, grain silos holding Canada's ransom.

Lance Berelowitz photo

BOTH VANCOUVER'S urban form and its public spaces have been profoundly informed by the view imperative. In Vancouver, this view is typically distant, panoramic and outward rather than inward-looking or overlooking the built environment, such as, for example, Manhattan's Central Park, long considered the prime real estate view location in New York City. In Vancouver, it is not the view of the city that is prized but rather the view of a distant Natural Tableau.

This phenomenon has affected the form and size of buildings at the periphery: most taller buildings are arrayed around the edges of the downtown peninsula. And it has also driven the market price of real estate in ways that are not typical of other cities: whereas in London, say, it is the square mile of the City that historically commands top dollar or, in New York again, the apartments facing onto Central Park, here it is the land around the waterfront edge that has the highest value.

The cult of the view has also skewed the more traditional, practical considerations in building design and layout, such as the orientation of buildings towards the sunlight (to the south in Vancouver), here largely reversed because the views of the mountains are primarily to the north.

The cult of the view has been codified by the City of Vancouver in a series of overlapping official "view corridors" laid over the map of the city. These view corridors, established from a somewhat arbitrary set of fixed locations around the city, are intended to "protect" public views of the distant mountain panorama from anything so crude as a building. They severely restrict the location and height of new buildings and as such are a major determinant of the emerging urban form.

However, the influence of the cult of the view in site-planning and architectural design is perhaps nowhere more explicitly illustrated than in the recent proliferation of slim high-rise residential towers. Out here on the West Coast, this newer generation of towers—dating back to the 1980s—has redefined the type. They have been distorted to address the view imperative in some very interesting ways.

High-rise Anxiety

Towers pierce the Vancouver skyline at unfamiliar angles and with unusual profiles, claiming a popular vista, terminating an axis or framing a familiar view. With their rooflines often completed by cupolas, turrets, spires and even sky trees, they present themselves proudly for the city to behold.

At first, the appearance of an odd new tower here and there, quirky, slim and unlike anything that had gone before, might have been dismissed as a one-off bit of architectural indulgence. But in the past two decades the number of these towers that has sprouted—like so many mutant trees in a New Age forest—makes it impossible to dismiss them as occasional aberrations. Sometimes whimsical, sometimes inspiring, occasionally clumsy or just silly, they are Vancouver's new generation of high-rise residential towers, and they have arrived.

What do these newer residential towers have in common? And what makes them, as a group, perhaps unique in North American—certainly Canadian—cities?

The first comment many observant visitors to Vancouver make about its built form is how slim so many high-rise residential towers are. The Vancouver tower footprint is usually much smaller than those in, say, Toronto or Montreal or New York. This is partly due to the historical patterns of development that resulted in Vancouver's West End evolving as one of the highest-density residential districts of any North American city. In the 1960s and '70s the city was growing fast. Families were moving out of the West End into the rapidly expanding single-family suburbs. At the same time, many new immigrants were arriving, often young and single, and more accepting of a high-density urban lifestyle. City Council encouraged urban growth in the West End by permitting densities of 2.75 to 3.00 floor space ratio (FSR is the maximum permitted floor area divided by the total site area) on narrow residential double lots. This, together with the small size of lots, 10 m (33 feet) or even 7.5m (25 feet) wide, quickly led to a multitude of narrow towers. Relatively low land and labour costs, combined with high demand from the many newcomers, did the rest. By 1980 the West End had some twenty-eight thousand units housing a population nudging forty thousand.

These slim new high-rise towers are not cost-efficient, however, so why do they continue to be built? The per-square-metre cost of constructing a twenty-storey tower of say 560 m^2 (6,000 square feet) per floor is significantly more than the cost of building one of 930 m^2 (10,000 square feet) per floor. The vertical circulation core (elevators, stairs and service ducts) is the same, for one thing, and thus the gross to net (that is, saleable) floor area

Vancouver's West End has evolved into one of the densest residential districts in North America.
Lance Berelowitz photo

ratio changes dramatically. What this means is that slim towers are more expensive to build on a saleable per square metre basis. The extra cost of this change must be borne somehow, and it is the end purchaser who does the bearing. Why?

He or she does it for the view.

The willingness to pay for spectacular views over the heads of the rest of the city to the sea and mountains beyond is what offsets the construction cost inefficiencies. People have always been drawn to Vancouver for its superb setting, waterfront location and seductive (relative to the rest of Canada) climate. Those endless sunsets (when it's not raining) over the Strait of Georgia sell the units that have views of them, and never more so than now. Buyers, increasingly from offshore or other—landlocked—Canadian provinces, are prepared to pay dearly for their piece of visual paradise.

Certainly, a little piece of paradise does not come cheap. For example, even the smallest one-bedroom units, which are less than 75 m^2 (800 square feet), in the then new 1000 Beach Avenue tower were listed at up to

The Tudor Manor con-
dominium tower, rising
behind the facade of
the fake Tudor original.

Derek Lepper photo

$368,500 back in 1991. Since then, the price has kept going up. Who nowa-
days can afford the price of the front-row view? Increasingly, and perhaps
inevitably, the new condominium towers offer a lifestyle and form of tenure
that only the wealthy can afford. The days of affordable rental units on the
waterfront are all but gone. Most new buildings are market-priced strata
title condominiums. Many residents, particularly in the West End, worry
about this apparent "Manhattanization." Part of the area's very success was
attributable to the rich mix of income levels, age and social groups, and
tenure options. If the bulk of the newer downtown condo development is
contributing towards the demographic homogenization of the West End
through gentrification, this can only be lamented.

In fact, however, the actual number of West End rental units lost to
condominiums is quite small. One reason is that these slim condominium
towers by their very nature generate quite small numbers of housing units.

For example, the three exclusive condominium tower projects designed by Henriquez & Partners Architects in the late 1980s (the Sylvia, the Eugenia and the Presidio) between them account for fewer than sixty units. Even a tower at the upper end of the size range, such as 1000 Beach Avenue, designed by the Hulbert Group, has only just over a hundred units. And in many cases a new tower replaced only a couple of old houses or non-residential uses, rather than rental housing units. Nevertheless, these luxury one-or-two-suites-per-floor high-rises raise a legitimate concern in terms of both density and demographic diversity.

Architecturally, certain themes are shared by this new breed of high-rises. Foremost is perhaps the postmodernist sense of displacement, a loss of authenticity in either design or construction; in its place is an architecture of reconstructed or "quoted" parts.

One of the earliest projects to display this disquieting sense of displacement and/or replication was the Tudor Manor condominium tower over-looking English Bay, designed by Paul Merrick Architects in 1988. With the self-conscious *savoir faire* of a fashion model on the runways of Paris, it rises, clad in its not-so-subtle references to its progenitor, out of the propped-up facade of the fake Tudor "original" low-rise apartment building—an unfortunate case of redoubled replication of the already dispossessed.

Richard Henriquez has argued that his work has as much to do with re-invention and recollection as displacement. His Sylvia condominium tower (1987), also on English Bay, was a benchmark for the new breed. In many ways, the project broke new ground and staked out the major elements of the new type: the very small footprint of only 260 m² (2,800 square feet), which the architects proved blocked fewer neighbouring views than a wider, lower form; the view-driven rotated plan; the historical references; the distinctive rooftop capping, and the introduction of the single unit per floor formula (which had been tried occasionally in the 1960s but not since).

Other elements that presented themselves in the Sylvia scheme and that found their way into subsequent tower projects by Henriquez and others were the extensive use of glass, open balconies on every floor and the treatment of the ground plane as a kind of *promenade architecturale,* an assemblage of invented historical patterns, references and recollections.

Henriquez takes this theme of invented recollection very seriously, if only as a starting point on which to hang a design. It is a neat conceptual device, a storyline that drives the architectural decisions, and it has produced some very evocative buildings. However, it takes a very literate public to understand the references. The reason for a living tree atop the Eugenia tower and precast concrete tree stumps at its base, or for a virtual reconstruction of Adolf Loos's famous Villa Karma at the base of the Presidio, eludes the average passerby, even as it informs the architect. Nevertheless, these three projects, with their deconstructed site plans and dichotomies of form, materials and memory devices, represent the mature work of a thinking, gifted architect and will long remain identified with the special Vancouver type.

Down the road from the Sylvia tower, at the foot of Burrard Street just before it cranks away to cross over False Creek on the piers of Burrard Bridge, is 1000 Beach Avenue. This project, on a waterfront site bisected by the visual axis of Burrard Street, consists of "terraces," "villas" and a twenty-seven-storey tower, all arranged around a marine plaza and marina. The original master-planning for the site was done by Henriquez. Two owners and two architects later, the office of Rick Hulbert was hired to design, among other parts, the tower.

The 1000 Beach Avenue tower frames one side of the southward axial view down Burrard Street and as such is acutely in the public eye, very visible from both downtown and the nearby bridge. The tower design has responded to this with an almost frantic accumulation of thematic elements. Its massing goes to extraordinary lengths to present a different response to each condition of orientation. The plan, essentially a simple square of about 600 m² (6,400 square feet), is manipulated with a series of projections—angular and curved—which at times define rooms and at other times form outdoor balconies. In fact, each corner unit (four of the typical five units per floor) has a balcony, even if it is not much more than a closet-sized angular prow. At the northwest corner, facing up towards Burrard Street, is an octagonal turret capped with the obligatory peaked hat. It's as if the design attempted to include every trick in the book of postmodernist devices. Many of the elements recall, especially from a distance, the Sylvia or Eugenia, which are themselves reconstructive exercises in part. And 1000 Beach Avenue has by no means been the only recent building to do this; the amorphous replication of borrowed elements characterizes many of these 1980s towers.

A much smaller project of this era, but with an equally prestigious address, is the diminutive thirteen-storey tower at 1668 Alberni Street by Hywel Jones Architect. Although this building exhibits almost all the by now typical themes, with a tiny footprint of around 170 m² (1,800 square

The 1000 Beach Avenue tower, framing one side of the axial view down Burrard Street.
Lance Berelowitz photo

feet), one unit per floor, a hinged plan and open balconies, etc., it neverthe-less achieves an unlikely degree of efficiency. The repetition of unit types throughout (except in the penthouse), the absence of shared elevator lobbies at each floor and the use of cheaper materials contributed to achieving a construction cost of a remarkable $1,130 per m^2 ($105 per square foot).

The ground plane was rendered as a passive, low-maintenance land-scape, terracing up to conceal the underground parking ramp that comes in off the higher elevation rear lane. As with the earlier Henriquez projects, a complicated set of formal landscape moves allude to the geometric genesis of the plan. In this case, a curved arc generates an elegant trellissed pergola that helps to screen the lane. This curve resonates up through the height of the tower in the north-facing balconies.

The developer's decision to use stucco over steel studs and the architect's loss of control over interior design decisions resulted in a building that never quite lived up to the full potential of its elegant proportions, restrained formalism, good neighbourliness and subtle colour scheme. Nevertheless, it is a prime example of the view imperative made manifest.

Finally, a project that seems to fly in the face of the aforementioned schemes in terms of its iconic philosophy is Matsuzaki Wright Architects' exclusive Les Terraces condominium tower (1991) on the water-front in West Vancouver. Partner-in-charge Eva Matsuzaki had spent several years in Arthur Erickson's office as one of his key designers, and Les Terraces displays Ericksonian influences. With its clarity of constructional order, restrained palette and eschewing of then current formalistic clichés, this tower offers a healthy antidote to its more excessive downtown contemporaries. However, this project does share with them many of the same elements: it too has one unit per floor, each averaging 280 to 370 m² (3,000 to 4,000 square feet), and is served by two elevators. A stepped section creates large terraces oriented towards the distant—and, it must be said, spectacular—views over the Strait of Georgia and the Gulf Islands. The top two floors combine to form the now *de rigueur* penthouse suite, and the ground floor, as with all the other examples, is given over entirely to access and circulation. In between these two extremities, a fully enclosed swimming pool and gym are offered for the exclusive use of residents, supervised by the building manager ensconced in his live-in suite.

Representing perhaps the apotheosis of its type even while offering a formalistic rebuttal to its downtown peers, Les Terraces demonstrates the vigour with which Vancouver has been able to promote a building form driven almost entirely by local geographic exigencies. In short, design driven by the view.

Since this earlier generation of Vancouver high-rise projects established the typology, the view imperative has continued to manifest itself in a range of design strategies in the many subsequent towers around town: the landscaping of the ground plane instead of actually inhabiting it, the skewing of floor plans, the recurrence of balconies to better capture views, the small floorplates, the formula of one or two units per floor and the distinctive penthouse rooftops. In the years since, many more high-rise towers have been built all around the downtown peninsula. Although not all these features are found in all projects and typical floorplates are creeping up to something closer to 650 m^2 (7,000 square feet), the majority of new towers still exhibit some of them.

In all, more than one hundred residential towers have been built in the downtown peninsula alone since 1991.[59]

The Cult of the View is here to stay.

Opposite page The 1668 Alberni Street mini-tower.

This page Vancouver towers overlooking Stanley Park: the cult of the view is here to stay.
Lance Berelowitz photos

12

The Domestic Tradition
The Search for an Indigenous Architecture

The architect's job is to interpret the life of the inhabitants. —GIO PONTI,
AMATE L'ARCHITETTURA (TITLE IN ENGLISH, *IN PRAISE OF ARCHITECTURE*)

VANCOUVER HAS ALWAYS borrowed from elsewhere when it comes to an architectural tradition. Perhaps this is due to the youth of the city, to its lack of history. Perhaps too to its peripheral status and geographic isolation from the centres of architectural culture in North America. Or perhaps the city has yet to fully shake off the cultural cringe of its frontier colonial origins and claim its place in the global sun. The lack of a sustained architectural avant garde, of cutting-edge architecture—a few notable exceptions notwithstanding—promoted and supported by the civic authorities no less than the private sector, is one symptom of this. Certainly there is far less patronage (or simple funding) of the art of architecture than in cities that have a much larger corporate presence. (Vancouver has fewer head offices than Toronto, Montreal or even Calgary, though that has not necessarily translated into better architecture in those cities.) Or maybe that is just how most Vancouverites prefer it in a place where the pursuit of private gratification over public life is central to the dominant ethos.

Whatever the reasons for its lack of a deep and sustained regionalist architecture, despite the output of some individual talents such as Patkau Architects, Vancouver has happily appropriated what it needed from the architectural canon, and continues to do so. And while there have been brief episodic spurts of indigenous creativity, and there is no questioning the abilities of local architects, the city is filled with half-assimilated architectural quotations from previous eras and other places. Thus, Vancouver has neo-Tudor Revival towers rising out of Tudor Revival apartment buildings, neo-gothic chateau mansard roofs that replicate the original pseudo-gothic chateau quotation, and its share of neo-traditional Arts and Crafts homes that quote the trappings of an architecture of Edwardian probity that was itself an invention of social reality. And latterly, the city has embraced a kind of pseudo "Heritage" architectural appliqué language that has become the officially sanctioned answer to the kitsch excesses of the postmodern "monster house" phenomenon of the 1980s and early '90s.

A perfect illustration of this enduring iconographic appropriation is also a particularly notorious example: when in 1991 the City of Vancouver held an architectural competition to select a design for its new central public library, it chose a scheme by Moshe Safdie & Associates that was, by most critical accounts, a simplistic (and cartoonish) quotation of the classic Roman Coliseum. What this particular iconography had to do with Vancouver (or a library) was anybody's guess, but it did not deter many Vancouverites from finding the tree-covered, blond-wood model of the Safdie design more compelling than those of his competitors and from voting for the Coliseum.

It is instructive to examine this episode in more detail, both as a cautionary tale (of the be-careful-what-you-wish-for type) and because it highlights many of the problems surrounding Vancouver's ongoing search for an indigenous architectural tradition.

In September 1991 the City of Vancouver announced a two-stage international competition to design a new central library. Consistent with its short and sordid history with regard to design competitions, the City set up a rigorous pre-qualification process and a long complex competition brief that hinted at a fair degree of nervousness at the prospect of a wide-open, winner-take-all design competition. Indeed, the competition was structured in such a way that the majority of architects would either be discouraged from responding or in fact would simply not qualify. This was to be no platform for launching the career of some talented young architect. No. The terms of eligibility were strenuous and devised to ensure the selection of a well-established, well-known firm that would be assured of possessing the daunting logistical and technical resources and experience anticipated by the brief. In addition, the pre-qualification phase of the competition was a two-stage process, resulting in a short list of eight teams, which then got narrowed to a final three-way choice, thus further reducing the likelihood of any unpleasant surprises.

On April 16, 1992, the submission dubbed Library Square by Boston-based Moshe Safdie & Associates, in association with local firm (another prerequisite) Downs/Archambault & Partners, was duly announced as the winner.

In many respects, this process worked well—certainly in its own terms—but whether it resulted in the most inspired creative choice is no longer an open question. Indeed, this type of competition structure, which is increasingly favoured by Canadian public sponsors, raises troubling questions about the nature of architectural competitions in general and about the level of respect and value that our society accords the science and art—not to mention the profession—of architecture. This exercise ensured that the current boundaries of establishment architecture were left unchallenged. There would be no Sydney Opera House or Toronto City Hall, both major public competitions that resulted in iconic buildings by relative unknowns. In addition, using the design competition as an opportunity for a younger or more provocative architect to establish a reputation was explicitly eliminated: certainly a Jörn Utzorn (Sydney Opera House), a Viljo Revell (Toronto City Hall), or even a younger Arthur Erickson and Geoffrey Massey (Simon Fraser University) would have been passed over.

The competition was further compromised by the confluence of two more wrinkles in the process: on the one hand, having a sizable majority of the Selection Advisory Committee made up of library board members and city councillors (not, it is worth noting, a jury of professional architects), and on the other, by soliciting in a random, unscientific way the lay public's responses to the three final submissions by putting them on display.

Given that the Selection Advisory Committee reported to City Council, whose members (including those same councillors on the committee) would make the final selection, and given that elected politicians are not inclined to vote contrary to the expressed wishes of their electorate, however arbitrary or uninformed those wishes might be, the result had a certain inevitability. This was despite the fact that the City's own advisory Urban Design Panel could not, on first review, recommend any of the three finalists, and notwithstanding the widespread discomfort with the winning design within the local architectural community. Indeed, in an unofficial straw poll by a gathering of local architects, the official winner was beaten out by the runner-up, KPMB Architects.

So much for the process. What of the product? Well, the winning scheme did nothing if not raise considerable public controversy. The media, both national and local, published a steady stream of articles and commentaries, many questioning the appropriateness of the winning form to both its program and place. But the obvious iconography of Moshe Safdie's design—widely referred to as the Roman Coliseum—did have an instantaneous recognizability, and this, in large part, helped explain its apparently overwhelming support in the general community. But enough non-architects raised troubling questions about the relevance of the dominant elliptical form, the overt references to that ancient historical venue for gladiatorial combats and Christian martyrdom, and the evident problems of contextual fit, that this was not just a question of the architectural community being out of touch with society.

Indeed, Safdie had to be commended for his knack of reading the populist sentiment so well and then reflecting that back on his particular audience in forms and images that both reinforced and succoured that sentiment. In fact, over the years Safdie has been remarkably successful at large-scale competitions in Canada, so much so that he can almost be said to have assumed the mantle of "court architect": the architect of choice for Canada's conservative cultural establishment.

Not that all was plain sailing with Library Square. In fact, the Selection Advisory Committee endorsed the wishes of the public and chose Safdie's scheme despite a long list of unresolved issues. In conditionally affirming this choice, City Council enumerated those issues in a lengthy list of requirements, some involving significant changes, which the architect was given twelve weeks to satisfy. Presumably an advance fee of $200,000 helped cushion the blow. Given that this list included some fundamental issues relating to the form, content and disposition of the chosen design, it is reasonable to conclude that this was not the most effective, nor the most inspirational, method of selecting an architect for one of Vancouver's most important and expensive public buildings in decades.

The scheme itself was compellingly simple. An elliptical double wall, eight storeys high, contains within its circumference the simple rectangular box of the library itself. The ellipse form is centred on its rectangular downtown city block, thus leaving the corners of the block open. The northeast corner is taken up by the government office tower that was an integral part of the brief, and the southeast corner is occupied by an agglomeration onto the outer curved wall, containing some retail stores and a daycare facility

The competition-winning design by Moshe Safdie
& Associates for Vancouver's central library.

Michal Ronnen Safdie photo

... and the library as built.

Robin Ward photo

upstairs. The library itself is entered obliquely by slipping around either side of the ellipse between the inner and outer curved walls, and then into a retail-lined, glass-roofed concourse that here conflates, in a telling way, the typologies of the shopping mall and civic forecourt.

The architects were required to address the design deficiencies of the original submission. First among these was the very feature that so many apparently found most compelling about the scheme: the elliptical form so reminiscent of Rome's ancient Coliseum. With its proportions of solid to void, its vertical layering of a repeated structural system and its neo-classical iconography, it manages both to mimic and trivialize its classical progenitor. Worse is the lack of definition or spatial enclosure that this centripetal form, disposed on a rectilinear grid, gives to the public open spaces that surround the building. As a result, these leaking spaces at the open corners of the site have an indeterminate quality of sameness, further confusing the already tricky reading of front vs. back, main entry vs. secondary entry, service vs. served.

When pressed on the issue of iconographic quotation, Safdie at the time claimed that the apparent literalness in the model would evolve through design development. But when the ship came in, nothing had really changed. Vancouver got its Coliseum.

In the final analysis, however, the client got more or less what it wanted: a non-threatening, feel-good architect whose credentials and creative calculus accorded perfectly with the limited spectrum of Vancouver's conservative civic and cultural elite. Whether Vancouver got what it wanted depends on whom you ask. And what it has to do with an architecture of the West Coast, let alone of Vancouver, is far less evident.

The chronicle of Library Square touches on many of the issues that bedevil the emergence of a genuine Vancouver architecture, let alone an avant garde. It is by no means an isolated example, however; the list is long.

Any such list would have to put the Cathedral Place office building (1993) pretty high up. Here, Vancouver witnessed the replication of a previously invented Canadian "Scottish baronial/gothic chateau" style. The irony is that this Canadian style had been created a hundred years earlier to brand the Canadian Pacific Railway company's hotels, which were erected at key stops along the transcontinental line as added inducements to get people to take the train. The CPR "chateau" style borrowed heavily from the sixteenth-century French country chateau, with liberal doses of gothic and Scottish baronial mixed in for good measure. To make the reference absolutely

Vancouver's "original" copper roof gothic icon (the Hotel Vancouver, right), and its recent replica, Cathedral Place.

Derek Lepper photo

explicit, many of these now-iconic CPR hotels were named "chateau" this or that, starting with the Chateau Frontenac in Quebec City (1892–93). It was a grandiose early example of corporate branding.

So when local self-made businessman Caleb Chan wanted to build a statement project, he acquired the site directly opposite the Hotel Vancouver with its distinctive chateau-esque copper roof and commissioned talented local architectural romantic Paul Merrick to design a homage to its historic neighbour.

Thus it came to pass that Vancouver now has two such distinctive roofs punctuating the city skyline, steeply sloped and in the iridescent green colour of oxidized copper. Except that just as the 1930s Hotel Vancouver is not a real chateau, Cathedral Place's roof is not actually copper but a painted simulation.

Dingbat Domesticity

> *The dingbat, left to its own devices, often exhibits the basic characteristics of a primitive modern architecture.* —REYNER BANHAM, *LOS ANGELES: THE ARCHITECTURE OF FOUR ECOLOGIES*

The evidence of Vancouver's insouciant willingness to embrace architectural styles from anytime and everywhere else is most pronounced in the realm of its residential buildings.

Historically, the emerging town's very earliest houses recalled the wooden row housing of San Francisco. This is not surprising: many of Vancouver's wood houses were assembled, Lego-like, from architectural pattern books shipped up from San Francisco, where their use had been widespread. They provided a handy menu of architectural styles for the new town's builders: the Queen Anne (for example, 451 East Pender, c. 1889), the widespread California bungalow (itself a reworking of an earlier house type invented by the colonial British in the imperial Indian Raj), the Craftsman Special, etc. Many of these surviving older houses, with their broad verandas, gables, exposed rafters, brackets and abundant wood-trim detailing, are today on Vancouver's official so-called Heritage A-List, lending them an architectural pedigree entirely unanticipated by their opportunistic—and in many cases anonymous—builders, and a telling commentary on our values.

A typical California
bungalow, a widespread
house style in Vancouver.
Robin Ward photo

Since those earliest days, Vancouver has inherited a veritable potpourri
of housing styles, including the English Cotswold/Fairytale Cottage, the
Spanish Colonial Revival, the Tudor Revival, the chateau, the Victorian, the
Edwardian, the Arts and Crafts Voseyesque, the neo-classical, the art deco,
the California moderne stucco box and so on.

These styles were intermingled, hybridized and often cross-referenced,
sometimes in one and the same building. And, just as cavalierly, these
various styles of domesticity appeared in no discernible chronological order
but rather in response to shifting public tastes. Just how cavalierly can be
illustrated by the design trajectory of a single local architect: Ross A. Lort.
Lort started off working with Samuel Maclure, the darling of Vancouver's
and Victoria's plutocracy and a master of the neo-Tudor picturesque.
Lort no doubt applied himself on many of the firm's half-timbered Tudor
knock-offs. Yet in 1936 he designed an elegant Vancouver rendition of the
streamlined moderne house then sweeping across the plains and up into the
foothills of Los Angeles. His house for Horace Barber on West 10th Avenue
is a compelling exercise in moderne austerity, with its smooth white-painted
concrete surfaces, abstract geometric form and flat roof. Lort appears to
have assimilated totally the modernist precepts of his contemporaries down
in Los Angeles, such as Rudolph Schindler and Richard Neutra. Yet less
than five years later, this same talented Lort was credited with designing the

Ross Lort was a master of architectural styles: the moderne Barber house (top) and an English Cotswold–style house for developer Brenton Lee.

Robin Ward photos

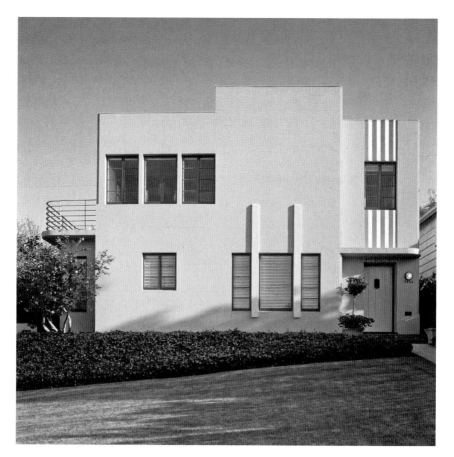

prototype for several speculative houses built in—of all things—the English Cotswold/Fairytale Cottage style.[60] His 1941–42 design is a fantastic conjugation of undulating shingle roof (imitating thatch), half-timbering, leaded windowpanes, rubble stonework and clinker-brick chimney. At least three examples of this house style remain around Vancouver. It is impossible to credit their design as coming from the same hand as that of the moderne Barber house (which also remains), or the Barber house design from that of the previous Tudor Revival work. But there they are: a case study in Vancouver's version of critical regionalism.

If this diversity of styles can be said to demonstrate the lack of an indigenously derived architectural vocabulary, they nevertheless—somewhat surprisingly—do reflect certain common underlying values. These can perhaps be best described as a kind of pastoral English charm and Anglo-Celtic modesty combined with Californian convenience. They also reflect the thrall of colonialism in which Vancouver was still then held. By means of the relentless repetition of similar housing types over large areas on a regular street grid with common frontage widths of typically 10 or 15 m (33 or 50 feet), a surprisingly consistent, if not homogenous, suburban residential streetscape spread across the city, right up to the Second World War.

The impulse to architectural appropriation continues today. As soon as some architect comes up with a vaguely clever new design idea that sells well, the rest of the developer herd will not be far behind. Take Nigel Baldwin's sawtooth gable roof. Many have.

In 1997 Baldwin, the talented then partner of Roger Hughes, designed a distinctive fifteen-unit multi-family townhouse project overlooking Connaught Park in Kitsilano for VanCity Enterprises. Located on a corner lot 30.5 by 38 m (100 by 125 feet), it was in many respects an exemplary example of sensitive residential intensification in what was a single-family neighbourhood in transition. The project was notable for the way it bridged the adjacent two- and three-storey houses and the higher density housing being developed on the nearby Arbutus lands, accommodating higher density while maintaining the "look and feel" of single-family housing. Baldwin achieved this, in significant part, through a clever device, accommodating the third floor within the form of a steeply sloping, finely scaled, double-sawtooth gable roof. This inverted roof form both minimizes the bulk of building and reinforces the single-family aesthetic. The design cleverly plays with the strong, sawtooth roof forms, offset by pop-out elements such as dormers and bays, all of which help to maintain a finer domestic scale and a sense of the individual

Nigel Baldwin's clever sawtooth roof device, now widely imitated.

Lance Berelowitz photo

identity of units. This is a trick of the eye of course, but it works remarkably well and goes a long way towards explaining why the project has been so well received in the neighbourhood.

Other developers were quick to take note. The double-sawtooth gable, to the best of my knowledge, had never been used before on a contemporary multi-family housing project. Now it is ubiquitous. Numerous housing developments have since employed the same device to similar effect, so much so that Baldwin must wish he had patented the idea. Or does he feel flattered? Vancouver's tradition of shameless architectural appropriation continues apace.

The multitude of domestic residential architectural styles in Vancouver included a robust local variant of what Reyner Banham referred to as the Los Angeles dingbat.[61] There, according to Banham, "It is normally a two story walk-up apartment block developed back over the full depth of the site, built of wood and stuccoed over." He goes on to note that these primitive modernist boxes, with their "simple rectangular forms and flush smooth surfaces, skinny steel columns and simple boxed balconies, and extensive overhangs to shelter four or five cars," are much the same around the sides and back. On the front facades, however, all hell breaks loose, with every competing architectural style imaginable applied to the basic type. Banham interprets this frenetic individualism as an extreme symptom of Los Angeles's promise of the individual urban homestead that it can no longer deliver.

In Vancouver, the dingbat has a well-established variant: the three-and-a-half storey walk-up apartment building that still exists widely in the West End and, to a lesser extent, in Kitsilano, Marpole and elsewhere. These modest buildings from the 1950s and early '60s, with their top-floor penthouse units, are a distinctive feature of the Vancouver residential landscape. The ubiquitous penthouse feature arose through the clever exploitation of an anomaly in the then zoning bylaw, which ordained that a fourth floor could be added only if it was a caretaker's flat and that this fourth floor area could be no larger than half the floorplate below it.

Interestingly, the Southern Californian culture of individualism was suppressed in its more buttoned-down neighbour to the far north, so, unlike their Los Angeles cousins, most of the Vancouver examples demonstrate a quiet conformism in their front facades. None of California's excesses of

A Vancouver version of the California dingbat style.

Lance Berelowitz photo

stylistic cant for it. But Vancouver does display many of the attributes of its Californian cousins: the simple planar massing and minimalist cubist forms; the impossibly thin steel pilotis (columns) that support the upper-floor mass to leave the ground plane clear for cars, entryways and manicured landscaping; the horizontal strip windows wrapping around the corners; the flat roofs and the two-tone pastel colour schemes. It is as if a bunch of Le Corbusier's students, having assimilated the ascetic Swiss master's Five Points of Modern Architecture, had headed for the West Coast, shed their clothes, parked themselves in the sun on the beach, and there, under the benign influence of some of Vancouver's local hallucinogenic stimulants, began designing. The results, refracted through the lens of the Californian experience, have proved surprisingly enduring. Vancouver's variant of the dingbat provided a cheap, quick and efficient way of building speculative residential developments on small lots, and it created a pool of affordable yet very livable domestic units.

There is also an inflated version of the Vancouver dingbat, where the building exceeds four storeys and is constructed in concrete. These larger siblings exhibit many of the same modernist avant-garde features, and a number of these exuberant dingbats on steroids can still be found in Vancouver's West End.

In what might be considered the apotheosis of the Vancouver dingbat, local builders in the early 1970s invented a mutant version that they called

A classic Vancouver Special house.

Robin Ward photo

the Vancouver Special. The Vancouver Special was, like the original dingbat, a crafty market-driven response to restrictive local zoning laws and rising demand for cheap housing. The Vancouver Special offered a new model of standardized housing that maximized the floor area and site coverage while still giving the appearance (barely) of a single-family house. It was also surprisingly affordable, and the design concept was simplicity itself: a two-storey rectangle that offered the option of either a single home on two floors or two separate units, one on each floor, sharing a common vestibule. This flexible arrangement perfectly suited the needs of many new immigrants, whose concepts of the extended family often were quite different from the traditional North American nuclear family. In effect, it meant that relatives could essentially buy two houses for the price of one, a significant consideration for newcomers with limited capital.

The Vancouver Special was an exercise in economy. It was built as a slab on grade, thus minimizing excavation costs. The wood-frame construction used minimum-sized 2 x 4 studs. Rooms were arranged along a narrow central corridor, thus maximizing their number. Dimensions were driven by off-the-shelf building products: for example, rooms were 3.6 m (12 feet wide) to match the standard carpet width. Windows were nailed on. The roof was angled to the minimum pitch that still permitted a cheaper tar and gravel roof. Thin brick veneer on the front facade provided a stand-in for real brick. The upper-level balcony across the width of the house was reduced to the narrowest depth possible, in effect providing just a railing for upper-floor sliding doors.

The traditional vertical stacking of domestic arrangements was inverted: living room, dining room and kitchen were on the second floor, while the ground floor was given over to a secondary kitchen and living area, more bedrooms and a covered carport out back. In practice, the Vancouver Special proved adaptable to suit a range of domestic arrangements. Small-time builders jumped on board in alarming numbers, and clusters of Vancouver Specials soon sprang up all over the place. The design establishment reacted with predictable outrage at this affront to the city's bourgeois aesthetic sensibility. The Vancouver Special quickly achieved widespread notoriety. Although aesthetically offensive to many people, the Vancouver Special has played an important role in densifying the city and providing a more affordable housing option for many.

There is a certain irony in the fact that while the Vancouver Special has long been an affront to the Vancouver architectural establishment, that same establishment frequently finds itself designing and living in equally kitsch architectural clichés and is increasingly involved in replicating a new pseudo "Heritage" aesthetic for housing. The pitched roofs, cutesy wood detailing and fake-traditional architectural geegaws are now the *de rigueur* language of contemporary residential design. It almost makes the Vancouver Special seem refreshingly honest in comparison.

All this makes it something of a relief to be able finally to report on one body of domestic architectural work that was (and remains) genuinely original.

Vancouver Modern

Vancouver's one indubitably indigenous style is what has come to be known as West Coast Modernism. Certainly, it was influenced by the pioneering Southern Californian modernists, who in turn had been directly influenced by their European mentors. But Vancouver's post–Second World War modernist heyday refracted the Californian experience through its own particular climate and geographic setting, producing a small but precocious body of domestic work whose originality is not in serious dispute.

The Modern Movement had grown out of social ideas emanating from central Europe in the 1920s and '30s. The post-revolutionary Russian constructivists, Germany's Bauhaus school, Adolf Loos, Eric Mendelson,

Mies van de Rohe, Walter Gropius and Le Corbusier developed and tested a new kind of architecture, one that presumed, even insisted, that architecture could and should be an agent of social change. New construction technologies—reinforced concrete, steel frames, tempered sheet glass and so on—were combined with contemporary social theories in an architecture of enlightenment: architecture would redeem society, would uplift living and working conditions, would pave the way for a cleaner, brighter, more egalitarian world. Then, with the onset of National Socialist fascism in Germany and Austria, several of these European architects found themselves exiled in the United States, including such established names as Walter Gropius, Marcel Breuer and Mies van der Rohe. A number, including Kem Weber, Rudolph Schindler and Richard Neutra, fetched up in Southern California.

The Vancouver connection to Southern California should not be underestimated. In 1944 a group of Vancouver artists and designers, led by Fred Amess and B.C. (Bert) Binning, formed the Art in Living Group to promote modernism in design and art. This group was instrumental in bringing up to Vancouver the transplanted Richard Neutra, who was then at the peak of his career in Los Angeles. Neutra stayed in Vancouver for just one week, giving talks at both the university and downtown about the mystery and realities of the site and his vision of an architecture that merged the outside and the inside, an architecture that dissolved into the landscape. He described how modernism could be reinterpreted to respond to the climate, materials and sites of the West Coast. His words fell on receptive ears and continued to resonate through the city's architectural community long after his departure. To local architects, Vancouver offered its own possibilities for modernism based on a reading of its wet climate, coniferous forests and dramatic geography. West Coast Modernism was born.

And in Vancouver, emerging out of the wartime era of restraint, a new breed of architect was ready to embrace the formalistic repertoire of liberation with the enthusiasm of the convert. Young, underdeveloped and distant from the old conservative establishment of the East Coast, Vancouver was to Canada something akin to what Southern California was to the United States: a place where young talent could begin careers and test new ideas. In short, while not quite offering Los Angeles's atmosphere of permissive extravagance, Vancouver, with its relatively benign climate and lack of pretension, offered a libertarian environment for the practice of modern architecture.

The best of that work was tested in that crucible of architectural experimentation, the single-family house. One of the modernism's chief character-

istics was the poetic suffusion of house into landscape and vice versa, most notably achieved in the early modernist homes built on Vancouver's North Shore, tucked into the rain forest or perched on the mountainside slopes overlooking Burrard Inlet.

With many young architects and artists deeply committed to the integration of architecture and art, a cross-fertilization of the disciplines began to make itself felt. This cross-fertilization had in fact been a notable feature of the progressive architectural scene as far back as the pre-war years. For instance, architect Ross Lort was president of the Vancouver Art Gallery from 1933 to 1949. And in 1941, even before he co-founded the Art in Living Group, local avant-garde artist B.C. Binning had designed what many consider the first truly modern house in Vancouver. It was, in a local context, a radical essay in modernist precepts and quite unlike anything built here previously. Designed in collaboration with architect Ned Pratt for Binning's own family and incorporating modernist murals that the artist himself painted, the house presaged subsequent collaborations of local artists (including Binning) and architects. The design was predicated on a simple yet powerful fusion of outside and inside, with large glass panels

The modernist B.C. Binning house in West Vancouver.

National Archives of Canada PA-132040, Jack Long photo

pivoting to let the space flow in and out. It was also one of the first house designs to explore what came to be known as West Coast post-and-beam construction, taking advantage of the plentiful structural timber then available locally.

The Binning house remains a high point of domestic modernism, all the more remarkable for having been designed not by an architect but an artist (Ned Pratt's assistance notwithstanding). Binning subsequently advocated for creating a School of Architecture at the University of British Columbia, under the direction of Swiss-born modernist Fred Lasserre, whose faculty he joined in 1947.

Modernist theories had come to Vancouver just as several young architects were building themselves houses, mostly on the forested slopes of the North Shore. Binning's seminal house was followed in 1948 by Ned Pratt's and Fred Hollingsworth's, two young architects beginning to make their mark. Ron Thom, an up-and-coming light in the Sharp and Thompson, Berwick, Pratt studio, designed an elegant, minimalist post-and-beam house for himself around 1955, and several more for clients. Roy Jessiman, another member of the firm, was responsible for the equally elegant Kennedy house that same year. Others, like Wolfgang Gerson and, most notably, Arthur Erickson, followed. By the mid-1950s, modernism had established firm roots in the North Shore rain forest.

This is not the place for a detailed history of Vancouver's modernist housing heritage. However, with the exception of the Canadian Centre for Architecture's 1997 exhibition "The New Spirit" and its excellent accompanying book by Rhodri Windsor Liscombe,[62] along with recent monographs on Ron Thom and Arthur Erickson, remarkably little has been documented about this body of work. The full story of Vancouver's early modernist housing legacy has yet to be told.

Fade to Modern

Almost as compelling as Vancouver's modernist custom houses, a small opus of commercial and institutional buildings that tested the precepts of modernism also emerged in the centre of the city.

After crossing the Atlantic to the United States, the Modern Movement became known as the International Style, a phrase coined by Henry-Russell Hitchcock and Philip Johnson. But by whatever name, in no Canadian city did the idealistic optimism of the Modern Movement find more fertile ground than in lush, temperate Vancouver. Modernism flourished—albeit briefly—in the rain forest, producing a small but highly considered body of classic modern work, both public and private. The rest of Canada, or at least those with architectural aspirations, looked on in envy.

Until very recently, the results could be widely seen across the city.

A curious amnesia surrounds the public's perception of Vancouver's modernist buildings; the unsung remnants of the city's heroic modern era are not generally considered to have "traditional" historic value. Vancouver society has not yet fully come to view modern architecture as a legitimate element of its built heritage, and several of the most important modernist works are either under threat of demolition or defacement through insensitive renovation, or are already gone. Perhaps the modern era is perceived as too recent or too linked to the urban renewal excesses of the 1960s and '70s for its buildings to be valued in the same light as, say, the Tudor Manor apartment facade. The latter, ironically, is a revivalist pastiche, whereas the best modern buildings in Vancouver represent the cutting edge of architectural thinking of their time.

Or maybe, in Vancouver's ongoing rush to reinvent itself, it is just too busy remaking the city to notice the intrinsic architectural merits and innovative, even prophetic, uses of materials, light, and space that these modernist buildings exhibited. They not only were sophisticated essays in contemporary architectural theory but had also become civic landmarks. These buildings, many now gone or barely recognizable, were some of the most innovative, forward-looking icons of the city's short history.

One of the first large-scale civic examples of the International Style was the Vancouver Vocational Institute (now Vancouver Community College), designed by Sharp and Thompson, Berwick, Pratt Architects and constructed in 1948–49. When young graduates Robert Berwick and Ned Pratt joined the established Sharp and Thompson in 1945, this local firm soon became one of the most progressive in Canada. In time, it was responsible for much of the best modern architecture in the city. Also deeply committed to architecture as art, the firm developed considerable connections with the local artistic community and explored modernism in art itself.

Next, the original 1930s-era art deco Vancouver Art Gallery on Georgia Street acquired a completely new modernist facade in 1951, designed by the ever-active Ross Lort. Large intersecting planes of concrete and glass were capped by a flat overhanging roof with a curved concrete cornice. This, perhaps more than any other commission, signalled the huge reach of modernism within the arts. The building has since been demolished.

Another precept of modernism was the celebration of technology and its benefits to society. Even the most utilitarian technological and industrial programs could be seen as vehicles for modernist expression. Factories, breweries and electrical stations were placed in this category.

The Dal Grauer electrical substation, built in 1953 by Thompson Berwick Pratt, was the first example of this in Vancouver, electrifying the startled city. It was designed as a giant glazed box, showcasing the interior electrical workings and making them visible from the street. Deliberately lit up at night, with internal elements like folded steel stairs and walls painted in bright primary colours, the building is an abstract composition resembling a modernist painting. The classical proportions of the facade, the subtle projection of the central bay and the allusive cornice formed by the window-cleaning track across the top contribute to a formal elegance and a sophistication that are way before their time.

The adjacent B.C. Hydro headquarters tower of 1955 is a testimonial not only to the high ideals of modernism but also to the inspired patronage of Dal Grauer, then chairman of the company. Spurred on by the innovative success of the substation, the architects—again Thompson Berwick Pratt, with Ron Thom leading the team—collaborated closely with both the enlightened client and B.C. Binning to produce a stunning essay in steel, glass and coloured mosaic.

The tower's lozenge shape was the result of a desire to get natural light as deep into the building as possible. Dal Grauer insisted that no desk be more than 4.6 m (15 feet) from a window. The extensive blue, green and black mosaic tilework around the base and entrance of the building, the colour coordination and the decorative motifs based on the tapered plan form are all products of Binning's collaboration with Thom.

With its sophisticated structural and mechanical systems and its giant coloured-light beacon (running up the west facade of the tower) that could be seen from ships in the Strait of Georgia, the building was both a monument to technology and an icon to the company's purpose of providing cheap electricity to all. There was nothing else quite like this ensemble in all of Canada, and its conversion to a strata-title condominium constitutes a major near loss of the nation's architectural legacy. But at least it was not demolished, and its renovation by Paul Merrick was done with great respect to the original and attention to detail, including the restoration of Binning's tilework so that, though the building has lost its original meaning, it remains a tribute to modernism.

The B.C. Hydro headquarters, designed by Thompson Berwick Pratt.

Selwyn Pullan photo

The late lamented federal
Customs House, designed
by C.B.K. Van Norman,
completed in 1955 and
demolished in 1993.

Jacques R. André photo

The next significant modernist building downtown did not fare so well. The federal Customs House was designed by C.B.K. Van Norman, another talented local architect. Opened in April 1955, the building was a sophisticated resolution to an awkwardly angled corner site. This angle was seized upon by the architect to animate the plan and was inflected by various devices throughout the design. The angled entrance canopy, corner piers and triangular stair echoed the sharp, angular context, providing crisp counterpoints to what would otherwise have been a bland monolithic building. The Customs House was also an essay in materials and their innovative use, another preoccupation of the modernists: local blue granite spandrels; aluminium windows, balustrades and canopy edging; Haddon Island stone end-piers; terrazzo floor surfaces and mahogany railings. With its abstract facades and cylindrical elevator penthouse pushing up through the flat understated roof, this was a sophisticated example of the International Style. Alas, it is gone, demolished in 1993 by the federal government to make way for a stodgy replacement.

Van Norman was also responsible for a number of other influential modernist buildings in Vancouver, including the 1955 Burrard Building offices, an exercise in glass curtain wall and metal minimalism that was among the earliest of its genre in the city. Sadly, when it was "revamped" several years ago, it lost the sophisticated curtain-wall cladding system and hence is now unrecognizable. Van Norman is one of those local architects whose contribution has yet to be fully recognized.

Finally, one of the best-known public buildings from this period is Vancouver's first Central Public Library, designed by Semmens and Simpson Architects and built in 1956–57. This carefully crafted house of knowledge, strategically located at the corner of Burrard and Robson, skilfully made the turn from primary boulevard (Burrard Street) to secondary street (Robson). The floor-to-ceiling glass expanses on the Burrard Street facade encouraged public permeability on the side of the building's primary entrance. Around the corner on Robson Street, glass gave way to more solid opaque materials, distinguishing between public and private areas. The four-storey building had a generous double-height atrium, thanks to a daring concrete structure and widely spaced columns. The library was capped with a set-back glazed top floor topped by a projecting tapered concrete cornice. The play of transparency and solidity neatly transmitted the building's twin messages of accessibility and profundity. The whole form was conceived as an elegant modernist paean to its functions of intellectual enlightenment and cultural repository. This project was described as "the best of a diminishing number of highly regarded Modernist buildings in Vancouver."[63] This can regrettably no longer be said of it, since the library has been relocated and the building radically altered. After a thorough commercial "renovation," the building does remain in a gussied-up reincarnation as home to a Virgin Megastore, a local television studio and, until it folded, a Planet Hollywood franchise restaurant. In the adaptation process, much was lost.

These, then, are some of the best remaining and lost examples of Vancouver's modernist legacy. Others have fallen or are under threat: the heroic Carling O'Keefe Brewery on Arbutus and Yew, with its extraordinary corner stair tower and faceted concrete wall, fell to the wrecker's ball; the massive full-block downtown central post office, with its rooftop helicopter pad and subterranean tunnels, still hangs on, as do the numerous unsung, simple three-storey walk-up apartments with their rooftop penthouses, strip windows and pastel colours.

These modernist works are important, not just aesthetically but historically. Modernism may be in danger of becoming extinct in the Canadian city where it reached its apex. This irony will not be lost on modernism's many out-of-town admirers. A city as young as Vancouver cannot afford, nor should it need, to ignore its recent past. So few of its older buildings are left that a broadened definition of built heritage to include the masterpieces of the Modern Movement was long overdue and finally has gained impetus at City Hall in recent years. Perhaps this was just in time: before long, our recent past may be the only built past we have.

The Livable City: Vancouver's Legacy of Social Housing

In the search for an indigenous architecture, an important but often overlooked aspect of Vancouver's contemporary residential architectural tradition is its rich inventory of social housing[64] (or "non-market housing," to use the now more politically correct term).

Vancouver must count as one of the few cities in any developed country that sometimes stands accused of having social housing that is "too good." What its accusers generally mean by this is that the quality of architecture of many social or non-market housing projects in recent years puts them on a level more commonly associated (in the layperson's eyes, anyway) with upmarket, private-sector housing. As such, the architects of these social housing projects could wish for no finer compliment than this criticism, born as it is of envy.

Vancouver has a large trove of such housing projects from the past twenty-five years. The conditions that produced such quality housing have their roots in the post–Second World War era. At that time, Canadian public housing (as it was then known) largely mirrored the British experience, with the federal government being directly involved through its Canada Mortgage and Housing Corporation (CMHC) in a national program that sought to address a rapidly expanding urban population, in addition to housing returning war veterans. The Canadian solution—large-scale modernist housing estates with a mix of ubiquitous slab-and-tower blocks and low-rise elements—resulted in many of the same social problems suffered overseas. By the end of the 1960s, this form of public housing was becoming increasingly discredited, and CMHC began taking its first tentative steps towards working with the nascent co-operative housing movement.

Vancouver, strongly influenced by social changes happening down the West Coast (specifically in California), rapidly became a leader in the co-op housing movement. The social upheavals of the time found fertile ground here, as the area's obvious climatic and physical attractions beckoned alternative lifestyle advocates, attractions that also drew many of the country's more innovative architects as well as those emigrating from elsewhere. This new crop of architects and civic figures, radicalized by the activist '60s and exposed to European urbanism through the increased mobility of an era of affluence, found in Vancouver those conditions that made innovative social housing a possibility.

Key political developments, such as the provincial Strata Title Act of 1972 and the election of a new reform-minded City Council in 1973, paved the way for major high-density, inner-city housing programs in Vancouver. By the end of the '70s, almost all non-market housing was being funded by CMHC, and the beginning of a golden era saw several exciting, groundbreaking projects get off the boards.

But while all seemed well in theory, the reality was somewhat different. What had been created as a national program to provide affordable quality housing for the socially disadvantaged became a victim of its own success. Housing co-ops were increasingly targeted at middle-income families, and the intended social mix failed to materialize. With soaring land costs, high inflation and interest rates of up to 20 per cent, CMHC was paying out an average of $8,000 annually per unit by 1981, while many of the poor remained unhoused. At the same time, the federal government was entering an era of escalating budget deficits. The response was to change the funding structure, with the provincial governments becoming the primary delivery agents of most social housing across Canada through newly created Housing Management Commissions, with 100 per cent targeting of the low-income sector. In British Columbia, this program emerged as BC Housing. In Vancouver, inner-city pressure groups, such as the Downtown Eastside Residents Association (DERA), began taking advantage of the new dispensation to launch social housing projects of their own. By the mid-1980s the first projects under the new provincial program were getting under way.

Although there were serious questions at the time about the efficacy and intent of the provincial housing program—the conservative Social Credit Party provincial government and radical left-wing DERA made for strange political bedfellows indeed—and federal social housing programs would dry up completely in the following decade, some of the most creative urban housing produced in Canada during the 1980s came out of the social housing sector in Vancouver. In this city of pre-eminent residential architecture, the architectural contribution made by social housing projects is considerable and offers some still salient lessons to other cities of the developed world.

Despite coming from many different hands with varied preoccupations, the range of design themes was consistent in most of the social housing projects of this era. These themes included a sense of urbanity and a focus on incremental densification, an interest in materiality, an awareness of street-scape, a celebration of the collective, a sense of exuberance and a complete rejection of post-war modernist housing theories as epitomized by the earlier high-rise tower and slab-block housing estates. Indeed, these newer projects, whose average height is just three or four storeys, achieved relatively high densities by building right to the site perimeters and addressing the street.

The first theme, a distinctly urban sensibility (by then current North American standards, at least), is common to all the projects discussed here. Much of Vancouver's original multi-family housing stock—the urban villa, the attached row house and the mansion block—achieved commendably high densities with distinctly urban typologies. Some of the city's first social housing projects in the 1980s involved the adaptation of these older structures, such as Barclay Heritage Square Park in the West End (planned by Downs/Archambault Architects and carried out by the Iredale Partnership), turn-of-the-century mansion blocks like Mount Pleasant's Quebec Manor (renovated by Henry Hawthorn Architect) and the Manhattan Apartments at Robson and Thurlow streets (renovated by Hotson Bakker Architects).

New projects that demonstrated this urban sensibility included the discreet street-making of Swiss architect Xavier Bellprat's Broadview Co-operative building which, though not located downtown, clearly addressed its location on Broadway, a major arterial axis. With its retail ground floor and housing above, this project was notable for being one of the first Canadian housing co-ops to include a commercial element.

The sense of street-making is strong in most examples, even where front gardens were retained. In the case of the Pacific Heights Co-operative by Roger Hughes, an existing row of individual old houses was retained and restored, with a new block of multi-family housing inserted behind. The space thus created between the two building elements serves to intensify the block and acts as a secure recreation space monitored by views from the overlooking units. A more suburban example is Bellprat's David Wetherow Housing Co-op, where the architects fought to obtain a reduction in the mandated streetfront setback from 6 to 2 m (20 to 6½ feet), thus achieving a street continuity with minimal front gardens—inner-city density housing in the suburbs.

In some cases, this street-making did descend dangerously close to mere facadism, due, perhaps, to a clash between architects' egos and very tight budgets. Indeed, this touches on perhaps the most significant criticism of these projects: that in some cases (though by no means all), most of the effort went into the exterior, with little grace or commodity remaining in the

The Broadview Housing Co-operative: discreet street-making architecture by Xavier Bellprat.
Lance Berelowitz photo

planning of individual units. A case in point may be the Helen's Court Co-op by Roger Hughes, where the somewhat frivolous entry pavilions and facade detailing ate up a sizable chunk of the overall budget, leaving less than ideal units within.

Closely linked to a distinctively urban sensibility was the introduction of much higher housing densities than were locally prevalent. Many of these projects represented a rediscovery of the virtues of inner-city living then overtaking several North American cities in the wake of the middle-class flight to the suburbs. Vancouver, in particular, had embarked on major reurbanization of the inner city core as industry, shipping and rail yards moved out of the downtown peninsula. For example, the DERA Co-operative, by Davidson Yuen Architects, was one of the first new residential complexes in the rundown Downtown Eastside area. Targeted at low-income, hard-to-house occupants, the design took advantage of its waterfront location by providing balconies for each suite, rooftop viewing decks and top-floor gaming rooms. The colourful layered front facade recalls the playful early Miami work of Architectonica, and, with its plastic, sculptural entrance bay, this project stands as a beacon of social optimism in the heart of old Vancouver.

Another downtown example by Davidson Yuen (in collaboration with Joe Wai) is Jubilee House (1985), built for a client that was one of many church groups involved in the city's social housing sector. The project includes single-person hostel units with shared facilities as well as suites, all within a brick-frame, blue-coloured stucco facade that presents an elegant addition to the public streetscape—again, a high-density, low-rise, urban solution to a perennial housing problem.

Indeed, these higher density projects often suggest, appropriately, a public facade to celebrate the inherent monumentality of the collective "place" as opposed to the individuality of the private house. This hierarchical sense of the public front versus the private rear is well developed in many of these schemes. Both of the Davidson Yuen schemes present a collective public facade, yet still allow for more varied private rear elevations onto secured courtyards.

In some instances, the aforementioned concerns were addressed primarily in formal terms (that is, the architectural massing of the building), but it is also interesting to note those built projects in which more solid masonry materials, notably brick, were used in a city whose residential buildings are constructed almost exclusively of wood. Keeping in mind that an economic premium is paid for choosing brick over stucco, it is evident

The DERA Housing Co-operative by Davidson Yuen Architects is a beacon of social optimism in the Downtown Eastside.
Robin Ward photo

that a deliberate decision was made about the sense of permanence of these projects, a decision that clearly, if subconsciously, echoes the fine early examples of brick-clad apartment blocks, such as Quebec Manor. Many of these housing co-ops eloquently demonstrate the point and distinguish themselves from their stucco-sea surroundings in the process.

This is not to say that all Vancouver social housing projects of the era raised themselves above the going construction standards. Some inevitably fell victim to the exigencies of tight budgets and the ingrained shortcuts of the construction industry, displaying the shoddy detailing and poor workmanship suffered by so many speculative development projects. For example, the Grandview Housing Co-op by Roger Hughes, while skilfully resolving a difficult, steeply sloping site above a major traffic artery and creating panoramic (if somewhat noisy) views over the False Creek basin to the North Shore mountains beyond, is sadly bedevilled by detail shortcomings, a case of trying to do too much with too little. It is by no means alone in this regard. Too many went the cheap stucco route and are now paying the price of major repairs.

The Lore Krill Housing Co-operative, designed by Henriquez Partners.

Derek Lepper photo

Nevertheless, in the final analysis, these social housing projects from the 1980s share a sense of optimistic enthusiasm, as in the Pacific Heights Co-op, and colour, as in Barclay Heritage Square—an optimism that belies conventional expectations about social housing. The ongoing pride with which many occupants still maintain their buildings fifteen years on and the envy that they continue to attract are strong indications that the refutation of the institutionalized sterility of earlier such housing projects signalled a positive break with the past while simultaneously reaching back to draw on deeper roots in the life of the city.

Much has changed since this heyday era of social housing. As mentioned, the federal government withdrew completely from social housing for starters (though there are current indications it may get back in), and there has been a decline in both the quantity and quality of projects across the country, reflecting the reduction in government funding. British Columbia did, however, remain one of the few provinces to continue its social housing program, albeit with little if any federal contribution, and Vancouver has somehow continued to produce social housing projects of a very high standard, if fewer than before.

Perhaps the most inventive of recent examples is the Lore Krill Housing Co-op by Henriquez Partners Architects, completed in 2002. This 108-unit project is located in the heart of the Downtown Eastside, which if anything has deteriorated even further in the decades since the housing projects already described were built. Funded through the very modest formulas of the BC Housing program, the project nonetheless manages to do so much more with less, thanks in large measure to the architects' design talents and their commitment to social housing.

Almost twenty years after the previous batch of social housing projects, the Lore Krill Co-op displays many of the same preoccupations that informed the earlier work, perhaps even more so. Here again is a robust streetwall architecture that picks up on and references the surrounding built context of older warehouses, apartments and particularly the now closed former Woodward's department store building one block away. The use of carefully modulated brick, masonry and concrete detailing bespeaks a serious commitment to getting the most bang for the public buck (the construction came in at a very modest $1,260 per m² ($117 per square foot). In fact, the architects went one further: in exchange for reducing the area of all units by 10 per cent, they were able to apply the saved money to better construction standards and more durable materials and finishes. To its credit, BC Housing went along with this innovative strategy, which also was endorsed by the co-op members themselves, and the project is much the better for it. In addition, this approach will no doubt result in lower long-term maintenance and repair costs.

The use of brick cladding is reminiscent of those earlier social housing projects, as is the high-density maximization of a tight urban site. And the collective is celebrated through a series of elements and facilities such as the communal courtyard, meeting spaces and rooftop vegetable gardens. The project has a sense of liveliness, too, especially on its inner sides, where two gently bowed facades greet each other across the tautly drawn central courtyard, tied together by two high-level pedestrian bridges.

As this and a few other recent projects demonstrate, Vancouver continues to benefit from the production of non-market housing of an exemplary standard. The social housing tradition continues as a vivid strand in Vancouver's evolving tapestry of an indigenous architecture.

13

A Brief History
of Zoning

EVER SINCE Canada's very first zoning bylaw was enacted by the Municipality of Point Grey in 1922, Vancouver has been using land-use zoning as a tool to shape its urban form. The earliest regulations were the first steps towards differentiating residential areas from commercial areas, thus protecting and enhancing the property values of both. The results, at least on the west side of Vancouver, are still evident: consistently uniform tree-lined streets, planted boulevards, regular setbacks for rows of houses, retail areas concentrated along key arterials that echo the long-abandoned streetcar routes. A liberal sprinkling of small parks completes the picture—largely still intact—of sylvan domesticity.

When Harland Bartholomew prepared his master plan for the City of Vancouver, one of the first things he did was to establish comprehensive zoning bylaws, thus endorsing the importance of zoning as a planning tool. Since then, the City has increasingly used rezoning to shift the balance of land use from industrial and commercial to residential.

A look at the map of Vancouver on page 216 illustrates the amount of land rezoned from industrial to other uses since 1968. It is startling to see that virtually the entire downtown peninsula waterfront and both sides of False Creek have been rezoned to non-industrial uses in this period. And the trend continues.

Rezoning industrial lands to high-density residential use has been a key tactic in Vancouver's ongoing strategy to become a more compact, higher density, sustainable community. For one thing, industrial areas do not usually have neighbouring constituencies to oppose densification in the way that established single-family residential neighbourhoods do. Thus, these "brown field" sites are easier areas for land-use intensification and have accommodated a disproportionate share of the city's recent growth. In addition to the

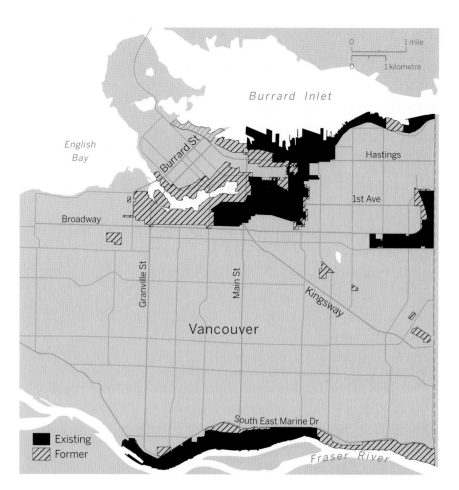

Vancouver's shrinking
industrial land base.
Eric Leinberger

Existing
Former

large-scale rezoning of industrial lands on the downtown peninsula and around False Creek, smaller pockets have been rezoned in the suburbs, most notably the former Carling O'Keefe brewery in Kitsilano (Arbutus Walk), lands along the SkyTrain line around Joyce Street (Collingwood Village) on the far east side of Vancouver and former sawmill sites along the Fraser River.

However, now that much of Vancouver's obsolescent industrial land base has been converted, less remains for economically viable rezoning. The City, rightly, also wants to maintain its industrial land base at an optimum level, both to provide jobs and the kinds of services required by the city and for tax revenue. With the inexorable diminution of industrial land available for rezoning, increasing pressure will be brought to bear on other areas for residential intensification. Vancouver's radical transformation of its waterfront accompanies the shift from waterfront-based industrial production and distribution to a knowledge-based, service-based and tourist-based economy. This story is still unfolding, and the future of the False Creek flats is a big part of the chapters remaining to be written.

Vancouver has also made effective use of the rezoning of industrial land to achieve public ends. For the city's first century, several hundred hectares of industrial and railway waterfront (the lands granted to the Canadian

Pacific Railway) virtually encircled the entire downtown peninsula. In the decades since Expo 86, huge swaths of this downtown waterfront have been converted to non-industrial uses, and as night follows day, the public waterfront walkway/bikeway system has followed.

The waterfront walkway/bikeway phenomenon is now virtually continuous right around the downtown peninsula and False Creek, with just a few gaps. The system was started by the completion in 1980 of the Stanley Park seawall. This extraordinary public amenity winds right around the promontory guarding the entrance to Vancouver's inner harbour, offering one of the world's great urban walks. Over the intervening time, the waterfront walkway has been extended beyond Stanley Park, along the edge of the West End and False Creek, and along Coal Harbour. It is also in place along large stretches of the Kitsilano and Point Grey waterfronts, so that it now totals some 20 km (12 miles) in length. As additional waterfront industrial lands are rezoned, the City's Planning Department, taking its direction from City Council, continues to insist on a broad zone for public perambulation, typically 10.5 m (35 feet) wide, to accommodate both pedestrians and cyclists. The waterfront walkway system stands as one of the City's proudest achievements; this seawall is one of the most tangible benefits that have accrued to the city as a result of this process.

One of the last remaining significant pieces of formerly industrial urban waterfront land that soon will come into play is the southeast shore of False Creek. Some 20 ha (50 acres) will be rezoned to facilitate a mixed-use development of up to five thousand housing units, jump-started by the awarding of the 2010 Olympic Winter Games to Vancouver: it is the site of the athletes village. And waterfront public access is of course integral to the plan. This will complete the entire False Creek loop, making it possible to walk or cycle from Coal Harbour right around the downtown peninsula and False Creek and all the way to West Point Grey. Ultimately, the City envisions extending it around Point Grey and along the north bank of the Fraser River, a plan that will require significant changes to the

A portion of Vancouver's growing waterfront walkway/bikeway system, along the north side of False Creek in Concord Pacific Place.

Derek Lepper photo

Vancouver's new relationship with the waterfront at Concord Pacific Place overlooking False Creek.

Derek Lepper photos

remaining industrial land uses along the river. But even here, there is already an ongoing shift away from heavy industry and towards waterfront housing, especially in the southeast corner of the city.

Through the widespread rezoning of traditional water-dependent industrial lands, Vancouver's urban waterfront has become one of its greatest physical assets, and many sections are now publicly accessible for the first time in the city's history. The process has dramatically transformed and extended the public realm.

The other major trend in the use of zoning to reshape the form of the city is the conversion of commercial lands to residential use. Again, the lion's share of this trend is taking place on the downtown peninsula, but it has also been an important strategy in densifying the suburbs.

A key move in the story of rezoning commercial lands was the City's "Living First" initiative to shrink the downtown commercial office district and to encourage residential densification in large parts of it. The second key move has been the very successful intensification of Vancouver's inner suburban arterial corridors through the creation of the so-called C-2 zone.

Rezoning Downtown: The "Living First" Story [65]

Since the mid-1980s, the City of Vancouver has been engaged in an ongoing project to densify the downtown peninsula's residential population. The population of about 40,000 back then had grown to some 70,000 by 2003; it continues to rise rapidly and is projected to reach 105,000 by 2021.[66] A big part of the reason for this athletic growth has been the manipulation of zoning policy. In achieving this, Vancouver has bucked the "flight to the suburbs" trend across North America in the post–Second World War years, a key factor in its perceived success.

In 1991 City Council approved a far-reaching policy to reduce the amount of land zoned for commercial use in the downtown peninsula and to rezone it to residential use. This policy, the 1991 *Central Area Plan,* saw nearly 750 000 m² (8 million square feet) of excess downtown office space converted to allow residential use. This initiative has been the road map for downtown Vancouver's residential growth ever since. As a result of this zoning change, several new neighbourhoods have emerged on the downtown peninsula in recent years.

Timing was important as well. The intersection of two trends—a shift away from railway-based waterfront industry and a shift in demographics—has been a major factor in this dramatic change. With the decline in industry, large tracts of hitherto undevelopable waterfront land became available. Increasing land prices and decreasing supply, coupled with changing local demographics, which has seen a significant influx of new residents from older cities and other cultures, and with different lifestyles, who would more readily accept alternatives to low-density suburban housing, have also played their part in the making of these high-density, high-rise communities.

These new neighbourhoods are part of a larger "Living First" sustainable development strategy championed by the City, which has sought to create a more compact, integrated, mixed-use community in downtown Vancouver. This strategy included the encouragement of housing intensification and diversity; the development of coherent neighbourhood structure plans; a focus on transportation alternatives such as public transit, walking and cycling; and the fostering of a more domestic urban design and public realm to mitigate the effects of high-density residential living.

A major first principle was to limit any increase in vehicle access to downtown by a policy of not building additional bridges or traffic lanes, so as to let congestion become an ally in creating conditions more amenable to urban living. This revolutionary (for North America at least) policy has reaped dividends, bringing intensified life to the streets of downtown Vancouver.

A second principle was to extend the existing urban fabric, the patterns and character of the built city, out towards the waterfront, rather than creating distinctly different environments. The street grid as well as the traditional street-reinforcing built form have been extended out to the edges of the peninsula wherever practical.

A third principle was to develop complete neighbourhoods at a pedestrian scale, with the full panoply of services and amenities such as shops, parks and community facilities. Many of these amenities have been "extracted" from developers in negotiated packages through the City's discretionary rezoning process.

The underlying theme in this "Living First" strategy was to bring into play the advantages of an urban lifestyle over a suburban one. Creating alternatives to the single-family home in the suburbs—which offer a rich mix of amenities, convenience, safety and comfort at a competitive price—has been key. The introduction of a relatively new (for Vancouver, that is) housing type, the attached townhouse, with its own front door onto the street, is one example. These streetfront townhouses, with their carefully modulated relationships between the street, sidewalk and building face, have had the effect of domesticating long stretches of downtown streets. They have also precipitated a surprisingly robust increase in families with children moving downtown for the first time. More than six hundred townhouses had been added to the downtown residential mix by the end of 2000, and the number is growing.

Giving credit where it is due, it must be said that City Hall itself has been a vital player in shepherding this transformation into being: a key challenge was to revamp the regulatory and planning processes to encourage a collaborative, negotiative development planning paradigm. This approach was based on a more discretionary zoning model that emphasized guidelines and incentives over hard regulations.

The strategy seems to be working. Vancouver is reversing North America's post–Second World War romance with the suburbs and, on the downtown peninsula at least, creating a lively urban environment in its place.

Remaking Main Street: The C-2 Story

Vancouver's early yet extensive streetcar network established an arterial street system that has become one of the most characteristic aspects of Vancouver's urban form, and today those streets serve as the centres of numerous local neighbourhoods. The streetcars may be long gone (largely replaced by trolley buses), but the shops and services that sprang up along their routes remain. And, increasingly, people are living on those streets too.

This latter development has been made possible by the City's C-2 zone, which permits up to four (though in practice most often three) floors of residential over a ground floor of commercial use. The concept of "living over the shop" has caught on in a big way, whereas in many other North American cities there is still widespread cultural and market resistance to this form of housing. But Vancouver has embraced it, and the residential densification of its traditional neighbourhood high streets has given them a new lease on life.

The projects in C-2 zones usually stretch along most of a block that fronts onto an arterial route, with streetfront shops, services, cafés and

restaurants that have residential units above. The residential units are often
split by a central courtyard, so that one row of units faces onto the street
and the other faces back towards the neighbourhood, which is typically
single-family housing. Often a mid-block lane separates the new projects
from adjacent residential buildings, and this device, coupled with building
setback and terracing, helps mediate between the four storeys of the C-2
zone and adjacent lower density areas.

Many, though by no means all, of the resulting projects have proved
handsome additions to their neighbourhood streetscape. The buildings
themselves, or at least the better designed ones, with their four-storey facades
framing the street, have helped to strengthen the public realm envelope
where before there were usually just one-storey buildings. They have injected
much-needed densification that in turn helps to support local businesses.
They also help to support higher use of public transit by locating more housing along bus routes. And they provide a broader range of housing options
at different price points than might otherwise be available in some of these
areas. In short, they are helping to build urban communities.

The C-2 zone has helped to re-establish a familiar building typology
in Vancouver that many other North American cities struggle to achieve. It
is a simple formula, really, a modest building type that reinforces the urban
fabric of the city as opposed to creating monuments. At their best, these
are polite background buildings, not "look at me" architectural statements.
The C-2 buildings are adding a new layer of urbanism across the city. They
are becoming common, in the best sense of the word, and Vancouver needs
more of them.

Vancouver's downtown
peninsula, a vibrant urban
environment offering a
compelling alternative to
the North American suburb.
Lance Berelowitz photo

Trafalgar Place on Broadway in Kitsilano: a successful C-2 zone mixed-use project, densifying Vancouver's high streets.

Lance Berelowitz photo

However, the C-2 zone is not without drawbacks. Where projects have been built without the benefit of an adjacent separating lane, there have been problems of overlook and scale impacts on adjacent single-family homes. As a consequence, the City embarked on a comprehensive review of its C-2 development regulations and guidelines, to try reduce these conflicts. Long delayed, the consultants' report was finally aired at City Council, and its recommendations adopted. However, a major shortcoming of this review is that, in response to neighbours' complaints, it was mandated to look only at reducing density, height and building massing. The terms of reference for the study did not permit any broader examination or indeed potentially upzoning adjacent residential areas either. In other words, an opportunity was missed to consider a much wider range of possibilities. The results are predictable: the recommended changes inevitably resulted in a reduction, albeit minor, in the total amount of housing that can be provided in this zone. There is something perverse in reducing, however nominally, the availability of a form of housing that has clearly addressed a demand and that has strength-ened Vancouver's urban form.

The C-2 zone has become a useful tool in the delivery of moderately priced rental and strata condominium housing in the city over the past decade as pressure has grown on affordable housing. It has also proved to be effective in building the kind of mixed-use neighbourhood centres and local high streets envisaged in CityPlan, a long-range city-wide frame-work for deciding programs, priorities and actions, and the closest thing Vancouver has to an official community plan. As such, the C-2 zone has become an important plank in the city's sustainable development platform. So it is ironic that one of the few real success stories in sensitive suburban residential densification just got more restrictive.

THIS BRINGS US BACK to the bigger issue of zoning *per se* as a tool for shaping the city. There is no question that land-use zoning has preserved many good things about Vancouver and has protected it from some of the worst excesses of unbridled development by mitigating the impact of market forces on the shape of the city. It has also been used creatively and power-fully in reshaping the downtown core in particular.

But the zoning bylaw, developed with the best of intentions as a means to an end, has over the years also become an end in itself, a sacrosanct system of thinking about and defining the city. It has, in short, become an impediment, even a crutch, too often stymying innovative urban planning and design, as many local architects will attest.

There is nothing inherently superior about land-use zoning as a mechanism for creating a better city. A city is a much more subtle, dynamic entity than any zoning bylaw can frame. The vast majority of cities worldwide have gotten along just fine for hundreds of years without formal land-use zoning, and it is only in the last seventy-five years or less that such regulations have been imposed. In those cases, the impact has been relatively minor, compared to the pre-existing urban fabric. The world's best-loved cities are the way they are not because of zoning bylaws but in spite of whatever zoning may now be in place.

The problem for Vancouver, young as it is, is that so little of the city was built before zoning was introduced that its more deleterious effects are much magnified. There is very little evidence of the organic city, the intricate web of urban spaces and built forms that arose before the heavy hand of zoning was applied. There is no "old town" core of narrow lanes and multiple layers of use. And there is very little unpredictability, no edge. At the risk of sounding simplistic, it is boring. Serendipity, complexity, conjunction, anticipation, surprise and delight: these very human experiences are what great cities offer. But zoning is a blunt, inflexible tool. Zoning is by definition exclusionary, limiting things to a preordained set of possibilities. It determines what cannot be done, rather than what can be. It does not anticipate nor nurture new, untried forms of city-building or habitation. It does not, in short, encourage the city of desire.

At recent local and national planning conferences, I have argued that what Vancouver needs is more flexible zoning. I have pointed to experiments in other cities such as Toronto, where certain areas have been set aside within which land-use rules are very permissive and development is controlled in other ways, such as by defining building envelopes and by setting up urban design guidelines. Vancouver's West End in particular, that high-rise, high-density residential precinct on the downtown peninsula, and the closest thing the city has to a zone of desire, is ripe for such an experiment.

The West End, which houses approximately forty thousand residents in what has been called North America's densest neighbourhood, has experienced significant demographic changes in the past couple of decades. It went from being inhabited by mostly single residents, including many young people, to a much more mixed, polyglot populace. Central to this has been the influx of substantial numbers of immigrants from all over the world, and since the fall of the Iron Curtain, particularly from Eastern Europe. There are now sizable communities of Serbs, Croats, Bosnians, Poles, Ukrainians and Russians, among others. It also has become the epicentre of Vancouver's flourishing gay community. And many people are staying in place, which is to say that the age profile of the area is shifting dramatically, much like most urban populations in Canada, to reflect the maturing baby boomers.

So what does this all mean for the West End? For one thing, it means far more demand for a greater range of goods, services and lifestyle options. It also means a surprising proliferation of families with young children and increasing numbers of residents who have very different sensibilities and expectations about what urban living means. They want and embrace a more complex, mixed-use, layered urban experience, where land is not zoned into separate geographic areas, but rather where they can live in and among a wide range of urban activities, from cafés and places of entertainment to schools to small factories, offices and shops. And it means an ever-widening range of lifestyles and alternative family arrangements. The physical and regulatory infrastructures have not kept pace with these social changes.

What if you could live and work in the same apartment tower? What if you could acquire a second apartment in your tower (without attracting capital gains tax) and convert it to an office, studio or cottage-industry workplace? What if the West End became rife with incubator businesses? And what if, instead of passive landscapes manicured to within an inch of their lives and empty lobbies on the ground floors of residential towers, there were coffee shops or bars, so that you could pop downstairs for a coffee or a glass of wine, buy the newspapers, meet your neighbours, play a game of chess? What if you could convert your underground parking stall into a place of business, or storage, or a beer cellar? What if you could sell it off? Or convert a top-floor apartment into a rooftop cocktail and sushi bar? Sounds far-fetched, perhaps even downright irresponsible, right?

But here's the thing. Such uses are not only permitted in many other great cities but add character, colour and value (both cultural and economic). Think of the *Bierstubes* in the basements of bourgeois Viennese apartment buildings. Or the cosy neighbourhood cafés on the ground floors of myriad Parisian apartment blocks. Or the rooftop cocktail bars and dance clubs of San Francisco. Or the dinner clubs, food counters and bars of Tokyo, Seoul and Hong Kong, tucked into every nook and cranny. Or the mixed-use skyscrapers of Manhattan, where in the same building a cinema, sports club, hotel, offices and apartments all happily coexist. Or the small businesses and services conveniently located in the basement floors of London's terraced Victorian houses. Or the souks and street markets of Mediterranean cities, infiltrating their way through Algiers, Lisbon, Nice, Tunis. By comparison with these examples, the West End seems starkly limited as an urban environment.

Fortunately, Vancouver is beginning to see some initiatives in this direction. The first, albeit limited, mixed-use towers have begun to emerge downtown (the Terminal City tower, the Wall Centre, the Shaw Tower). And certain parts of the city have been moved towards what the City Planning Department coyly refers to as "choice of use" or "swing" zones. For example, the Triangle West neighbourhood zoning in theory permits the inclusion of both office and residential uses within the same building, though in reality very little of this mixed use has been built. Although the innovative, flexible zoning approach developed for Triangle West could be a model for other areas in the city, this has not yet happened, and it remains a promising model without emulations.

Which brings us back to the West End, where the judicious introduction of more flexible zoning could have an immediate benefit. More importantly, it would contribute to the enhancement of a richer and more complete community, without overthrowing the many virtues the inhabitants already enjoy. The West End would deliver on the promise of urbanism. It might then even earn its latest sobriquet: Little Sarajevo. And it could indeed lay claim to becoming a City of Desire.

THE ADOPTION of more flexible, less restrictive land-use zoning will also be the key to eventually shifting the almost 70 per cent of Vancouver's zoned land base away from exclusively single-family detached homes towards more sustainable, affordable and diverse housing options. Indeed, it is in the suburbs that the true limitations of traditional zoning, and the challenges it poses, are most manifest. It is here that the next chapters in the history of zoning will be written.

14

Hollywood North

This place is too new!—DOUGLAS COUPLAND ON HOW VANCOUVER IS
PERCEIVED BY VISITING EASTERN CANADIANS, FROM *CITY OF GLASS*

WHEN VANCOUVERITES LOOK over their shoulders at other places that might
presage their own future, they do not look at Calgary on the other side of the
Rocky Mountains and certainly not even more distant Toronto, which might
just as well be on another continent. Rather, the view is southward, down
the coast to Seattle. Seeking a somewhat broader perspective, they might cast
their eyes even farther south to Portland.

Seattle, Portland: these are understandable cities, places to which Vancouverites can relate. They are nearby, share many features in common and
are similar enough, yet, being American, are that much more well endowed
and energized: they suggest what might happen in Vancouver if it plays its
cards right. They also offer object lessons in what Vancouver should avoid.
But their problems are not too much worse than Vancouver's and are therefore within the bounds of imagination: freeway impacts, congestion, inner-
city decay versus gentrification, skyrocketing property values, declining
resource industries and so on. These are things Vancouver also has had to
grapple with and continues to do so.

A few Vancouverites may even look as far south as San Francisco, rec-
ognizing something in common with that West Coast city's smugness about
its personal wealth, its spectacular setting and its self-ascribed role as the
nation's natural home of radical social experiments. There, they might see a
vision of what Vancouver is becoming: an aestheticized centre of much-
polished charm settled comfortably within a pacified landscape and an outlying hinterland where the majority of lives are actually lived but that people
do not talk about too much. It is a sobering prospect, this view of ferocious

gentrification at the precious centre and ragged, rampant, uncoordinated sprawl at the periphery.

But if Vancouverites really want to scare themselves, they look at Los Angeles.

Los Angeles is Vancouver's worst nightmare. Yet in so many ways there are remarkable parallels, real echoes of the Los Angeles that Vancouverites love to hate, right here in Lotus Land.

Take that name, "Lotus Land," bestowed on Vancouver by a scornful yet envious rest of Canada and gratefully, even smugly, accepted by the locals. The implications behind the moniker are analogous to those implied when Americans speak of Los Angeles as the "Land of Sunshine" or "Surfer City": a conjugation of indolence and sybaritic hedonism under the sun. Except that in the Canadian context, it is not the prospect of endless sun that Vancouver tempts with but rather that of an endless lack of "real" winter. Vancouver has one of the softest, mildest, least extreme climates north of the 49th Parallel. Like Los Angeles is (or once claimed to be) for America, it is the promised land. In this sense, Vancouver and Los Angeles are eerily similar, and the comparisons by no means end there.

Of course the two cities are places of vastly different scale. Although Los Angeles might well claim to be the world's first supercity and Greater Vancouver's entire population could fit snugly into a very small part of the Los Angeles conurbation, the comparables are worth considering, if only to get a glimpse of Vancouver's darker underside potential.

Both Vancouver and Los Angeles owe their nineteenth-century growth largely to a remarkably similar (and well founded) fear of being left behind and bypassed by the emerging transcontinental railway networks. And both places were founded on a deal with the devil in the form of railway companies. These parallel stories took place within fifteen years of each other.

When it became apparent that the Southern Pacific Railway line between San Francisco and Yuma on the border with Texas was likely to bypass Los Angeles altogether and leave it disconnected from the transcontinental railroad, the local business leaders foresaw economic disaster. They struck a deal with the railway company to reroute the line to Los Angeles in return for large tracts of land to develop. From the moment that the deal was made, Southern Pacific began to shape the future supercity in profound ways, laying out from central Los Angeles a series of radiating spur lines in several directions. By 1880 the five lines out to San Fernando, San Bernardino, Anaheim, Wilmington and Santa Monica had established the structural skeleton on which Greater Los Angeles was to grow. They precipitated the subdivision and development of adjacent land almost as quickly as the rails were laid. Moreover, these lines became in short order the basis of future interurban routes—the Big Red Cars—that rapidly connected the constituent parts of the city. And of course the railway brought in the floods of settlers who created the City of Angels.

In Vancouver, meanwhile, the Canadian Pacific Railway had planned to terminate its transcontinental line at Port Moody at the easternmost head of Burrard Inlet. However, the savvy owners of real estate farther west down the inlet (today's City of Vancouver) knew their land values would stagnate and fade away without the railway. The provincial government was the biggest landowner of them all, so it struck a deal with the CPR to extend the line westward as far as Coal Harbour: Vancouver would become the terminus. The cost was high: the CPR got thousands of hectares of land granted outright to develop as it saw fit, including ownership of much of the waterfront. But it seemed cheap at the price to those early civic boosters, whose own adjacent land values would now soar.

Thus, both cities were essentially founded on land speculation based on deals made to ensure the coming of the intercontinental railroad. And unquenchable land speculation has remained central to their economies ever since.

As with early Vancouver, Los Angeles was laid out in a series of street grids of brutal efficiency to optimize land development. However, scattered through both cities, there are subtle inflections of master-planned layouts, delicious examples of what Reyner Banham characterized as the Art of the Enclave:[67] compare the sinuous hillside redoubts of Palos Verdes Estates and the British Properties, both laid out by the celebrated Olmsted Brothers, or the elegant layouts of Beverly Hills and Shaughnessy Heights, which were developed at exactly the same time (1906) for privileged markets and had similar exclusionist ownership restrictions to protect land values and social cohesion. In point of fact, both cities commissioned far-reaching urban planning studies by the same authors during the same period: Harland Bartholomew had barely finished his seminal plan for Vancouver[68] in 1928 when he, in association with the aforementioned Olmsted Brothers, was retained to prepare a key report on Los Angeles.[69] Their recommendations drew on many of the same lessons Bartholomew had applied to Vancouver. Both plans called for an enhanced public realm, expanded parks and public beaches, and extensive greenway belts ("pleasureway parks" in the awkward terminology of the reports). And, in both cases, the plans were never fully implemented. For both Vancouver and Los Angeles, the Depression-era Bartholomew/Olmsted plans, with their extraordinary optimism and belief in the primacy of the public commons, represented "a window into a lost future."[70]

With their endless grids, low-density settlement and preponderance of stand-alone single-family homesteads, both Greater Vancouver and Greater Los Angeles have the sense of being cities in outline, awaiting the next layer of infill to flesh out their grid skeletons.

The story of Los Angeles's surprisingly extensive early interurban railway network was paralleled by Vancouver's own equally extensive inter-urban/streetcar system. The interurbans played a decisive role in the early expansion of both cities. And both let their rail-based systems wither in favour of the road-based car and bus, and are now spending large fortunes to rebuild public rail-transit systems.

Vancouver and Los Angeles are cities of the future: with so little history, they are future-focussed to an extent incomparable with almost any other city in North America. The two are making it up as they go along. The ahistorical impulse is a central feature of both their social cultures: with barely one hundred years of urbanization apiece, neither is overburdened with a long history, permitting them to embrace the future with a sense of limitless possibility. This of course is part of the allure, especially for people coming from the more established eastern seaboard, let alone from tired old Europe. The two cities are the urban experiments of the future for their respective nations.

Their citizens are largely immigrants, so that a disproportionately high number are first-generation residents. And their demographic mix has shifted dramatically in recent years, creating new cultural realities, new forms of social and physical expression. The dominance of earlier European settlers is breaking down, challenged and increasingly usurped by the Latino wave in the case of Los Angeles, and by Asians in Vancouver. What old Establishment elites there were are rapidly being replaced by elites of new wealth and new centres of power from unpredictable sources. With no real Establishment, both cities are more open to new ideas, to experimentation.

As cities of experimentation, Los Angeles and Vancouver have been loci of architectural inventiveness, the preferred homes of architectural exiles. This is particularly true of the modernists, who found in them a fertile receptivity to the new. Both places represent the end of the line, Terminal

City, the place of dreams where everyone can own a house on a piece of land. It is not surprising therefore that these two cities have produced the most sustained, inventive bodies of custom residential architecture. The single-family house has a power here that is unmatched in the more collective, denser models of Midwest and East Coast cities. Vancouver and Los Angeles represent the North American pinnacle of the custom-designed house as an architectural thesis. It is no accident that the most provocative, challenging residential architects chose either Los Angeles or Vancouver in which to practise their art: Frank Lloyd Wright (for some of the time), Irving Gill, Rudolph Schindler, Richard Neutra, Ron Thom, Ned Pratt, C.B.K. Van Norman, Arthur Erickson, Fred Hollingsworth, et al. If the latter names are less familiar to the general reader, it is only due to Los Angeles's far more confident self-promotion, and Vancouver's correspondingly insecure self-effacement. It is no reflection on the quality of the work. The two cities have the richest opus of twentieth-century modern residential work in their respective countries.

Vancouver and Los Angeles are major ports: indeed, they are the largest Pacific Ocean ports of the United States and Canada, respectively, and the entrepôt ethos is central to their economies. They are thus also the biggest illegal drug gateways into their nations from Asia and the Pacific Rim. Drugs are big in both cities, but the drug culture is just one manifestation of a shared reputation for experimentation and illicit permissiveness.

The disparities of wealth that immigrant cities manifest are on full display in Los Angeles and Vancouver. Both are home to sizable populations of wealthy immigrants and global citizens, as well as economic refugees. On the one hand, the "fat cat" Los Angeles foothill communities of Hollywood, West Hollywood, Beverly Hills, Bel Air, Brentwood and Pacific Palisades find their topographic and economic Vancouver equivalents in Westwood Plateau, the British Properties, Hollyburn Heights, Cypress Park Estates, Upper Caulfeild and Whytecliff. And on the other hand, the plains of South Central Los Angeles, filled with millions of people from Mexico and Central America, has its Vancouver analogue in the flat swaths of suburban Richmond, Delta, Surrey, Cloverdale and Langley, where entire communities of Chinese, Southeast Asian and Indian newcomers struggle with the hard scrabble of a new life in a foreign land.

Those disparities are mirrored in the aesthetic ethos of both cities as well. The built urban environments are very familiar to visitors from one city to the other: simple stucco-clad or wood-sided houses (Vancouver even calls one style of these the "California bungalow"), while in the outlying suburbs the cacophony of strip-mall franchises, auto lots, ever-wider streets and oversized commercial signage is almost equally ubiquitous.

Vancouver and Los Angeles are the logical termini of internal migration within their respective countries as well. Many people fetch up here at the end of the line, and this has had a direct impact on their social and political cultures: many homeless street people, lots of hard drugs easily available through their seaports and from across their nearby borders, significant poverty concentrated in transient inner-city areas such as Los Angeles's Westlake and Vancouver's Downtown Eastside, notorious for being Canada's poorest postal code. Both cities face significant social challenges as a result of these extreme inequities, and their political leaders have from time to time tripped up over these challenges. Listen to former Vancouver City Councillor Jennifer Clarke on the hustings as a mayoral candidate for the incumbent party in the 2002 municipal election: "My Vancouver does not have any ghettos. As your mayor, I am going to take back the Downtown Eastside one block at a time."[71] How exactly this was to be done was left unexplained, though it no doubt involved sizable doses of private-sector land development. Unfortunately for Ms. Clarke, she did not get the opportunity to test her surprisingly original approach to addressing social dysfunction. The denizens of the Downtown Eastside, as with other voters, declined in droves to vote for her party, and she lost her seat on City Council.

Now listen to former Los Angeles City Councillor Mike Hernandez, who represented the First Council District that includes that city's poorest neighbourhood, speaking about his council's record on Westlake:[72] "We are still light years away from per capita equality in city facilities or services." He went on to tell reporters that "The mayor continues to cater to that population he believes votes." Westlake, Hernandez's former constituency, has twenty-five times the population density of Brentwood, Bel Air or the Palisades.[73] Meanwhile, Ms. Clarke's own natural constituency, the west side of Vancouver, is the least dense in the city, while the Downtown Eastside continues to squeeze people in. Two sides of the same coin?

In this economic-geographic disparity, too, Vancouver and Los Angeles are strangely alike. Both strongly exhibit the northern-hemisphere city phenomenon of land values being higher in the west and lower in the east: the most exclusive, wealthiest suburbs of each city are typically to the west, while the poorest, least desirable are downwind to the east.

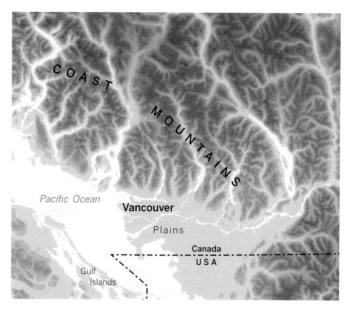

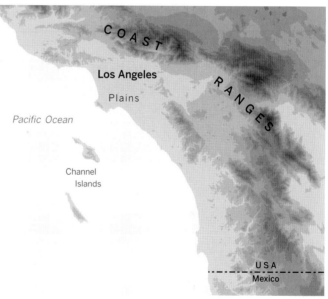

THE PARALLELS between Los Angeles and Vancouver are not just historical, social, political and economic. There are also topographical, geological and ecological similarities.

Both cities are rimmed by mountain wilderness to the north and east, ocean to the west and flat plains stretching away to the south, terminated to the far south by an international border (the Canada–U.S. border and the U.S.– Mexico border). Thus, they have broadly (if superficially) similar topographically driven urban features: foothill settlements rising up the mountain slopes to the north and looking down over the city below; low-density plains of suburbia stretching out towards the southern horizon; beach zones along the western edge, and a cross-cultural transition zone along an international border that is just beyond that southern horizon but nevertheless makes its presence felt in many tangible ways.

But the superficially similar topographies of Los Angles and Vancouver hide a more profound factor in common. Both are located on major fault lines: they share the seismically active Pacific Rim of Fire. Los Angeles is situated right over the notorious San Andreas fault, among others, and Vancouver is situated right beside a major subduction fault line that, when it gives way, could well bury the city. This shared intimacy with geological Armageddon has bred a certain fatalism in their residents: there is not a lot they can do about it, so they have adopted an easy come easy go attitude. Collective denial finds a common home in both places.

Vancouver and Los Angeles also exhibit many aspects of the Edge City phenomenon: they both share the view imperative, with homes along the waterfront being the most desirable. Compare, for example, the exclusive properties on Point Grey Road with Malibu's beachfront homes.

Vancouver and Los Angeles: topographical and geographical similarities.
Eric Leinberger

Top Vancouver's seismic neighbourhood.

Eric Leinberger

Bottom Los Angeles's seismic

neighbourhood, from Mike Davis, *Ecology*

of Fear. Cartography by Dave Deis

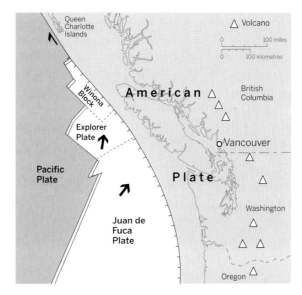

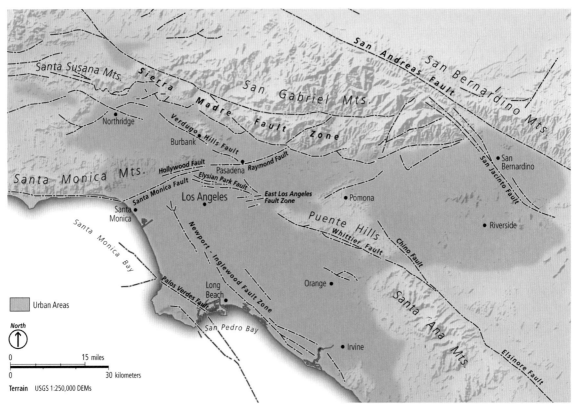

And back from the edge, the hillside properties are the most desirable. Altitude equals wealth.

The concomitant truth for both cities is that the daily reality for the vast majority of their residents, who live neither along the waterfront nor on the sunlit uplands, is banal suburbia. Their common truth is that few actually get to enjoy the good bits: most live out on the plains/delta, far away from the nice edge. Yet it is the edge that defines each city in the public eye. Who does not imagine Santa Monica when conjuring up an image of Los Angeles, or Kitsilano when doing the same of Vancouver?

Los Angeles represents the mythic beach culture of the United States. This role is played in Canada by Vancouver: it is the only city in the country that can lay claim to even the semblance of such a thing. The beachfront is the locus of public life in both Los Angeles and Vancouver; it is the zone of highest urban intensity. To the extent that more traditional Eurocentric public spaces are suspiciously absent in both cities, the corresponding forms of public space have bent to this reality: Vancouver's waterfront walkway system with its myriad strollers, joggers, cyclists and skaters is directly analogous to the beachfront route that takes Southern Californians through Santa Monica, Venice Beach and beyond.

The two cities have a culture of the pursuit of private gratification, a culture that favours active, sporty lifestyles, well-toned bodies. They are, respectively, the spandex and Gore-Tex capitals. This is obviously due in part to their permissive climates but also to their locations at the extremes of the social and geopolitical spectrums: so different from bustling New York or buttoned-down Toronto (both far more Eurocentric). And while their climates make this possible, the two West Coast cities are obviously different: Vancouver is the more modest, temperate, northern version of the let-it-all hang-out Southern Californian lifestyle.

Los Angeles and Vancouver belong to the small and exclusive group of large cities that face the ocean sunset. Their location on the West Coast overlooking the Pacific Ocean and their particular geographies orient them towards the west, where each night the sun drops into the sea. This might seem like a superficial fact, but there are very few large cities (Perth, Cape Town and Valparaiso come to mind) that share this sense of being at the edge of the world, nightly witnesses to the end of the day, in such a literal sense as these two cities do. It has a direct effect on the collective psyche of both, making them feel somehow more directly connected to the cycles of nature. It seems to have encouraged a heightened sense of spiritualism, mysticism and self-reflection. Is it any surprise to learn that they have disproportionate numbers of psychologists, psychiatrists, therapists? Lotus Land indeed.

The residents of both cities are in love with mobility. Los Angeles openly revels in this fact, has even created its central mythology around it. Although Vancouver may be reluctant to admit its association with the automobile, the myth of personal mobility runs deep here. Whether this is expressed in the many lovingly maintained 1950s and '60s sedans, coupes and convertibles that cruise the city's beachfront pleasure drives or in the remarkable array of personal transportation devices—bicycles, roller blades, skateboards, scooters—that locals embrace with relish, Vancouver is about freedom of movement as much as Los Angeles is. Vancouver, with its forgiving climate, has more collector convertibles than any other city in Canada. An Angeleno in his 1963 Camaro convertible would fit right in amongst the old Valiants, Triumphs and MGs that brighten up the streets of Vancouver. Although Vancouverites like to believe that they favour environmentally friendlier public transit, the reality[74] is that the number of cars is growing faster than the region's population.

And the car is having a disproportionate impact on the environment of both cities. Consider how they experience severe smog as a result of temperature inversion, caused primarily by a similar confluence of onshore maritime winds, topological factors and the ubiquitous car. Just as in Los Angeles the San Gabriel and San Bernardino mountains that ring the city to the north and east trap the pollutants in the lower atmosphere and funnel them inland, so do the surrounding Coast Mountains in Vancouver. Up the Fraser Valley, Abbotsford—with the highest smog levels every summer—is Vancouver's Fontana. An Angeleno driver making his way through the hazy soup of August in the Fraser Valley would feel disconcertingly at home. Although Vancouver's air pollution is not as extensive as Los Angeles's, it nevertheless is a very visible reminder of the uncomfortably similar ecological stresses that affect them.

Ecological comparables go beyond air pollution to embrace the very act of human settlement. Los Angeles and Vancouver were tamed for urbanization by the imposition of the grid. Where that street grid ran into inconvenient topographical impedimenta, it tended to simply ignore them. Landscapes were severely modified to facilitate development, especially along the more dramatic strips of slope, shoreline bluff, hillside. These ecologically distinctive places offered the most prized, valuable sites for homes,

Vancouver's beach scene, compared to …

Derek Lepper photo

… the Los Angeles beach scene.

Jeffrey Stanton photo

and neither city hesitated when it came to reordering the natural landscape to better suit land speculation.

Both cities rub up against a rich yet deeply imperilled natural ecology, in Los Angeles's case the desert, in Vancouver's case the rain forest. There is almost nothing left of the chaparral ecology in the Los Angeles basin, just as there are almost no first-growth trees left around Vancouver. As a further consequence of this ecological clash where chaparral or rain forest meets suburb, the residents of the two cities uneasily cohabit with a surprising array of wildlife: mountain lions (cougars) live on the edges, as do bears and coyotes, and smaller urban species in common include skunks, raccoons and ground squirrels. As both cities continue their apparently inexorable

A film shoot in Vancouver, with
the city standing in for Los Angeles.

Derek Lepper photo

expansion into what remains of proximate habitat for the larger predators, the incidences of conflict are rising. Every year, local stories about the tragic intersection between young suburbanite and hungry cougar are interchangeable between the two cities. And in common, the usual response is to shoot the "transgressing" animal rather than rein in the growth.

FINALLY, both Los Angeles and Vancouver are substitutes for reality, stand-ins for other places: as movie industry centres, they are invented environments (though in yet another eerie echo, the real money is based in the East), and Los Angeles's sub-genre pornography movie industry finds its Vancouver analogue in the stripper-club scene for which it is widely known.

As sublimations of other real places and invented environments, both are the natural home of escapist fantasy for each of their respective cultures: Dream City. They are what we want them to be, endlessly mutable, reinventable: simulations of everywhere and anywhere else. In a pinch—and this is what scares Vancouverites the most—they might even stand in for each other.

15

Public Life
or Spectacle?
The Culture
of Public Space

SOONER OR LATER the urban detective in search of clues to understanding Vancouver will reach the edge. Understanding the peculiar culture of Vancouver's public life and the centrifugal spaces where it takes place, at the edges, and which is so often based on spectacle rather than active collective participation, is central to piecing together the story of the city's emergent urban form.

As noted previously, Vancouver's public realm has some unique characteristics, including its apparent lack of traditional public spaces: it is missing the town squares of most older established cities in the New World, let alone the varieties of *platz, piazza, place* and *plaza* of European cities.

Historically however, Vancouver did have at least a couple of such traditional spaces where collective public activities were focussed: the square at the provincial court house and Victory Square. Although these spaces have mutated and been degraded over time and lost much of their strength as civic condensers, they are vestigial reminders of what once was. The square in front of the former provincial court house (now the Vancouver Art Gallery) has already been examined.[75] As a point of reference as Vancouver's most intact exemplar of a traditional centripetal space, Victory Square is described briefly below. Thereafter, we move quickly out to the edge and a review of the city's more eccentric range of contemporary public spaces.

Victory Square

Victory Square is one of Vancouver's earliest public spaces and was once at the centre of the booming frontier town. As early as 1890 (that is, four scant years after Vancouver's incorporation as a city), the square shows up in the famous 1890s bird's-eye view map of Vancouver (pages 98–99). At that time Victory Square was called Court House Square, after Vancouver's first court house built here in 1888 (and long since demolished).

In the 1910s this square became the centre of Vancouver's newspaper publishing industry, when both the *Daily Province* and the *Vancouver Sun* had headquarters in the area, the former in the Province Building overlooking the square and the latter in the spectacular Sun Tower on nearby Beatty Street. The square was even overlooked by the tallest building (briefly) in the British Empire, when the Dominion Building was constructed on the north side of Hastings Street in 1908–10.

Sometime after the First World War, the space acquired its current name of Victory Square, reflecting the Allied victory in the war. In 1924 a three-sided cenotaph was erected near the northern edge of the square, at the intersection of the two centreline axes of Hastings Street as it bends past the square. After the Second World War, the square gained increasing significance as the site of the annual November 11 Remembrance Day parade, which today remains one of the city's last truly unmediated public events.

Victory Square has an irregular, wedged quadrilateral shape, resolving the transition between the original Granville Townsite street grid and the subsequently dominant downtown peninsula grid. The space has a wide base along the higher south side, and it slopes down and narrows towards the north, where Hastings Street cranks at Cambie Street from one grid alignment to the other. The tapering shape and the older buildings that still surround it—all of them built right out to the streetline—help create a reasonably well-defined urban space. Most of the square is planted with grass, shrubs and flower beds, a traditional Vancouver response to public open space, however urban. A small hard-surfaced level area surrounds the cenotaph.

In recent years, with the westward shift in the city's economic centre, this part of town declined. Victory Square was virtually abandoned by Vancouver society and increasingly appropriated by more marginal people and the homeless. Faced with this situation, the Park Board quietly decided to redesign the square, primarily to reduce its use by "undesirables" (read drug dealers and pimps), mostly through more lighting and the elimination

of low-level vegetation that restricted the view into the square from passing police cruisers. In 2003, after a lengthy confrontation between the City and a group of homeless people who set up a squatter camp on the square to protest its gentrification, the improvements went ahead. The space has been cleaned up, shrubbery reduced, new street furniture and lighting installed. And, at least for now, the squatters are nowhere to be seen.

Meanwhile, the annual Remembrance Day ceremonies struggle on, working around the limited ability of the square in its current incarnation to accommodate large numbers of people. On this one day of the year, Vancouverites reclaim the space, including the surrounding streets, however awkwardly it works as a place of public assembly. Although still an important event in Vancouver's calendar, the civic and military ritual of remembrance—with its blessed utter lack of commercialization—has a whiff of its days being numbered.

Victory Square at the height of its function as Vancouver's pre-eminent public space in the early twentieth century. City of Vancouver Archives #Str P57, Leonard Frank photo

Victory Square, for all its physical shortcomings and virtual abandonment by Vancouverites, is still one of the city's very few functional traditional public spaces. Its future remains to be seen.

From Factor 15 to *Feu d'Artifice*: Life's a Beach

Vancouver's true culture of public space is evident on the waterfront. Not only are the apparent populist notions of a public space culture in this city highly codified there and therefore subject to an overwhelming romanticization but it is also true that Vancouver, in its emphasis on public activity at its edges as opposed to the centre, illustrates a variant of well-established forms of public life of the waterfront city.

The formalized waterfronts of such New World examples as Bondi Beach, Sydney or Santa Monica, not to mention such Old World examples such as Brighton, Nice or Venice, display the rich heritage of places whose locus of public life is on the waterfront. In these examples, at least the Old World ones, there is a highly formalized architecture of public space, supported and in part defined by an appropriate scale and use of surrounding buildings: Brighton's pavilion and pier, Nice's grand hotel–lined Promenade des Anglais and the great palazzos of Venice's Riva degli Schiavoni. Indeed, an entire architecture of the waterfront—reflecting the well-defined cultural practices associated with the beach in Western culture—has evolved and developed from these and other examples, to be replicated and reinvented across the world in seafront cities.

In Western industrialized cultures, the beach has historically been more than just a neutral place, as Robert Shields points out:

> [The beach] became the locus of an assemblage of practices … which, attached to the notion of "Beach," transformed its nature into a socially defined zone appropriate for specific behaviours and patterns of interaction outside of the norms of everyday behaviour. "Beach" became the topos of a set of connected discourses on pleasure and pleasurable activities … It was territorialised as a site fit for leisure, and the story of its transformation over time … amounts to a social history of the Beach.[76]

While a detailed social history is beyond the scope of this book, Vancouver's case is intriguing in that the apparent "natural" experience of socially neutral waterfront public space masks a highly contrived, ideologically controlled and commodified reality, in which the city's beaches can be understood as a series of discrete public spaces, in terms not only of built environment but also in social formation, use and regulation. Moreover, the translocation of public life away from the traditional sites of political activity (town square, city hall, court house, etc.) has been accompanied by a corresponding change in the emphasis of use of public space to one of personal leisure.

Why is this important? Because a society that allows its true public spaces to be turned into benign venues of consumption and leisure, as beaches are typically portrayed and thus perceived, is in danger of losing the will and ability to appropriate those spaces as theatres for vital, legitimate political expression. And the role of public space in this context in the metropolitan city's history is essential to the democratic impulse. Look, for instance, at the symbolism and central role of Beijing's Tiananmen Square, or the Velvet Revolution's use of Prague's Wenceslas Square, or Nelson Mandela's rally in Cape Town's Grand Parade after his release from incarceration. Every society and every city needs its public spaces for the exercise of democracy.

By titling this section, only somewhat facetiously, "From Factor 15 to *Feu d'Artifice*," I am suggesting that it is between the apparent dipoles of the so-called "natural" beaches and the "artifice" of events such as Vancouver's annual fireworks spectacle, where the city's public culture can be found.

The cultural, social and political functions typically fulfilled by the more traditional public spaces of the Western city are, in Vancouver's case, primarily performed by the spaces associated with the shoreline, waterfront park and seawall promenade. In Vancouver, these spaces, far from being the "natural" accidents of geography, are as artificially contrived, as architecturally constructed and as socially deterministic as the most articulated public space in any European city. The beaches, waterfront parks and seawall promenades of Vancouver are as culturally determined in their own way as, say, an Italian piazza is ineluctably a product of that culture. Vancouver has a particular *genius loci,* in which the spaces of public discourse are coded like no other's.

The second aspect of interest is the increasing commodification of Vancouver's public spaces and how this is reflected in the spaces themselves on the one hand, and in the cultural codes of behaviour of citizens on the other. Certain public spaces are formally associated with certain modes of public expression, and these modes are constrained and manipulated by the forces of authority and commerce to a high degree. This is by no means a phenomenon in Vancouver alone; indeed, it has been noted in other contexts by some of the most respected commentators on urbanism. The

contraction and usurpation of the public realm in North American cities
has been documented for some time. Vancouver exhibits but a variation of
this increasingly global phenomenon.

Vancouver's public space has been increasingly appropriated by commercial and promotional interests, often at the expense of truly ethnic-based,
community-based or class-based activities. Manipulation and dispersal are
creating a paradigm that is increasingly hostile to traditional public space.
In Vancouver, this paradigm is couched in the seductive terms of "natural"
leisure, making it extremely difficult to express the inherent threat to a populace in danger of pleasuring itself into civic marginalia.

On arriving in Vancouver in the mid-1980s after a decade spent in Europe,
I found myself searching in vain for the kinds of grand public spaces that
I had come to expect of the Western city. There were, at first glance, a very
few existing older public spaces which bore a vague resemblance to the great
spaces of the European city. There was Victory Square, with its cenotaph
and formal layout, and Robson Square. But neither of these seemed to fulfil
the same traditional cultural functions as social condenser, place of public
gathering or even just a foil to set off great civic or cultural buildings.

English Bay in the 1930s:
the "beach territorialized
as a site fit for leisure."
Vancouver Public Library
48576

More curiously still, Vancouver's municipal seats of power are located not in the centre of the city but rather at the fringes, what with City Hall rising imposingly out of an inner suburban neighbourhood and the Park Board headquarters (a not insignificant municipal power base in Vancouver), tucked into the edge of the city's 400 ha (1,000-acre) Stanley Park.

The location of the Park Board offices—an elected and powerful civic body—within the city's largest park rather than in the city centre is a clue as to the true nature of public space in this city of seductive simulations. But it was only while pondering the issue over the course of many summer days on the beach (a not unremarked irony) that it slowly dawned on me that these were Vancouver's only truly democratic public spaces: the beaches, waterfront parks and seawall promenades. And the more I examined these places of apparent leisure as analogous public spaces, the more comprehensible they seemed as the locus of public life in the city.

From its earliest days, Vancouver seems to have sought its most public cultural expression at the edge of, or even in, the surrounding water. Remember Thomas Mawson? Barely two decades after its founding in 1886, the city was contemplating the visionary urban designs of the noted British landscape architect, who proposed the following as the central public space for the city: "In Coal Harbour I would have my Grande Rond Pond, and the park beyond as the Tuileries, though not humanised."[77] Remember how this "Grande Rond Pond" water body, surrounded by a promenade and with a statue of Captain Vancouver atop a tall column at its centre, would become, to quote Mawson again, "the great social centre of Vancouver"? It was to form the foreground for a great civic building, perhaps the Natural History Museum of British Columbia. The museum never did get built, but the Rond Pond survives in its current form as Lost Lagoon, at the entrance to Stanley Park from Georgia Street. And instead of a statue at its centre, there is a programmed water fountain, located on axis with Georgia Street, a primary ceremonial route. The fountain is one of the few visible examples of a public space design that has successfully integrated the urban and the natural. It is also perhaps the clearest example of the marginalizing tendency of public space in Vancouver, where the central space is in fact a void: in this case, water.

Eighty years later, the notion of the city as an amphitheatre surrounding a public space of water is stronger than ever, conflated to the scale of False Creek or English Bay. Today, one of the city's most spectacular events is the annual Celebration of Light (formerly Symphony of Fire), in which

Top English Bay beach in 2 00, an example of the beachfront as an architecturally constructed public space.

Bottom Vancouver's City Hall rising out of its inner-suburban neighbourhood.

Lance Berelowitz photos

competing "national" fireworks displays are staged from a barge in the centre of English Bay and watched by hundreds of thousands of people gathered on the surrounding edges of the city. This is, in some respects, the most significant public event in the annual calendar, and yet a closer examination of the phenomenon reveals some disturbing trends.

However, let us first look at the nature of Vancouver's beaches and their highly articulated, increasingly commodified characteristics. On examining a map of the city, it is not entirely far-fetched to note a kind of sliding scale of relative public use of each beach in relation to its geographic location: a social geography of the city.

The most central beach is on English Bay, at the foot of Denman Street in the heart of the West End on the downtown peninsula; this beach demonstrates some of the most urban characteristics. It is used by a wide variety of people, representative of the diverse and dense West End population. The beach is highly formalized and in fact is virtually an artificial creation, the sand having been mechanically deposited and secured with rock groins. On the landward side is a formal urban edge, consisting of paved walkway, cut-stone retaining walls, street furniture and the English Bay Bath House, which now serves as public change rooms, toilets, beach administration and concession outlet. The area is surrounded by some of Vancouver's most popular cafés, restaurants and nightspots, and is used twenty-four hours a day throughout the year. It is not surprising, too, that the bath house structure is a favourite haunt of Vancouver's gay men. On a hot summer's day, with its cosmopolitan crowds, street vendors, musicians, taxi drivers, gay cruisers, tourists and police, this is about as urban as Vancouver gets. The waterfront is a great social condenser.

Moving out from the downtown core, the next significant strand is that of Kitsilano Beach in trendy singles territory, with the inner-city suburbanite apartments of Kits marching up the hill to the hip scene of 4th Avenue. The emphasis here is on physical appearance, manifest health and hedonism, and the form of the beach reflects this. The sand itself is gridded with a series of volleyball nets neatly aligned in a row of conspicuous consumption of the body. Behind this, and across the heavily trafficked pedestrian/bicycle path, the close-cropped grass mediates between a range of other sports facilities and functions from basketball to tennis. The beach is flanked at one end by Vancouver's largest, most elegant outdoor swimming pool, with its attendant devotees of the Zen of lap swimming.

The other significant structure (until its recent demolition) on Kitsilano Beach was the 1960s-era concession outlet, change rooms and lifeguard headquarters. Even this complex, with its rakish control tower and service

Opposite page Early Vancouver as amphitheatre surrounding a public space of water, English Bay. Vancouver Public Library 6609

This page The urban beachfront promenade on English Bay. George Vaitkunas photo

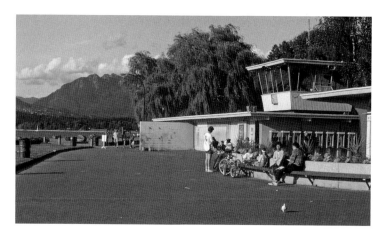

Kitsilano Beach's recently demolished rakish control tower, reflecting the culture of this place.

Lance Berelowitz photo

counter advertising cappuccino, seemed to suggest a certain affinity with the hedonistic culture of this beach. However, in one of Vancouver's more nasty recent public battles over the opposing visions of the beachfront's public role, the courts finally gave approval in 2004 for the Park Board to demolish the old facility and erect a swank new restaurant, paid for and operated by the successful private leasehold bidder.

Even the carefully placed rows of logs (a distinctive feature of Vancouver's beaches) along the length of the sand support a finely calibrated range of public poses and performances. Kitsilano Beach, with its body beautiful and volleyball culture, highly programmed uses and busy events calendar, is a thoroughly commodified public space holding a very well-articulated position somewhere between downtown urbanite and inner suburbanite in the spectrum of the city's public life.

Farther westward out from the centre are the beaches of Jericho, Locarno and Spanish Banks. A certain exotic quality begins to inform these places, reflected even in their foreign-sounding names. There is a whiff of wildness, or at least less urbanity, in the unkempt bushes and dunes of Jericho, the windswept openness of Locarno and the tumbling forested bluffs of Spanish Banks. The patrons here are accordingly equipped: they come well dressed and kitted, usually in large social groups, often family oriented, and with all the accessories of an expedition. Here are the picnic banquets of extended Italian, Greek or Central American families, the organized brio of office parties, the shifting alliances of student groups from the nearby University of British Columbia. The patterns of behaviour, while indisputably ritualized, are looser, somehow more regionalized. The softer, more informal scallops of beach and undulations of landscape support and mould this pattern. We are here encountering the public life of the inner suburbs.

Finally, at the outer edge of the peninsula, is the corresponding extreme of public permissiveness. Wreck Beach is located at the foot of the crumbling bluffs of Point Grey, at the most westerly geographical point of the city. It has no road access and is difficult to get to, reached by steep, rough paths hacked out of the wooded cliffs. The form of the beach is somewhat ephemeral, shaped and shifted over time by the tides, currents and variable deposits f om the adjacent Fraser River mouth. It is in many ways the least formal of the beaches, testing the limits of dissent in the city. Nudity is the

A picnic banquet at
Spanish Banks beach.

Lance Berelowitz photo

norm, and all manner of marginal behaviour is exhibited, from meditat-
ing in the lotus position to sounding the last post at sunset, from sex and
voyeurism in the bushes to drug deals in the open.

Even here, however, the ethos of dissent has to some degree been
commodified or at least exploited: a section of the beach called Main Street
is lined with wooden stalls offering a broad range of services, including
food, booze, drugs, massages, equipment rentals and so on. This activity is
self-policed by the denizens of the beach, though not for want of trying by
the official forces of authority.

Wreck Beach may be at the social and physical periphery of the city, but
in some ways it is the most public of Vancouver's public spaces. It is perhaps
the clearest prototype for the inversion of central public space, where the
farther out you get from the centre, the more vital and unrestrained the
public culture.

The same phenomenon has been observed previously on the Stanley
Park seawall, the heroic waterfront promenade that represents the apotheosis of public space as *promenade naturelle,* in perfect expression of the
paradox of a city whose most active public life is at its edges.

Each of Vancouver's beaches plays a finely calibrated role in the spectrum of the city's public life. These waterfront edges, far from being the casual result of geographical happenstance, are in fact carefully constructed and managed to fulfil a well-defined range of public functions. And to the extent that so many of Vancouver's more successful organized public spectacles take place at or near the water, these spaces are increasingly targeted for the use and consumption of various market niches, to borrow from advertising terminology.

To see the paradox inherent in this phenomenon, look at the success of Granville Island. There is a rich irony in the fact that while it is, quite rightly, considered to be perhaps the most exciting part of the city, with its mixed-use and dynamic urbanity, nevertheless underneath all that apparently spontaneous activity, Granville Island is a contrived, tightly managed physical and social construct. Granville Island offers itself as a palette of public pleasures moored to the south shore of False Creek, yet it is an exercise in invented history.

In the 1970s the industrial functions on this False Creek sandbar that had been built up to support them were in decline. The factories, shipyards and iron foundries had closed one by one, leaving a landscape of abandoned old industrial sheds. In an inspired move, local architects and representatives of the federal government (the island's landlord) came together to develop a master plan for reinventing the island. Their urban design approach, radical for its time, focussed on retaining much of the former industrial character, recycling the older buildings and insisting on a careful integration of new structures and a simple kit of streetscape elements. Central to this plan was the notion that people and cars would share the public spaces between buildings, something that had never been done before in Vancouver. There were to be no sidewalks, just a continuous, undifferentiated public realm.

The Granville Island project is a huge success. A series of public spaces, both contrived and found, mediate between water and land. Building forms are strictly controlled, and their uses are programmed to achieve a careful balance of attractions for the consumer and profits for the vendor. Every new addition or alteration is subject to the scrutiny of the federally owned island's consultant architect and Canada Mortgage and Housing Corporation landlord management team. The centrepiece of the island is the so-called Public Market, where everything has been carefully designed to convey the sense of being in a traditional, organically evolved space. The aisle widths are deliberately undersized. Stall leases in the market are assigned

Top The beach at Spanish Banks is softer, more informal, reflecting the public life of the suburbs.

Bottom Sunset Beach from Burrard Bridge, an example of Vancouver's highly contrived, carefully calibrated beach spaces.

Lance Berelowitz photos

Granville Island,
Vancouver's hugely
successful yet invented
waterfront theme park.

Lance Berelowitz photo

according to a strict set of guidelines to maximize product variety and profits. Vendors are required to abide by an equally strict set of regulations concerning the display of their produce. Even the buskers are programmed. It is the closest thing Vancouver has to a theme park, complete with taste police. And yet ... and yet everyone loves it! Granville Island is the most visited attraction in all Vancouver.

The most successful part of the waterfront is also then, apparently, the most commodified. This lesson has not been lost on the city's cultural arbiters and is nowhere more evident than in the recent proliferation and shifting emphasis of so-called festivals. Some of the older community-based festivals, which interestingly enough are not by the sea, such as the Powell Street (Japanese) Festival in Oppenheimer Park at the centre of the former Japanese quarter, or the Greek Festival centred on that community's long association with Kitsilano's West Broadway, have either changed their names or shifted their emphasis in recent years to reflect the move away from ethnic celebration to a more ambiguous, homogenizing event. For example, the Powell Street Festival, one of the few remaining east-side community-based events, which since 1977 has celebrated Vancouver's long-standing Japanese community, has in recent years come under increasing pressure from the change in social character and community demographics around Oppenheimer Park, now frequented by a sizable number of drug dealers, prostitutes and the homeless, and far fewer Japanese; the Greek Festival has become the Kits Days Festival, no doubt reflecting the changing demographics and buying power of the Kitsilano neighbourhood as it increasingly gentrifies.

Although there are a few exceptions—the Public Dreams Society's Illuminares lantern parade at Trout Lake and its Parade of Lost Souls at Grandview Park being two of them—these changes signify the increasing commodification of community-based, class-based or ethnic-based public ritual, as expressed through the rampant proliferation of so-called festivals. Vancouver now has, in addition to the above, the Folk Music Festival, the Fringe Festival, the Film Festival, the Children's Festival, the Jazz Festival, Festival Vancouver, the Comedy Festival, the Writers Festival, the Dragon Boat Festival, the Dancing on the Edge Festival, the Wine Festival, the Shakespeare Festival, the Gay Pride Festival and the previously mentioned, and hugely successful, Celebration of Light. Vancouver is truly in danger of being festivalled to death! The commercialization of society through the co-option of many of these formerly community-based events is well captured in this quote from local writer/filmmaker Joel Bakan's recent book, *The Corporation:*

> The annual Vancouver Children's Festival was once a respite from commercialism. So I was taken aback when, on a recent visit to the festival with my son, we found ourselves in the middle of a mock Kia car dealership after entering the grounds through the main gate. Shiny new vehicles were seductively positioned on the grass, banners with Kia logos fluttered in the breeze, and chippy young Kia staff roamed the grounds giving away free stuff to kids. The festival had permitted the display in exchange for Kia sponsorship dollars.[78]

What all this means is that highly organized, tourist-oriented and thus socially approved public spectacle is increasingly replacing genuine spontaneous public life. The fact that many people seem not to recognize the difference is all the more cause for concern. Vancouverites are being turned into consumers of, rather than participants in, their own culture, tourists in their own city, and the forms of public space are quietly being appropriated. Meanwhile, more self-generated, unregulated expressions of public life are being increasingly marginalized, both physically and socially.

As an indication of this phenomenon, the annual Celebration of Light fireworks festival is instructive. In recent years, this commercially sponsored "free" event has assumed metropolitan proportions, attracting huge crowds even as it appropriates large parts of the city from its citizens. At the height of the summer season, some 350,000 people per night converge on the waterfronts of central Vancouver for each of four separate displays,

The annual Celebration
of Light fireworks
display in English Bay.

Heather Dean photo

jostling for a view out over English Bay, epicentre of the fireworks. Numerous roads are barricaded and barred to car traffic from all but those with proof of local residency. Extra public transit is laid on, and scores of police officers on crowd control duty earn extra cash working overtime. The fireworks, which are set to music broadcast on a local radio station, continue for approximately thirty minutes. As seabirds flee their nightly nesting places and hundreds of pleasure craft encircle the firing barge, the show builds to a Wagnerian crescendo over English Bay. At the moment of climax, everyone stands facing out to sea, their backs turned to the city, transfixed by the explosive finale. The sky is alive with coloured light, illuminating thousands of gasping spectators. As the spectacle ends, the satiated thousands stream back to their homes in awed excitement or pile into their cars for the long drive out to the ever-expanding suburbs …

The Celebration of Light is not some grassroots civic celebration or collective cultural expression or commemoration of historic significance but rather an exquisitely choreographed, sophisticated, expensive public spectacle. On the other hand, maybe this is the apt cultural expression of a community as diverse and recent as Vancouver's, apparently hell-bent on obliterating its own short though significant civic history. The triumph of spectacle over substance, artifice over *civitas*, seems exultantly complete.

If it can be said that Vancouver has a curiously distorted public culture, as represented by the architecture and uses of its public spaces, then it must also be said that, in its own peculiar way, and with barely a nod to traditional Western notions of formal public space, this culture is as vibrant and alive as any. For proof, if such is needed, you need only go down to the beach.

That's what everyone else does.

Epilogue

VANCOUVER HAS ALWAYS BEEN a seductress, a city of desire. It is now consciously selling itself as such on the global marketplace of cities. And many are buying. In the process, Vancouver is reinventing itself in hyperreal time. Every month, the view of downtown Vancouver from across False Creek changes yet again. There is a disorientingly transitory feeling to the place: city as moving target, a work in progress. It stands still for no one. If Paris is a movable feast according to Hemingway's famous homily, then Vancouver is a dream in motion. Today's breathless issue is tomorrow's old news, overtaken by successive improvisations. This is one of the fastest changing cities in the world. Cityscapes emerge, and disappear, with alarming alacrity. There are entire chunks of the city in which not a single building was there a decade or two ago. At the same time, Vancouver retains an air of insouciant innocence, stubbornly (happily?) clinging to an independent, even isolationist, mentality, defying all offers and inducements of metropolitanism.

Yet in this farrago of urbanization, Vancouver has moved from frontier entrepôt to metropolitan gateway within a mere generation. In the process, it has somehow retained, re-created or reinvented many of the elements that characterize civilized urban living but that have eluded so many other cities in North America. Its American cousins have taken note: interpretations of the "Vancouver model," however incompletely assimilated, are emerging in cities as diverse as San Francisco, San Diego (Vancouver with better weather?), even Fort Worth.

Meanwhile, Vancouver continues to reinvent itself. The downtown is utterly transformed, the city's inner suburbs are poised for change and some of the outlying bedroom municipalities are just beginning to take on the airs of regional town centres. And over the last couple of years, the changes have been even more dramatic and profound. This epilogue is really a prologue to Vancouver's future.

In retrospect, the period 2003 to 2004, during which I wrote much of this book, might be viewed as a watershed for the city, due to the number and variety of significant events.

First, the end of 2002 saw a wholesale change in the local political landscape, with the incumbent Non-Partisan Association (NPA)–dominated Vancouver City Council being almost completely annihilated at the polls in the municipal elections. An alliance of mostly political neophytes under the left-wing Coalition of Progressive Electors (COPE) umbrella assumed control of council for the first time since 1985–86. Change was in the air. A populist new mayor, former chief coroner and sometime television drama series advisor Larry Campbell, swept into power. Campbell seemed to offer a leadership style that focussed more on a vision for the future rather than the cautious law and order governance of previous administrations. Perhaps this was a harbinger of bigger changes to come.

Early in 2003 some important urban planning ideas came out of the City's Planning Department. These included housing alternatives that bridge the gap between the single-family detached house and the typical apartment building, such as row housing, new infill strategies, clustered housing and semi-detached duplexes, four-plexes and six-plexes. All these options would densify traditional single-family neighbourhoods while maintaining their overall look and feel. The densities explored ranged from a floor space ratio of 0.7 (the upper density limit of traditional detached homes) up to 1.2. Curiously, there is currently no residential zoning in Vancouver permitting housing in this range. If applied across all residential areas, this approach could add significant densification while retaining much of the city's single-family housing character. Another important policy change in early 2004 finally allowed, for the first time ever (and after years of advocacy), secondary suites in all single-family houses anywhere in Vancouver, further advancing urban sustainability. Remarkably, the sky did not fall down.

In May 2003 the City of Vancouver released the first version of the *Official Development Plan* for its 20-ha (50-acre) Southeast False Creek lands, which called for a model sustainable community, with myriad strategies and requirements for getting there. However, many questioned the specifics of the plan, in particular the proposed high-rise form of development, and in 2004 it underwent substantial changes to reflect these concerns. It is still being revised. Although some have questioned the depth of the City's commitment to sustainable development, the release of the first ever *Official Development Plan* that consciously aims for a sustainable urban environment was a significant milestone in the life of the city. It remains to be seen whether the underlying sustainability principles are honoured in the main or the breach.

Meanwhile, back in February 2003, Vancouver, led by the Sheltair Group, had made a submission to the international Sustainable Urban Systems Design Competition organized by the International Gas Union (IGU). The IGU's goal is to explore the role that cities and the energy sector can play together in developing sustainable solutions to global urban environmental problems. Vancouver had been selected to represent Canada against submissions from eight other cities around the world, and its entry, dubbed cities[PLUS], posited a vision of urban sustainability that looked a hundred years into the future. With contributions from a broad range of local interest groups and stakeholders, it was a visionary document, supported by some heavy hitters. The Vancouver cities[PLUS] team chair was Lloyd Axworthy, former Canadian Minister of Foreign Affairs, and Mike Harcourt, former mayor of Vancouver as well as former premier of British Columbia, was vice-chair. The Greater Vancouver Regional District endorsed and helped sponsor it.

In June 2003, much to Vancouver's delight, the cities[PLUS] submission was awarded the grand prize by an international jury at the IGU conference in Japan, beating out entries from Goa (India), San Diego/Tijuana (United States/Mexico), Tokyo (Japan), Mishima (also in Japan), Buenos Aires (Argentina), Changshu (China), Berlin (Germany) and Vologda (Russia).

Vancouver had arrived on the global cities map.

The recycled dust had barely settled when, on July 2, 2003, five years of hard work and furious lobbying finally paid off when Vancouver was awarded the 2010 Olympic Winter Games by the International Olympic Committee. This was a huge boost to the city's international profile, and for a brief moment Vancouver made news headlines around the globe. The world started to take notice.

It remains to be seen how effectively Vancouver uses the Olympic Games as a catalyst for leveraging urban improvements: certainly the potential of a hallmark event such as the Olympics to help generate long-term legacies is enormous, as demonstrated by previous host cities such as Barcelona and Sydney. Plenty needs to be done, however, for Vancouver to fully capture the potential benefits that go way beyond the actual seventeen-day event, and the real work is still ahead. And there is always the risk that things will come unravelled. Just ask Atlanta. But the payoff could be significant: metropolitan Vancouver can expect to become a quite different place post-2010: new and improved roads; better and more public transit; new community and recreation facilities; the completion of the wholesale transformation of False Creek into a more sustainable community and urban waterfront; an enhanced public realm and public spaces; a cultural critical mass and raised standards. But even more than these physical changes, impressive as they might be, is the prospect of Vancouver's developing a culture of excellence. And the ineffable, empowering sense of pride and self-confidence that citizens of all great cities evince. That is the real prize in Vancouver's grasp.

In early December 2003, TransLink, Greater Vancouver's regional transportation authority, approved the contentious $4-billion *10-Year Outlook* plan for substantial expansion on several fronts. This ambitious program calls for two new rapid transit routes (the Richmond-Airport-Vancouver RAV Line and the Coquitlam Line); new and wider bridges over the Fraser River; substantial expansion of the trolley bus fleet; new and wider regional roads and truckways; increased cycling, walking and transit capacity as alternatives to driving, and a new passenger commuter ferry network. Finally, Vancouver seemed to be serious about catching up with other metropolitan areas in terms of building the transportation infrastructure it desperately needs. It is not a moment too soon.

Then came the RAV line fiasco. Four times the vote was called at the TransLink Board, with approval being twice denied before some serious political arm-twisting, and a last-minute infusion of extra public cash, resulted in enough of the local politicians being persuaded to change their vote, thus allowing the project to proceed. But not without much rancour and debate, and there are still many credible commentators who believe that the RAV line will be a dangerously expensive Cadillac where a Chevy would do just fine.

Next, in the dying days of 2003, a change took place at Canada's political epicentre with potentially profound impacts on Canadian cities in general and Vancouver in particular: Paul Martin's accession as leader of the national Liberal Party and the new prime minister heralded a major new federal government focus on the increasingly acute investment deficit in Canada's major cities. Within weeks of assuming office, Martin announced a New Deal for cities: the elimination of the federal Goods and Services Tax for all municipalities and the return to cities of a portion of the gasoline tax that the federal government collects. Taken together, these two measures should add up to a substantial increase in the ability of Canadian cities to fund the new physical and cultural infrastructure investment so critical to their ongoing well-being and global competitiveness.

Finally, in June 2004, Canada went to the polls in a hard-fought general election as Paul Martin sought a mandate to advance his agenda. He got it, but only by the slimmest of margins: a Liberal Party minority government that needs the support of other political parties, most notably the left-leaning New Democratic Party (NDP), to survive. Where does this leave Martin's New Deal for cities agenda? Ironically, probably strengthened: reinvestment in urban Canada is also high on the list of NDP priorities. This, in conjunction with the election of some high-profile urban Vancouver Liberal Party candidates who are now key cabinet ministers, suggests that the city will have a stronger say at the federal government head table in coming years. And with the 2010 Olympic Winter Games now rapidly approaching, Vancouver is going to get increasing attention from the rest of Canada.

THERE IS something exhilarating about living in a city on the ascendance, a city that is getting demonstrably better by the year. Not too many cities can make this claim. Every morning, Vancouver wakes up to something new, yet another project underway or a shift in the way it permits itself to be governed. New construction rises up from the ground at a frenetic pace, in a parody of the rate of natural growth in the Pacific Northwest rain forest. Buildings are also demolished, in most cases instantly forgettable ones. The pace of change is breathtaking.

The overwhelming majority of new projects, so often initially opposed, have improved the urban fabric of the city rather than detracting from it, as is often feared by those who oppose new development. But most people still instinctively resist change. Perhaps this says something about the nature of design, and something also about a deeply buried strand of the Vancouver psyche that is profoundly anti-urban. Yet Vancouver is held up more and more as a model of contemporary urbanism.

In the introduction to the catalogue for the "Vancouver ReVisions" urban design exhibition at the Vancouver Art Gallery in 1986, I wrote: "At 100 years old, the city of Vancouver is at once unmade and complete. Unmade in content, complete in outline." When I wrote those words nearly twenty years ago, they were indeed true and, I thought, telling of a place that had been incorporated as a city barely a century previously. The shape

Stanley
Park

Burrard Inlet

English
Bay

False Creek

■ Built form in 1987

■ Built form added
   since 1987

of the city was clearly visible in outline, though it still awaited the filling in
that comes with the second wave of urbanization when virgin land runs out
and layers of urbanism begin to accrete.

Two decades later, the physical armature, the outline, is indeed well in
place. More importantly, Vancouver is now getting round to filling in the
urban content. The second wave of development is rolling out from the
centre. Vancouverites are starting to build a city that is commensurate with
its spectacular setting and that relies less and less on that setting to get away
with second-rate urban design.

There are many exciting aspects to Vancouver's emerging urban form.
Its skyline is not one of them, however, at least not yet. This too may be
about to change. Vancouver is growing up, literally. For many years the City
enforced strict height controls on buildings in the downtown peninsula,
primarily with the commendable goal of preserving public views of the
North Shore mountains. But one consequence of this policy was a flattening
out of the skyline, a kind of self-effacement of the profile of the city, in sharp

A figure-ground map of Vancouver's downtown

urban form, showing new construction since 1987.

Eric Leinberger

contrast to the dramatically vertiginous mountain setting. Another consequence is that there is really no tall structure that symbolizes Vancouver in
the way that, say, the CN Tower does Toronto, or the Empire State Building
does New York, or the Eiffel Tower does Paris. The closest thing Vancouver
has to an iconic structure are the fabric roof "sails" of Canada Place jutting
out into the harbour.

Ever since the *Downtown Official Development Plan* was approved in
1975, the maximum height limit for high-rise towers was 137 m (450 feet).
Then, in 1997, City Council approved the recommendations of a detailed
Skyline Study Report. The study identified seven sites that it concluded could
support taller buildings, with just two of these sites allowing a maximum
height of 183 m (600 feet), and the other five between 137 and 168 m (450
and 550 feet), all subject to stringent design conditions.

There matters stood until the third Wall Centre tower was erected in
1999, becoming, at 146 m (480 feet), the tallest building in Vancouver. Since
then, only two of the *Skyline Study Report* sites have been developed, both
with buildings that did not break the regular 137-m (450-foot) height limit.

In the past two years, however, two more of the selected sites have been
approved for taller buildings. One is a distinctive, crystalline fifty-storey
hotel tower beside the Hotel Georgia, and the other is a mixed-use fifty-
seven storey tower of 196 m (642) feet at the corner of Georgia and Thurlow.
However gingerly, a Rubicon has been crossed in the history of the city's
form of development.

THESE AND OTHER less obvious signs indicate that Vancouver really is
changing, in ways that potentially will have profound and exciting consequences for its urban form.

In its release of data from the 2001 census, Statistics Canada confirmed
that for the first time English dropped below 50 per cent of the total
population as the mother tongue of Vancouver residents. At the same time,
Vancouver's national share of corporate head offices dropped to fourth place
for the first time (behind Toronto, Montreal and Calgary), in terms of both
the number of head offices and the total number of people working in them.

Yet Vancouver appears to have an energetic small-business sector,
thriving "green" research and development, and a growing creative class. It
is moving towards a new "creative economy," away from a traditional one
based on resources and manufacturing. And it is doing so on its own terms.
This is new territory, the deliberate and concerted willing into being of a

new mythology for the city and the emergence of a new model of urbanism. Vancouver's focus on quality of place and quality of life is increasingly attracting the knowledge workers, the global citizens and the "cultural creatives" whom the new city states are targeting.

The old paradigms are shifting. A new urban ecology is emerging for this city on the edge. In addition to simply getting bigger and taller, the city is becoming more complex, more layered and nuanced. And it is becoming self-consciously smarter. The poster-child city is growing up.

In the opening years of the twenty-first century, Vancouver has insinuated itself into the consciousness of the world in a calculated seduction of the global imagination. The ecology of the city is being adjusted and recalibrated accordingly, to respond to this new *Zeitgeist*. The past two decades have been witness to a remarkable reinvention. The coming decades will prove whether this willed reinvention of the city is durable, or as ephemeral as our dreams.

Notes

1. Several portions of this book have appeared previously in a different form in the following publications: *Architecture/Research/Criticism* magazine; *Metropolitan Mutations: The Architecture of Emerging Public Spaces,* edited by Detlef Mertins; *Boulevard* magazine; *Canadian Architect* magazine; *Competitions* magazine; *Stadt Bauwelt* magazine and *Vancouver's New Neighbourhoods,* a brochure published by the City of Vancouver Planning Department.

2. Reyner Banham, *Los Angeles: The Architecture of Four Ecologies,* 23.

3. 2001 Statistics Canada census, rounded numbers.

4. Peter Carey, *30 Days in Sydney,* 3–4.

5. For example, Ujjal Dosanjh, from Vancouver, was Canada's first ever Indo-Canadian provincial premier; in 2004, he was elected to Parliament.

6. Reyner Banham, *Los Angeles: The Architecture of Four Ecologies.*

7. See William Rees, "Ecological Footprints and Appropriated Carrying Capacity: Measuring the Natural Capital Requirements of the Human Economy."

8. Parts of the southern Fraser River delta suburbs of Richmond and Ladner are below sea level, and are protected by a series of dykes and levees.

9. Mike Davis has described this same paradox with respect to Los Angeles: how many of the best and most sensitive natural parts of that city have also been the most degraded, precisely because of the same speculative impulses. He points out in *Ecology of Fear* that as long ago as the 1930s, urban planners were warning Los Angeles that its "future prosperity was directly threatened by the increasing discrepancy between tourists' buoyant expectations and their disillusioning experiences in the Land of Sunshine."

10. The Garden City Movement had its genesis in Great Britain around the beginning of the twentieth century with the publication in 1898 of Ebenezer Howard's seminal *Garden Cities of Tomorrow.* Its most notable proponents were English architects such as Raymond Unwin and Edwin Lutyens, both of whom worked on the iconic Hampstead Garden Suburb. The Garden City Movement was disseminated throughout the British Empire and showed up in designs for new capital cities such as Canberra (Walter Burley Griffin) and New Delhi (Lutyens again).

11. See Graeme Wynn and Timothy Oke, eds., *Vancouver and Its Region,* 268.

12. See the Greater Vancouver Regional District's *Livable Region Strategic Plan 2001 Annual Report,* 32.

13. *Transportation Plan,* City of Vancouver, 1997.

14. Andrew Scott, "Aboriginal History," in *The Greater Vancouver Book: An Urban Encyclopaedia..*

15. As Eric Nicol describes it in *Vancouver,* the colonial British pre-emption process "was a method of land acquisition permitting a [male] British subject to obtain a grant of land not yet surveyed," at no cost. Until the land was actually surveyed, no payment was required. However, the land had to be permanently occupied by the pre-emptor. Needless to say, this system proved singularly attractive to Vancouver's earliest colonial speculators.

16. Much of the background on early District Lot pre-emptions and subdivisions comes from Bruce Macdonald, *Vancouver: A Visual History.*

17. Graeme Wynn and Timothy Oke, eds., *Vancouver and Its Region,* 118.

18. See Graeme Wynn and Timothy Oke, eds., *Vancouver and Its Region,* 122.

19. David Ricardo Williams, *Mayor Gerry,* 167.

20. *Greening Downtown,* by Baird Sampson Associates, 1–14.

21. Reyner Banham, *Los Angeles: The Architecture of Four Ecologies.*

22. The award-winning Central City project was designed by the talented architectural firm headed up by local wunderkind Bing Thom.

23. *A Plan for the City of Vancouver, British Columbia:*

Including Point Grey and South Vancouver, and a General Plan of the Region, 192, by Harland Bartholomew and Associates.

24. TransLink's *10-Year Outlook* (approved in 2004) envisages, among many other regional transit improvements, a much increased commuter passenger ferry service around Burrard Inlet, but it remains to be seen if this actually comes to pass. There is currently no funding in place for this service enhancement, and it is very much an open question as to how much of this far-reaching plan will actually be implemented.

25. *Price Tags,* an electronic newsletter put out by Gordon Price, focusses on Vancouver urban issues and achievements. Recent issues are online at www.northwestwatch.org/publications/price-tags.asp.

26. Much of the background for this chapter and on the first capital of British Columbia in particular comes from Graeme Wynn and Timothy Oke, eds., *Vancouver and Its Region.*

27. The recent decision by local government representatives on the TransLink regional transportation board to approve a deal that will see the federal government contribute up to $450 million towards the proposed RAV rapid transit line between Richmond, the airport and Vancouver is a recent case in point. See Chapter 6.

28. Douglas Coupland, *City of Glass.*

29. The initial project was managed by local developer Michael Geller on behalf of Aoki Corporation and includes buildings by Hotson Bakker Architects, Hancock Bruckner Eng & Wright Architects, and Henriquez Partners Architects, all of whom have done better work elsewhere.

30. Robson Square, 1972–79, by Arthur Erickson Architects with landscape architects Cornelia Oberlander and Raoul Robillard.

31. The lower levels of Robson Square were taken over in 2002 by the University of British Columbia as a downtown satellite campus.

32. See Chapter 4.

33. The Irish Guinness family built the Lions Gate Bridge as a way of unlocking the development potential of their vast yet inaccessible North Shore land holdings, which have subsequently increased in value many fold.

34. Refers to Grace McCarthy, former provincial cabinet minister in charge of installing decorative lighting along the suspension cables of the bridge in anticipation of Expo 86.

35. Douglas Coupland, *Polaroids from the Dead.*

36. Designed by the author.

37. Colin Rowe and Fred Koetter, *Collage City.*

38. See Léon Krier's award-winning entry in the Paris La Villette Park Competition, *Architectural Design* 47, no. 3 (1977).

39. Frankie Goes to Hollywood was a 1980s British glam-rock band with a reputation for sexual explicitness.

40. See Madelon Vriesendorp's illustration *Flagrant délit* in Rem Koolhaas, *Delirious New York.*

41. Mark Potter, "Expo 86; An Expensive Party," *Section a* 3, no. 1.

42. A term coined by Antoine Grumbach in "La Villette Redevelopment 1976," *AD Profiles 15,* 1978.

43. See Antoine Grumbach, editorial, *Ad Profiles 15,* 1978.

44. Aldo Rossi, *The Architecture of the City* (Italian edition).

45. Rowe and Koetter, *Collage City,* 102–5.

46. Sinclair Centre by Henriquez and Partners in association with Toby Russell Buckwell & Partners, completed in 1986. See *Canadian Architect,* March 1987.

47. *"Sous les pavés, la plage …"* (Beneath the pavers, the beach) was the anonymous graffiti slogan taken up as the battle cry of protesting students in the Paris riots of May 1968.

48. Charles-Pierre Baudelaire, *The Flowers of Evil,* ed. by Marthiel and Jackson Mathews (New York: New Directions, rev. ed. 1963); *Les Fleurs du Mal* originally published Paris, 1857.

49. See various novels and stories by Raymond Chandler.

50. Camillo Sitte, *The Art of Building Cities: City Building According to Artistic Principles.*

51. Frederick Gibberd, *Town Design.*

52. Richard Sennett, *The Fall of Public Man.*

53. Portal Park, Vancouver, 1987, Thompson Berwick Pratt Architects.

54. Granville Island Public Market, Vancouver, 1975–88, Hotson Bakker Architects.

55. Rem Koolhaas, *Delirious New York,* 104. Koolhaas coined the phrase "Culture of Congestion" to describe one of the ideals of Manhattanism.

56. The Sinclair Centre, Vancouver, 1986, Richard Henriquez Architect and Toby Russell Buckwell Architects.

57. The Canadian Pacific Railway station, built 1912–1914, renovated 1976–78, Hawthorn Mansfield Towers Architects.

58. Original building begun 1905, The Landing renovation 1988, Soren Rasmussen Architects.

59. According to City of Vancouver Planning Department staff sources, ninety-four residential towers were built downtown between 1991 and 2003.

60. According to Harold Kalman, Ron Phillips and Robin Ward, *Exploring Vancouver.*

61. Reyner Banham, *Los Angeles: The Architecture of Four Ecologies.*

62. Rhodri Windsor Liscombe, *The New Spirit,* published in conjunction with the exhibition "The New Spirit: Modern Architecture in Vancouver, 1938–1963," organized by the Canadian Centre for Architecture. Professor Liscombe's thoroughly researched, engagingly written and profoundly informative curatorial and accompanying catalogue text is by far the most impressive writing on Vancouver modernism and is essential reading for any student of the architecture of Vancouver.

63. Harold Kalman, Ron Phillips and Robin Ward, *Exploring Vancouver,* 91.

64. By "social housing," I mean housing built with partial or complete public subsidies, as opposed to market housing, and that includes a range of tenureship models such as co-operative housing, co-housing and special-needs housing.

65. The "Living First" story is drawn from City of Vancouver sources, such as the regular newsletter put out by Central Area Planning, *Planning for a Downtown in Transition* (autumn 1999); the *Central Area Plan* (1991); and Co-Director of Planning Larry Beasley's article " 'Living First' in Downtown Vancouver," *Zoning News.*

66. I am indebted to John Madden, planning analyst with the City of Vancouver, for providing many of the statistics quoted in this chapter.

67. See Reyner Banham, *Los Angeles: The Architecture of Four Ecologies.*

68. See Chapter 5 for a detailed discussion of Harland Bartholomew's *A Plan for the City of Vancouver, British Columbia, including Point Grey and South Vancouver, and a General Plan of the Region, 1929.*

69. Olmsted Brothers and Bartholomew & Associates, *Parks, Playgrounds and Beaches for the Los Angeles Region* (Los Angeles: 1930).

70. See Mike Davis, *Ecology of Fear,* 67.

71. As recalled by the author, who was present at this speech delivered by Ms. Clarke at the Vancouver Aquarium.

72. Quoted by Mike Davis in *Ecology of Fear,* from which much of the background on contemporary Los Angeles is drawn.

73. Mike Davis quoting the Los Angeles City Planning Department, *Population Estimate and Housing Inventory,* in *Ecology of Fear,* 138.

74. See Chapter 3.

75. See Chapter 9.

76. Robert Shields, *Places on the Margin.*

77. Thomas Mawson, "Vancouver: A City of Optimists," in *Town Planning Review.*

78. Joel Bakan, *The Corporation,* 118.

Bibliography

Books

Bacon, Edmund. *The Design of Cities.* London: Thames & Hudson, 1972.

Bakan, Joel. *The Corporation: The Pathological Pursuit of Profit and Power.* Toronto: Viking Canada, 2004.

Banham, Reyner. *Los Angeles: The Architecture of Four Ecologies.* University of California Press, 2001.

Berelowitz, Lance. "Places at the Edge: Public Space as Platform for the Contemplation of the Natural Tableau," in *Metropolitan Mutations: The Architecture of Emerging Public Spaces,* ed. by Detlef Mertins. Toronto: Little Brown Canada, 1989.

Carey, Peter. *30 Days in Sydney: A Wildly Distorted Account (The Writer and the City).* New York: Bloomsbury Publishing, 2001.

Conn, Heather, and Henry Ewert. *Vancouver's Glory Years: Public Transit 1890–1915.* North Vancouver: Whitecap Books, 2003.

Coupland, Douglas. *City of Glass.* Vancouver/Toronto: Douglas & McIntyre, 2000.

Davis, Chuck, ed. *The Greater Vancouver Book: An Urban Encyclopaedia.* Surrey, BC: Linkman Press, 1997.

Davis, Mike. *City of Quartz: Excavating the Future in Los Angeles.* New York: Vintage, 1992.

———. *Ecology of Fear: Los Angeles and the Imagination of Disaster.* New York: Vintage, 1999.

Delale, Alain, and Gilles Ragache. *La France de '68.* Paris: Editions du Seuil, 1978.

Delany, Paul, ed. *Vancouver: Representing the Postmodern City.* Vancouver: Arsenal Pulp, 1994.

Gibberd, Frederick. *Town Design.* London: Architectural Press, 1953.

Kalman, Harold, Ron Phillips and Robin Ward. *Exploring Vancouver: The Essential Architectural Guide.* Vancouver: UBC Press, 1993.

Kelly, Brian L. "History of Transit," in *The Greater Vancouver Book: An Urban Encyclopaedia,* ed. by Chuck Davis. Surrey, BC: Linkman Press, 1997.

Kloppenberg, Anne, Alice Niwinski, Eve Johnson and Robert Gruetter, eds. *Vancouver's First Century: A City Album 1860–1960.* Vancouver: J.J. Douglas, 1977.

Koolhaas, Rem. *Delirious New York: A Retroactive Manifesto for Manhattan.* New York: Oxford University Press, 1978.

Liscombe, Rhodri Windsor. *The New Spirit: Modern Architecture in Vancouver, 1938–1963.* Vancouver/Toronto: Douglas & McIntyre and Montreal: Centre canadien d'architecture/Canadian Centre for Architecture, 1997.

Luxton, Donald, ed. *Building The West: The Early Architects of British Columbia.* Vancouver: Talonbooks, 2003.

Macdonald, Bruce. *Vancouver: A Visual History.* Vancouver: Talonbooks, 1992.

Maiden, Cecil. *Lighted Journey: The Story of the B.C. Electric.* Vancouver: Public Information Dept., British Columbia Electric Company, 1948.

Mertins, Detlef, ed. *Metropolitan Mutations: The Architecture of Emerging Public Spaces.* Toronto: Little Brown Canada, 1989.

Meyer, Ronald. "The Evolution of Roads in the Lower Fraser Valley," in *Lower Fraser Valley: Evolution of a Cultural Landscape,* ed. by Alfred H. Siemens. Vancouver: Tantalus Research, 1968.

Nicol, Eric. *Vancouver.* Toronto: Doubleday Canada, 1970.

Punter, John. *The Vancouver Achievement: Urban Planning and Design.* Vancouver: UBC Press, 2003.

Rees, William. "Ecological Footprints and Appropriated Carrying Capacity: Measuring the Natural Capital Requirements of the Human Economy," in *Investing in Natural Capital: The Ecological Economics Approach to Sustainability,* ed. by AnnMari Jannson, Monika Hammer, Carl Folke, Robert Costanza. Washington: Island Press, 1994.

Rowe, Colin, and Fred Koetter. *Collage City.* Cambridge, Mass.: MIT Press, 1978.

Roy, Patricia E. "The Changing Role of Railways in the Lower Fraser Valley, 1885–1965," in *Lower Fraser Valley: Evolution of a Cultural Landscape,* ed. by Alfred H. Siemens. Vancouver: Tantalus Research, 1968.

Roy, Patricia E. *Vancouver: An Illustrated History.* Toronto: Lorimer and Ottawa: National Museum of Man, National Museums of Canada, 1980.

Scott, Andrew. "Aboriginal History," in *The Greater Vancouver Book: An Urban Encyclopaedia,* ed. by Chuck Davis. Surrey, BC: Linkman Press, 1997.

Sennett, Richard. *The Fall of Public Man.* New York: Knopf, 1977.

Shields, Robert. *Places on the Margin: Alternative Geographies of Modernity.* New York: Routledge, 1991.

Siemens, Alfred H., ed. *Lower Fraser Valley: Evolution of a Cultural Landscape.* Vancouver: Tantalus Research, 1968.

Sitte, Camillo. 1889. *The Art of Building Cities: City Building According to Artistic Principles.* Translated by Charles Stewart. New York: Reinhold, 1945.

Sorkin, Michael, ed. *Variations on a Theme Park: The New American City and the End of Public Space.* New York: Hill & Wang, 1992.

Vancouver Art Gallery. *Vancouver, Art and Artists, 1931–1983.* Vancouver: Vancouver Art Gallery, 1983.

——. *Vancouver ReVisions.* Vancouver: Vancouver Art Gallery, 1987.

Vogel, Aynsley, and Dana Wyse. *Vancouver: A History in Photographs.* Banff, AB: Altitude Publishing, 1993.

Walker, Elizabeth. *Street Names of Vancouver.* Vancouver: Vancouver Historical Society, 1999.

Williams, David Ricardo. *Mayor Gerry: The Remarkable Gerald Grattan McGeer.* Vancouver/Toronto: Douglas & McIntyre, 1986.

Wilson, Ethel. *The Innocent Traveller.* Toronto: Macmillan of Canada, 1949.

Wyman, Max, ed. *Vancouver Forum 1: Old Powers, New Forces.* Vancouver/Toronto: Douglas & McIntyre, 1992.

Wynn, Graeme, and Timothy Oke, eds. *Vancouver and Its Region.* Vancouver: UBC Press, 1992.

Zukin, Sharon. *The Cultures of Cities.* Cambridge, Mass.: Blackwell Publishers, 1995.

Periodicals and Published Papers

Beasley, Larry. "'Living First' in Downtown Vancouver." *Zoning News,* April 2000.

Berelowitz, Lance. "Edge City: Vancouver, Repository of Form and Style." *Canadian Architect,* October 1985.

——. "Fade to Modern." *Boulevard Magazine,* November 1990.

——. "Fitting a Square Peg into a Round Hole: Vancouver's Library Square Competition." *Competitions,* winter 1992.

——. "From Factor 15 to Feu d'Artifice." *Architecture/Research/Criticism,* January 1995.

——. "Highrise Anxiety." *Canadian Architect,* January 1992.

——. Introduction in *Vancouver ReVisions.* Vancouver: Vancouver Art Gallery, 1987.

——. "The Liveable City: Social Housing in Vancouver." *Canadian Architect,* February 1988.

——. "Reinventing Vancouver's Waterfront." *Stadt Bauwelt,* March 1998.

——. "Remaking History." *Canadian Architect,* July 1993.

——. "Urbanists in the Garden City." *Canadian Architect,* May 1987.

——. *Vancouver's New Neighbourhoods.* Vancouver: City of Vancouver Planning Department, 2003.

——. *Vancouver's Urban Design: A Decade of Achievements.* Vancouver: City of Vancouver Planning Department, 1999.

——. "Yaletown on the Edge." *Canadian Architect,* March 1995.

Hlavach, Jeannette. "A Shoreline Path Grows in Vancouver," *California Waterfront Age,* n.d.

Mawson, Thomas. "Vancouver: A City of Optimists," *Town Planning Review* 4:1 (April) 1913.

Reports and Policy Documents

Central Area Plan. City of Vancouver Planning Department, 1991.

Downtown Transportation Plan. City of Vancouver, 2002.

Greening Downtown, Baird Sampson Associates Architects, et al., City of Vancouver Planning Department, 1982.

Livable Region Strategic Plan. Greater Vancouver Regional District, 1996.

Livable Region Strategic Plan 2001 Annual Report. Greater Vancouver Regional District, 2001.

A Plan for the City of Vancouver, British Columbia: Including Point Grey and South Vancouver, and a General Plan of the Region, 1929, by Harland Bartholomew and Associates. Vancouver: Vancouver Town Planning Commission, 1930.

Skyline Study Report. City of Vancouver, 1997.

Southeast False Creek Official Development Plan. City of Vancouver, 2003.

Streetscape Design Standards, by Urban Forum Associates (Lance Berelowitz) and City of Vancouver staff. City of Vancouver Engineering and Planning Departments, 2001.

10-Year Outlook Plan. TransLink (also known as the Greater Vancouver Transportation Authority), 2003.

Transportation Plan. City of Vancouver, 1997.

Index

Page references to captions appear in *italic type.*

References to endnotes are by page number, the letter *n* (for note) and the note number.

C

California bungalow style, 190, *191*
Cambie Bridge, 67
Cambie Street, 62, 63, 66, 67, 135
Campbell, Premier Gordon, 125
Campbell, Mayor Larry, 280
Canada, government of, 91–92, 207–8, 255, 262–63
Canada Gate, 153
Canada geese, 29
Canada Mortgage and Housing Corporation (CMHC), 156, 207, 256
Canada Place, 92, 101, 104, 265
Canada Place Way, *104*, 104
Canadian Centre for Architecture, 200
Canadian National Railways station, 148
Canadian Pacific Ltd., 105
Canadian Pacific Railway (CPR): hotels, 189–90; land, 44–45, *45*, 60, 95–96, 216–27, 229 (*see also* Coal Harbour; Shaughnessy Heights); piers, 85, 86, 101; station, 96, 97, 148, 152, 171; terminus, 12, 14, 96, 229; tracks, 76, 79, 107, 110
Capilano Estates, *123*
capital of British Columbia: New Westminster, 89, 90; Victoria, 90–91
Cardew, Peter, 152, 155
Carey, Peter, 9
Carling O'Keefe Brewery, 116, 119, 206, 216
carpenter ants, 30–31
Carrall Street connector, 81, 82
cars, 36–37, 47, 71, 74–76, 85, 219, 236
Cathedral Place, 189–90, *190*
Cedar Cottage, 74
Celebration of Light, 249–50, 257–58, *258*
Centennial Plaza, 132–33, *133*
Central Area Plan, 218n65, 218–19
Central Area Planning, 218n65
Central City, 78
Central Park Line, 76, 78
central post office, 59, 206
Central Public Library (1956–57), 205–6. *See also* Library Square
central public library design competition (1991–92), 184–89, *187, 188*
Central School, 63, 64
Central Valley Greenway, 84
Centre Street, 97
chain (measurement), 45–47, *46*
Champlain Heights, 134
Chan, Caleb, 190
Chandler, Raymond, 162
chaparral, 238
chateau style, 189–90
cherry trees, 18–19, *19*
Chillwack, 86
Chinatown, 81, 83, 151
"choice of use" zoning, 225
cities[PLUS], 261
City Beautiful Association, 58, 60
City Beautiful movement, 58, 100

city hall building, 63–66, *249*, 249
"City of Destiny," 62–63, 65, *66*
City of Glass, 95, 95n28, 227
CityPlan, 222
City Square, 67
civic arts centre, 101–2
civic centre design competition, 58–59, *59, 60, 64*
Clarke, Jennifer, 232
climate, 9–10, 15–16, *17–18,* 22–23, 228
Cloverdale, 231
CMHC (Canada Mortgage and Housing Corporation), 156, 207, 256
Coal Harbour, *iv,* 27, 28–29, 40, 83, 100–106, *103, 104, 106,* 147, 217
Coalition of Progressive Electors (COPE), 260
Coast Mountains, 10, 20, 22, 236
Coast Salish First Nation, 10
Collage City, 147n37, 153n45, 163
Collingwood, 74
Collingwood Village, 119–22, *120, 123,* 123, 216
commercial rezoning, 218. *See also* C-2 zone
community-based planning, 120
community police station, 120
Concert Properties, 116
Concord Pacific Place, 83, *101,* 107–15, *108, 110,* 150, 218
Connaught, HRH the Duke of, 131, *133*
Connaught Park, *117,* 117, 193
co-operative housing, 155–56, 207, 208–13. *See also* affordable housing; non-market housing; seniors' housing; social housing
COPE (Coalition of Progressive Electors), 260
Coquitlam Line, 262
Cordova Street, 44, 171
corner sites, 147, 151–52
Corporation, The, 257
cougars, 238, 239
Coupland, Douglas, 95, 139–40, 227
court house, 131, 134; square, 131, 132, *133. See also* Centennial Plaza; Robson Square
Courthouse Square (1890), 242. *See also* Victory Square
Covent Garden, 149
coyotes, 29, 238
CPR. *See* Canadian Pacific Railway
CRAB Park, 164
Craftsman style, 190
"creative economy," 265–66
C-2 zone, 119, 218, 220–22, *222*
Cunningham, James, 166
Curtis, Bill, 114. *See also* Bill Curtis Square
Customs House, *204,* 205
Cypress Mountain. *See* Hollyburn Mountain
Cypress Park Estates, 231

D

Dal Grauer electrical substation, *203,* 203
Davick, L.E., 100
David Lam Park, 128
Davidson Yuen Architects, 210, *211*

David Wetherow Housing Co-operative, 156, 209
Davis, Mike, 26n9, 230n70, 232n72, 232n73, *234*
Delale, Alain, *160*
Delirious New York, 149n40, 170n55
Delta, 35, 86, 231
Delta Group, 116
Denman Street, 148
DERA (Downtown Eastside Residents Association), 208, 210
DERA Housing Co-operative, 210, *211*
design competitions, 60, 64. *See also* civic centre competition; central public library design competition
Design of Cities, The, 163
development history, 25–26, 95–125
diagonal shortcuts: Point Grey, 50, *51;* Kingsway, 40, *72,* 72
dingbat style, 190, 194–96, *195*
District Lots, 40, *42,* 42, *44,* 44, 49
Dominion Building, 242
Dosanjh, Ujjal, 13n5
"double cross streets," 68
Douglas Road, 72
Downs/Archambault & Partners, 185, 208
Downtown Eastside, 210, 213, 232
Downtown Eastside Residents Association (DERA), 208, 210
Downtown Official Development Plan, 265
downtown peninsula, *iv, 5,* 11, 28–29, 42, *43, 44,* 44–45, 48, 82–83, 100, 136–37, 164, 181, 216–17, 218–20, *221,* 250, 264
downtown rezoning, 218–20
Downtown Transportation Plan, 36, 83
Dunsmuir Viaduct, 81

E

earthquakes, 35–36, 233, *234*
Eastern European community, 224
Eburne, *48,* 48, 76
Eburne/New Westminster Line, 76, *77*
"Ecological Footprints and Appropriated Carrying Capacity," 17n7
ecology, 15–16, 26, 30, 233, 236–39
Ecology of Fear, 26n9, 230n70, 232n72, 232n73, *234*
11th Avenue, 117
Eliot, T.S., 145
English Bay: Bath House, 166, *167,* 251; beach, 128, *129,* 167, *247,* 249, 250–51, 258, *258*
English Cotswold/Fairytale Cottage style, 191, *192*
Erickson, Arthur, 130, 162, 180, 200. *See also* Arthur Erickson Architects
Eugenia Place, *155, 177,* 178
exotic species, 18–19, 30–33
Exploring Vancouver, 4, 193n60, 206n63
Expo 86, 78, 92, 101, 138n34, 150, 153
"Expo 86: An Expensive Party," 150n41
Expo lands. *See* Concord Pacific Place
Expo Line, 78, *79,* 79